Sport, Racism and Ethnicity

Edited by

Grant Jarvie

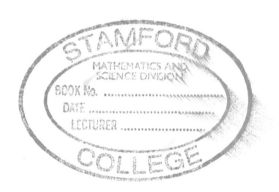
 Falmer Press

(A member of the Taylor & Francis Group)
London • New York • Philadelphia

UK   The Falmer Press, 4 John St, London WC1N 2ET

USA   The Falmer Press, Taylor & Francis Inc., 1900 Frost Road, Suite 101, Bristol, PA 19007

First published 1991. Reprinted 1995

British Library Cataloguing in Publication Data
Sport, racism and ethnicity.
  1. Sports. Sociological perspectives
  I. Jarvie, Grant
  306.483

  ISBN 1–85000–916–3
  ISBN 1–85000–917–1 pbk

Library of Congress Cataloging-in-Publication Data
Sport, racism, and ethnicity/edited by Grant Jarvie.
  Includes bibliographical references and indexes.
  ISBN 1–85000–916–3: — ISBN 1–85000–917–1 (pbk.):
    1. Discrimination in sports. 2. Racism. 3. Minorities.
  4. Ethnic relations. I. Jarvie, Grant, 1955– .
  GV706.32.S74 1991
  305.8—dc20   90–25669
                                          CIP

Set in 11/13pt Bembo by Graphicraft Typesetters Ltd., Hong Kong.

Printed in Great Britain by Burgess Science Press, Basingstoke
on paper which has a specified pH value on final paper
manufacture of not less than 7.5 and is therefore 'acid free'.

Sport, Racism and Ethnicity

For Colin

Contents

Contents

Acknowledgments

I am grateful to a number of people for their comments, encouragement and advice. The idea of *Sport, Racism and Ethnicity* grew out of a one day conference held at Warwick University in June 1989. Our objective was to consider not only the racism experienced by various sportsmen and sportswomen in Britain, but also the way in which various racisms have been articulated in South Africa, the Caribbean, Canada and the United States of America. To this end we believe that *Sport, Racism and Ethnicity* makes an important contribution not only to the existing sports literature, but also to the area of racism in general. Falmer Press are to be thanked for their encouragement with this project. I am indebted to the *International Journal of Sports History* for permission to reprint Richard Burton's contribution to this text. The research and production of this manuscript would not have been possible without small research grants provided by Warwick University and the West Midlands Sports Council. Hammie and 'Bazza' have provided critical constructive advice on sections of the book. Above all I should like to thank the contributors for making my job as editor relatively easy and Carolyn Ison for her meticulous preparation of the final manuscript.

List of Tables

List of Abbreviations

ANC   African National Congress
AWG   Arctic Winter Games
COSATU   Congress of South African Trade Unions
FAS   Fitness and Amateur Sport
FEDSAW   Federation of South African Women
GNWT   Government of Northwest Territories
IOC   International Olympic Committee
NSC   National Sports Congress
NWT   Northwest Territories
SACOS   South African Council of Sport
SAN-ROC   South African Non-Racial Olympic Committee
SASA   South African Sports Association
SASF   South African Sports Federation
SASPO   South African Non-Racial Sports Organization
UDF   United Democratic Front

Introduction

Sport, Racism and Ethnicity

Grant Jarvie

Over the past decade or more there has been a notable growth of interest in the study of sport, racism and ethnicity. Numerous developments have undoubtedly contributed to stimulate this interest, but three sets of considerations appear to have been of decisive importance. First, black sportsmen and sportswomen within various countries have experienced remarkable 'successes' in international sport. In May 1990 a British television documentary indicated that at least 50 per cent of Britain's athletic squad and 50 per cent of current British boxing champions were black. Second, such a disproportionately high level of athletic participation by various ethnic minority cultures has often been used by liberal-minded sports enthusiasts and certain academics to argue that sport itself is relatively free from racism and that sport, more than any other sphere of society, enjoys a certain degree of democratization and equality. As such, it has been, and continues to be, necessary to challenge certain cherished sporting beliefs that sport itself is inherently free and voluntary. Finally, the development of the non-racial sports movement in South Africa, the Olympic Project for Human Rights, which led to the 'Black Power' demonstration at the 1968 Mexico Olympic Games, and other self-consciously political protests such as the national-popular protests which have characterized English cricket tours to the West Indies, are but three examples of the way in which sport itself has been central to struggles of popular resistance against dominant groups. Modern developments, not least of which is the work of the late C.L.R. James, provide numerous examples which might be used to refute Ralph Miliband's statement of the early 1960s that sport itself is not conducive to any form of consciousness (James, 1963).

What is common to all of these considerations is that they dramatize sport as an arena through which various groups actively re-work their relationships and respond to changing social conditions as a whole. Sport, then, is first and foremost a social activity involving a complex set of primary relationships and, as such, sporting practices themselves are far too complex and diverse to be viewed as simple products of voluntary behaviour. The contributors to *Sport, Racism and Ethnicity* have no quarrel with the idea that sporting participation may open up a great number of possibilities and choices for some people and that sport has the potential for bridge-building. Collectively, however, the authors would take issue with any kind of argument that did not recognize the social and cultural contexts which exert pressure on people's choices, options, experiences and actions. We might all be equal on the starting line, but the resources (political, economic and cultural) that people have and the hurdles that people have to leap to get there are inherently unequal. Sporting relations themselves are vivid expressions of privilege, oppression, domination and subordination. As such, there may be a strong element of voluntarism and freedom of choice in sport, but it is only within a range of negotiated and socially produced limits and pressures (Gruneau, 1983).

To date, much of the focus on sport, race and ethnicity has tended to focus on black athletes. As Susan Birrell has recently indicated, such an approach is essentially problematic (Birrell, 1989). In the first instance, it tends to reduce and obscure the diversity of sport by equating race with black and consequently obscures other cultural identities such as Native Americans, Asians, Chicanos and Africans. In the second instance, the term 'black athlete' usually refers to black male athletes and, therefore, is not only gender blind, but obliterates the experiences of such sportswomen as Judy Simpson, Tessa Sanderson, Florence Joyner, Anna Quirot and Grace Jackson. In the third instance, the question of social class is almost completely obscured through the practice of reading race as race/class. Thus the complex interaction between racial and class dynamics as a way of understanding both state-socialist and western, liberal democracies is completely lost. For instance, Archer and Bouillon have argued that soccer in South Africa cannot be understood purely in racial terms, but as the most popular sport in South Africa; it draws upon a significantly black African culture but also facets of white working-class culture (Archer and Bouillon, 1982). Finally, and perhaps more importantly, the whole issue of sport, race and ethnicity should not stand in the way of the analysis of racism(s) which will vary both in terms of specific social formations and historical conjuncture. One of the strengths of *Sport, Racism and Ethnicity* is that collectively, it not only considers the racism(s) experienced by various ethnic minority sportsmen and sportswomen in Britain, but also the way in which various racisms have been articulated in, for example, South Africa, America, the Caribbean and Canada.

A further feature of much of the research on sport, race and ethnicity has been a failure of the researchers to differentiate adequately between the changes that have taken place at the level of athletic participation, and those which have occurred at the level of organizational leadership (Cashmore, 1982). Even more misleading are those accounts of sport and social differentiation which make general inferences about the changing nature of racial or gender relations in any society based upon a consideration of athletic participation rates. Not only do such accounts tend to overlook the broader issues of power and domination in society, but at a more concrete level, they tend to ignore the changes that have or have not taken place at the level of organizational control. A similar failing permeates those accounts of sport and social differentiation which tend to emphasize the 'distributive' as opposed to the 'relational' aspects of sporting inequality. Such a pragmatism concerning distributive resources and sports participation rates fails to take on board the structural arrangements which tend to guarantee privilege and social self-recruitment not only into preferred activities, but perhaps more importantly, into positions of power and influence both in sport and society. Thus it must be said that in terms of primary relationships such as class, gender or race, athletic participation rates and quantifiable allocations of resources are poor criteria by which to gauge either the dissolution of racial barriers, or the apparently democratic character of any particular nation-state.

Many of the personal troubles which Afro/Caribbean, Asian, Native American, or African sportsmen and sportswomen experience are in fact related to broader structural dynamics and meanings such as those articulated through racism. If one individual black British coach is not invited to manage the Olympic, Commonwealth or International athletic squads, the problem might be nothing more than a personal trouble, but if successful black British coaches in general cannot find representation at managerial or board level, then this personal trouble transcends from the level of individuality to being a more public issue. If up until the late 1950s no black West Indian cricketer had captained the national cricket team, the problem might be nothing more than personal choice, but if black West Indian cricketers in general failed to find representation within the most powerful positions of responsibility, then the problem transcends from the level of individuality to being a more public issue. If one Asian housewife does not seem able to find the opportunity to train or participate in sport, the problem might be nothing more than a personal trouble, but if Asian women in general cannot develop healthy, recreational lifestyles, then this personal trouble again transcends from the level of individuality to being a more public issue. The value of such a critical approach to sport does not deny the pleasurable dimensions of sporting experience, but it helps individuals understand that the social and political dimensions of sporting activity may be closely related to one's own personal troubles. Thus for a broader understanding of why things are the way they are, it is necessary to relate sport to general features of social organization and ultimately political action.

The following questions are indicative of some of the key issues which appear in this general text:

1 To what extent has the West Indies' growing prowess in international cricket stimulated the rise of nationalist and racial self-consciousness in the Caribbean?
2 What is the relationship between racism, patriarchy and the sporting experiences of women?
3 As a mode of resistance, what is the role of sport within popular struggle in South Africa?
4 How do young children of South Asian origin experience sport?
5 Does sports participation affect the academic progress of African-American students?
6 Does the notion of meritocracy explain the sporting experiences of black people?
7 To what extent are Native Americans accommodated within sport in Canada?
8 What is the relationship between the African National Congress and various sporting organizations in South Africa?
9 To what extent have various cultural and sporting traditions in the Caribbean been comprehensively creolized?

These and many other questions are merely illustrative of the potential richness of any text which revolves around the experiences of sport, racism and ethnicity within various cultural contexts.

A further concern with much of the literature on sport, race and ethnicity, is that it has tended to ignore basic questions concerning power arrangements and the role of sport in either consolidating or challenging the racist values of various dominant groups. At least three notable measures of the power of different groups to construct and negotiate sporting practices might be briefly mentioned: first, the power to structure sport in preferred ways and institutionalize these preferences in set rules and organizations; second, the power to establish selective traditions and rituals as being those which count; finally, the power to define a range of legitimate practices and meanings associated with sport again reflects certain social arrangements. Various forms of racism permeate all of these processes by which decisions concerning sporting practices are made. What is at stake, it seems, is the monopolistic capacity of certain dominant groups to define what sport is or what sport should be like within various racist social formations. Again it is important to distinguish between idealized conceptions of what sport should be like and how it is actually experienced at different levels by various groups who have to suffer such racism. The resources which allow particular groups to exert their power are socially produced and consequently negotiable and yet the same resources have not been universally available in any of these sporting struggles or quests for excitement.

It is hoped that by using the term ethnicity, the central term of racism(s) is not marginalized or reduced to that of secondary importance. Indeed one of the major reasons for producing this text lies in the fact that so many of the sociological and historical accounts of sport have been essentially ethnocentralistic. Marx (1986) himself used the term 'ethnicity' to refer to an originating feature of communality in all human societies. Ethnicity, in this sense, was an expression of the basic social identity needed to permit a sharing of skills and resources that could be historically cumulative. While ethnicity itself is a social construct which allows us to identify different social, cultural and sporting identities, it is not synonymous with racism and should not obscure the way in which racism permeates sporting experiences. The terms sport, racism and ethnicity collectively are indicative of the complexity of the task that faces sociologists, cultural critics and historians alike who attempt to challenge the conventional wisdom on sport and question the underlying values and assumptions that operate in this sphere. It is hoped that collectively, *Sport, Racism and Ethnicity* not only makes a small contribution to the void of literature on this topic, but more importantly, challenges many of the racist cherished beliefs surrounding sporting culture.

References

ARCHER, R. and BOUILLON, A. (1982) *The South African Game*, London, Zed Press.

Introduction

Birrell, S. (1989) 'Racial relations theories and sport: Suggestions for a more critical analysis', *Sociology of Sport*, **6**, pp. 212–17.

Cashmore, E. (1982) *Black Sportsmen*, London, Routledge.

Gruneau, R. (1983) *Class, Sports and Social Development*, Amherst, University of Massachusetts.

James, C.L.R. (1963) *Beyond a Boundary*, London, Hutchinson.

Marx, K. (1986) '*Economic Manuscripts of 1857–58*' *Collected Works, Volume 28*, London, Lawrence and Wishart.

Chapter 1

Cricket, Carnival and Street Culture in the Caribbean

Richard D.E. Burton

Taking its inspiration from C.L.R. James's classic *Beyond a Boundary*, serious discussion of the relationship between cricket and society in the Caribbean has focused on three closely connected issues.[1] First, and most straightforwardly, it has dwelt on the way in which the changing racial and class composition of West Indian teams since 1900 (the year of the first West Indian tour to England) has mirrored with almost preternatural precision the evolution of West Indian society over the same period, as non-white cricketers came first to challenge and eventually to overthrow the almost complete domination of West Indian cricket by members of the white plantocracy that had obtained before 1914 and which, in a modified but still perceptible form, continued into the 1950s; in this perspective, the crucial event is the appointment, in 1960, of Frank Worrell as the first non-white captain of the West Indian Test team, thus consecrating the black cricketing supremacy that had existed *de facto* since the mid-1940s at exactly the same time that the West Indies were painfully and with much uncertainty, attaining to political independence. Secondly, much attention has been devoted to the manner in which the West Indies' growing prowess in international cricket has not merely reflected but may actively have stimulated the rise of nationalist (and, to some extent, racial) self-consciousness in the British Caribbean. It was, some have argued, only when they saw their cricket team locked in combat with that of their English colonial masters that Jamaicans, Barbadians, Trinidadians and Guyanese came to see themselves as West Indians possessing a common historical, cultural and political identity transcending the insularity, isolation and inter-territorial competitiveness that many West Indians see as among the most baleful legacies of British colonialism in the Caribbean. In this view, the key date is without question 1950, the year that, to the accompaniment of steel bands, calypsos and mass enthusiasm among the newly installed West Indian migrant population, the West Indies defeated England in England for the first time, thanks to the formidable batting of the 'three Ws', Worrell, Weekes and Walcott, and to the scarcely credible bowling feats of 'those two little pals of mine, Ramadhim and Valentine',[2] thereby emerging as a world cricketing power on a par with England, Australia and South Africa. It was as though — to use an image that a number of West Indian writers have applied to the colonial context[3] — Prospero had taught Caliban the use of bat and ball only to find himself comprehensively 'out-magicked' by his upstart colonial pupil, thus betraying on the cricket field the vulnerability and fallibility that were becoming more and more evident in his governance of the West Indies as a whole: after 1950, it is argued, the 'mother country' would never be quite the same again in West Indian eyes. Finally, and more tentatively, West Indian cricket has been shown to present a dualistic structure corresponding to the dichotomous (or 'plural') character of West Indian society and culture as a whole,[4] a structure in which two traditions — that of the white élite and its coloured imitators, on the one hand, and that of the black masses on the other — have co-existed throughout the history of West Indian cricket, distinct in methods, aims and values, now clashing, now interacting creatively, but never wholly merging, with the 'Afro-centric' tradition of the white and coloured élite. An English game introduced into the Caribbean by Englishmen, West Indian cricket has, in this view, become progressively more and more 'African' in character, so that the 'black-wash' of English cricket in the summer of 1984 was accomplished not only by an overwhelming black team but, so to speak, by 'black' cricketing methods (notably the unrelenting use of bowling of exceptional pace and aggression) reinforced by and reflecting 'black' values and mores and giving rise to unforgettable displays of black triumphalism both on the field and off. West Indian cricket, in other words, has retained its English form while being injected with a new and specifically West Indian content and meaning. In the course of its transposition to the Caribbean, cricket, like so much else, has been comprehensively creolized.[5]

The Broader Context

The present study — the provision and tentative character of which I happily admit — takes as its starting-point these three related themes but seeks to go beyond them in its attempt to situate West Indian cricket within the broader contexts of West Indian culture as a whole. In particular, it dwells upon certain marked similarities — or so it seems to me — between the history, evolution and underlying meaning of West Indian cricket and the parallel development and significance of that other quintessentially Afro-Caribbean cultural phenomenon, carnival. In its turn, carnival will be shown to embody and crystallize in a particularly memorable form the intricate patterns of West Indian street culture, so that cricket, carnival and the street corner become overlapping expressions of a single underlying social, cultural and psychological complex. In everything that follows, players and spectators are seen as co-participants in an organic ritual, 'a social drama in which', as the Jamaican novelist and sociologist Orlando Patterson has written, 'almost all of the basic tensions and conflicts within the society are played out symbolically'.[6] Whereas in England it is not uncommon for players and officials to outnumber spectators at county matches, and even Test matches at Old Trafford, Edgbaston or Trent Bridge do not lose their meaning if they are watched by only a few hundred spectators, cricket in the West Indies is almost inconceivable — certainly at Test level — without massive and vociferous spectator involvement. What gives West Indian cricket its unique creole character is, in a very real sense, just as much participants as the players themselves, so that the frontier between players and spectators — the boundary-rope which, in England until a few years ago, represented a quasi-sacred limit that no spectator would dare transgress — is, in the West Indies and in matches in this country in which West Indians are involved, continually being breached by members of the crowd to field the ball, to congratulate successful batsmen and bowlers and, in not a few instances, to express their disgust at umpires' decisions, the tactics of the opposition, and so on.[7] On occasions, as is well known, this disgust has ceased to be simply an empty gesture on the part of irate individuals to become a collective outburst of outrage and resentment on the part of whole sections of the crowd, culminating in the riots that have occurred from time to time on West Indian cricket grounds, not, I think, as regularly or as predictably as is sometimes claimed, but none the less with sufficient frequency for riots and rioting to be seen as an ever-present potentiality in West Indian cricket at its most intense and passionate; it is with a consideration of the circumstances and meaning of these riots that the present study concludes.

The constant and indispensable involvement of the crowd in West Indian cricket can be paralleled in many other Afro-Caribbean cultural institutions where there is no absolute clear-cut separation between 'performers' and 'spectators': in cock-fighting, for example, in all forms of Afro-Christian worship with its highly charged and passionate inter-play between 'priests' and 'congregation' or, still more, in such African-derived possession cults as voodoo, pocomania or shango where again celebrants and congregation merge and co-participate in a manner foreign to most European religious practice.[8] Similarly, in carnival in Trinidad, the crowds that follow bands and masquerades are, in their way, just as much performers as the performers themselves so that, at its climax, Trinidad carnival becomes an immense, all-embracing festival acted out by the people for the people. It is, as I shall try to show, as just such a popular fiesta, a mass carnivalesque collective rite, that West Indian cricket can best be appreciated and understood.

In order to understand the place of cricket in contemporary West Indian society, it is necessary first to say something of the role of play, recreation and entertainment in the West Indies from the slave epoch onwards. We so associate slavery with manual labour of the most crushing and dehumanizing kind imaginable that we may fail to take fully into account the extraordinary variety and vitality of slave entertainments and pastimes whose function, it seems needless to add, was precisely to rehumanize the lives of men, women and children who were in other respects reduced to the level of animals, even of objects. There are numerous accounts in the literature of slavery of how slaves who, during the working day, appeared to be reduced to zombie-like insensibility and passivity would, when they returned to their own huts and yards at nightfall, suddenly become alive again and how music and dance, in particular, would almost magically revive and revitalize men and women who, in the fields, have moved about like barely animate spooks.[9] Correctly identifying dance and music, especially drumming, as potential sources of slave resistance, slave-holders repeatedly tried to curb, even to repress completely, such activities, though always, it goes without saying, to no avail.[10] Many slave dances were, of course, of African origin, though others were clearly satirical imitations of the gavottes, pavanes and quadrilles that slaves would see their masters and mistresses performing in the Great House; mimicry and parody have long been recognized as one of the main sources of Afro-Caribbean culture, and it is not impossible that some such satirical intention lay behind the initial adoption of cricket by black West Indians in the early 1800s.

Interestingly, music, dancing and their associated ritual activities were often referred to as 'plays' or 'playing' by the slaves. In 1729, a certain A. Holt wrote that slaves in Barbados held gatherings on Sundays

> which they call their plays ... in which, their various instru-
> ments of horrid music howling and dancing about the graves
> of the dead, they [give] victuals and strong liquor to the souls
> of the dead.

In 1788, again referring to slaves in Barbados, one Peter Marsden noted that

> every Saturday night many divert themselves with dancing
> and singing, which they style plays; and notwithstanding their
> week's labour, continue this violent exercise all night.

These 'plays' would reach their height at Christmas when, traditionally, rigid supervision was relaxed somewhat and slaves were for once
free to move about from plantation to plantation. In 1790 the well-
known Jamaican planter William Beckford wrote that

> some negroes will sing and dance, and some will be in a
> constant state of intoxication, during the whole period that
> their festival at Christmas shall continue; and what is more
> extraordinary, several of them will go ten or twelve miles to
> what is called a play and will sit up and drink all night, and yet
> return in time to the plantation for their work the ensuing
> morning.[11]

It is no accident, of course, that many of the most significant
slave uprisings in the Caribbean took place, precisely, at Christmas,
most notably in Trinidad in 1805 when slaves organized resistance
under the cover of drumming and dancing societies with quasi-
military names like the Regiment Macaque, the Regiment Danios and
the Couvri de Sans Peur;[12] still more significant was the largest single
slave uprising in the British Caribbean, the so-called 'Baptist War' or
'Christmas Rebellion' that took place in Jamaica in December 1831
and January 1832 under the leadership of the celebrated black Baptist
minister, Samuel 'Daddy' Sharpe.[13] A number of other examples
could be given; let us merely retain the long-standing association
between 'play' in the broad sense which slaves gave to the term —
music, dancing, drinking, sociability — and latent, potential, symbolic or actual subversion of the established order of slave society.

Carnival and Street Culture

The link between 'play' and resistance is still more marked in the case of carnival in Trinidad.[14] Before the abolition of slavery in 1834 it is clear that carnival in Trinidad was celebrated exclusively by the white élite, particularly the white French-speaking Roman Catholic élite, and some members of the coloured, again principally French-speaking and Catholic, middle-class: blacks, free and unfree, were present, if at all, only as spectators. After abolition, however, carnival was swiftly taken over by the now free black population. The whites who had hitherto dominated the street processions henceforth celebrated carnival 'behind closed doors' in their own homes or in private ballrooms and theatres, leaving the streets to the mass of the population, and particularly to those members of the black lower classes known in nineteenth-century Trinidad as 'badjohns' or 'jamets', from the French *diametre*, the 'other half', in other words the criminal or semi-criminal underworld.[15] There are, it seems to me, very definite parallels between this 'take-over' of carnival by lower-class blacks in nineteenth century Trinidad and the similar, though more gradual, 'take-over' of cricket by black West Indians since 1900. As it was taken over by blacks, so carnival in Trinidad changed unmistakably in character. Before 1834, it appears to have been much the same kind of pre-Lenten festivity that it was in Roman Catholic societies throughout Europe and Latin America; after abolition, however, it clearly becomes a popular black festival of liberation with such rituals as the 'canboulay' (*cannes brulées*) procession at midnight on the Sunday of carnival celebrating in a veiled, symbolic form the deliverance of the black population from the yoke of slavery.[16] Not surprisingly, carnival in Trinidad, especially in the capital Port of Spain, was often an occasion of confrontation between, on the one hand, black revellers and masqueraders and, on the other, the forces of law and order, local policemen and British soldiers alike. There were major clashes at carnival time in 1881 and 1883, leading to repeated attempts by the colonial government supported by the local élite to control the festivities and even to suppress them completely; a particular target of official ire was the 'tambour-bamboo' bands from which the modern steel band is ultimately derived.[17]

By the late nineteenth century, carnival had been to a large extent 'domesticated', and white and coloured Trinidadians who had shunned the street festivities for sixty years or more gradually began to venture out of their houses on the three days preceding Lent and tentatively and cautiously to mix once more with the black revellers on the streets. At one level — what we might call the ideal or mythical level — all racial, social and political hostilities in Trinidad are supposedly suppressed and forgotten for the duration of carnival; normally divided, even antagonistic, the whole population, says the myth, comes together as one. Yet very often, in bringing normally distinct and distant groups of the population together, carnival serves only to highlight the differences and hostilities between them; as recently as 1970, at the time of the so called 'February Revolution', major political, social and, to some extent, racial confrontations occurred in Trinidad at carnival time.[18] In much the same way, an enthusiasm for cricket is shared by all sections of the (male) West Indian population, whites, coloureds, blacks and East Indians alike; indeed, an enthusiasm for cricket is, arguably, the only enthusiasm that truly cuts across social and racial dividing-lines in the Caribbean. Cricket brings people together in the English-speaking West Indies as nothing else — religion, politics, or whatever — does, but precisely because it does so, it reveals the differences and hostilities between them. The dozen or so 'cricket riots' in the Caribbean are only the most extreme manifestation of West Indian cricket's unique capacity both to unite and to divide.

Other aspects of carnival have a direct bearing on the character of cricket in the West Indies, particularly the scope that it gives to forms of ritualized or stylized conflict that anthropologists have shown to be endemic in Afro-American culture in general.[19] Competition is at the very heart of carnival in Trinidad. There are, in the first place, organized competitions between calypsonians for the title of Calypso King in which there may be 200 or more contestants each singing two or three calypsos and each accompanied by bands of enthusiastic supporters;[20] there is, too, the nationwide competition for the title of Carnival Queen which always involves passionate and sometimes violent controversy, in part because of the importance commonly attached to the winner's ethnic identity and skin colour. On a less organized but no less formalistic or ritualistic level, there are the conventional confrontations, challenges and exchanges of abuse, derision and defiance between different bands of masqueraders who often represent different localities, different professional categories or different social and ethnic groups; all of these confrontations have the effect of externalizing and, at the same time, of channelling and sublimating tensions and hostilities between individuals and groups which, during the rest of the year, normally remain suppressed.

During the nineteenth and early twentieth centuries, a particular importance attached to the ritualistic and stylized conflicts between bands of so-called 'stick-fighters' who, armed with hardwood sticks variously known as poui, gasparee, balata or anare, would confront each other on the streets at carnival-time, hurl abuse and defiance at each other and then engage in mock — and sometimes not so mock — stick combat; introduced into Trinidad by slaves from the French-speaking islands, stick-fighting, otherwise known as calenda or calinda, is clearly of African origin. In an island culture otherwise deprived of indigenous heroes and heroism, leading stick-fighters or batonniers such as the celebrated Mungo the Dentist — so called for his skill in 'fixing' the teeth of opponents![21] — reigned as virtual kings of the districts and peoples they represented; the reputation of a locality or street-gang became identified with the reputation of its batonniers who would both repel rivals from other areas and lead periodic sorties into enemy territory.

It is interesting that stick-fighting and the cult of the batonnier entered into decline at much the same time that black enthusiasm for cricket and the accompanying cult of black batsmen and black fast bowlers began to emerge, and it would be interesting, too, to know how far street sodalities such as the Jacketmen, the Hirondelles and Jockey Boys (from San Fernando), the Sweet Evening Bells and Tiepins (from Tunapuna) and Peau de Canelle, the Cerfs-Volants, the Bakers, Bois d'Inde and the s'Amandes (from Port of Spain) formed the nucleus of the black cricket clubs — themselves notoriously undisciplined and aggressive — that would emerge in the 1890s and early 1900s.[22] Whatever the answer, there are, it seems to me, possible continuities between the figure of the champion batonnier or 'kalinda king' and that of the champion black batsmen, and I was, to say the least, fascinated to come across the following description of how batonniers practised in nineteenth-century Trinidad:

> In practising, one of the best methods for quickening the eye, steadying the nerves and improving one's judgement was 'Breaking' [i.e., parrying a blow with your stick]. It consisted in having one or two fellows stand 15 or 20 yards off and hurl stones at you in rapid succession, and it was your business — and, of course, to your interest — to 'break' these stones successfully. A very proficient 'breaker' would often have three men hurling stones at him, and it was seldom, indeed, that he got hurt (*Trinidad Guardian*, 2 March 1919).[23]

To my knowledge, not even the most diehard member of the 'Africa or bust' school of Afro-American anthropology has tried to trace back West Indian prowess at cricket to the people's African 'roots'. Calenda, though, could just constitute a link, and the possibility of some submerged continuity between the African past and the Afro-Caribbean present should not, perhaps, be discounted in its entirety.

The world of carnival is, as many writers on the theme have stressed,[24] a negation or subversion of the structures, hierarchies and values that obtain in society during the rest of the year. Carnival is 'the world turned upside down', a make-believe counter-society over which the pauper or madman is king and the servant-girl queen, and it is noticeable in this respect how carnival societies in Trinidad — as, no doubt, elsewhere — have their own elaborate hierachies of kings, queens, princes, princesses, dukes, captains and sergeants-at-arms, just as, one might further note, secret societies among slaves had their elected kings, queens, dauphins and dauphines.[25] Even today, Trinidadian calypsonians give themselves, or are given, mock-royal, mock-aristocratic or mock-heroic sobriquets such as Lord Kitchener, Mighty Sparrow, Lord Beginner, Black Stalin and Mighty Chalkdust (the *nom de carnaval* of schoolteacher Hollis Liverpool)[26] as though to underline carnival's symbolic subversion of the structures of every-day life. The last shall be first, the first shall be last: during carnival, the popular imagination throws up its own hierarchies of prestige, achievement and charisma which, at every point, challenge and fictively negate the hierarchies and norms of established society.

And so it is, I tentatively suggest, with West Indian cricket. Often springing shaman-like from the lowest strata of black society, the Constantines, the Headleys, the Walcotts, the Soberses, the Richardses are the carnival kings and princes of the people, symbolic subverters and destroyers of a world where white is might and, as such, embodiments of a dream-world in which, by identification and projection, every black West Indian, be he never so poor, is monarch for the day:

We was only playin' de MCC, man;
M — C — C
who come all de way out from Inglan.

We was battin', you see;
score wasn't too bad; one
hurren an'ninety —

seven fuh three.
The openers out, Tae Worrell out,
Everton Weekes jus' glide two fuh fifty

an' jack, is de GIANT to come!
Feller name Wardle
was bowlin'; tossin' it up

sweet sweet slow-medium syrup.
Firs' ball ...
'N .. o .. o'

back down de wicket to Wardle.
Secon' ball ...
'N .. o .. o'

back down de wicket to Wardle.
Third ball comin' up
an' we know wha' goin' happen to syrup:

Clyde back pun he back
foot an' prax!
is through extra cover an' four red runs all de way.

'You see dat shot?' the people was shoutin';
'Jesus Chrise, man, wunna see dat shot?'
All over de groun' fellers shaking hands wid each other

as if was they wheelin' de willow
as if was them had the power

(Edward Kamau Brathwaite, 'Rites')[27]

Carnival is a phenomenon of the street, and it is also to the street that, in the first instance, West Indian cricket belongs. If English boys learn to play cricket in back gardens, parks, playing fields and on village greens, it is on the street — or, in the smaller islands, on the beach — that West Indian boys develop their batting, bowling and fielding skills. As such, cricket in the Caribbean partakes of the immensely complex street culture of West Indian males, a culture whose main features we can, with the help of the writings of anthropologists such as Roger D. Abrahams[28] and Peter J. Wilson,[29] define, again very tentatively, as follows. According to Abrahams and Wilson, there is a marked contrast in West Indian cultures between the female-centred and female-dominated culture of the home or 'yard' and the male-centred, male-dominated culture of the street and its adjuncts, the rum-shop, betting-shop and barber's. The gynocentric ity and respectability, while the androcentric world of the street lays emphasis rather on the counter-values of individualism, competition and reputation; the yard is an enclosed enclave of seriousness while the street is an open, mobile world of play. Though there is a tension between the two worlds and their associated values, there is, according to Abrahams and Wilson, no necessary conflict between them: complementarity rather than antagonism is, in normal circumstances, the order of the day. The values and qualities most esteemed on the street are style, flair, 'cool', defiance, reputation and, in extreme instances, aggression, though both Abrahams and Wilson are at pains to stress that, again in normal circumstances, street hostilities between individuals and groups (or, to use Wilson's suggestive term, 'crews')[30] are commonly expressed in semi-ritualistic, sublimated forms; both writers, for example, attach great significance to the marked stylization and hyperbolization of verbal insult and defiance in the Caribbean and among Afro-Americans in general.[31] In the analysis proposed by Abrahams and Wilson, the values of the yard, based as they are on the concepts of order, respectability and seriousness, are closer to the established European-derived or European-influenced values of the dominant élite — closer, in other words, to the values traditionally embodied and enshrined in English cricket — whereas, says Abrahams, the play ethos of the street 'means not only switching styles and codes characteristic of all types of play, but also switching downward to roles and behaviours regarded from household (and Euro-American) perspectives as "bad" or improper'; 'in the Afro-American order of behaviours', he continues, '"play" is not distinguished from the "real" or "work" but from "respectable" behaviour ... playing then means playing bad, playing black, playing lower-class'.[32]

If Abrahams and Wilson are correct, I would suggest, again with great caution, that the values, mentalities and ways of behaving in evidence among West Indian cricket crowds are an extension — even a heightened, exaggerated and stylized form — of the already stylized values, mentalities and ways of behaving characteristic of West Indian male street culture in general: expansiveness, camaraderie, unruliness, jesting, joking, verbal and bodily bravado, clowning, in a word, playing. Not only this, but it would seem that the qualities that West Indians most prize in their cricketers are essentially 'street qualities': what counts is not the mere scoring of runs, but scoring with style, panache, flamboyance, an ostentatiously contemptuous defiance of the opposition.

Similarly, fast bowling must not simply be fast but look fast. West Indian fast bowling confronts batsman and spectators alike with an all-out exteriorization of the methods and signs of attack: a run-up of (usually) exaggerated length and speed, a momentous heave of arms, legs and torso at the instant of delivery, with the ball unleashed at colossal speed straight at batsman and/or stumps, either bouncing half-way or two-thirds down the pitch and rearing up to around the batsman's chest and face — the 'throat ball' as it is reputedly known in the contemporary West Indian dressing-room, firing into the batsman's block-hole (the 'yorker' at which Charlie Griffith and Joel Garner have so excelled) or — a mode of attack apparently commonplace in black West Indian cricket in the 1920s and 1930s,[33] perfected (if that is the word) by Roy Gilchrist in the late 1950s, and now banned — 'beaming' on the full at the batsman's (until recently) unprotected head. No concealment or mystery here: just aggression projected in a pure and naked state, a total spectacle complete in itself and instantly understood, all to the accompaniment of a percussive crescendo of rattling beer-cans, clapping, hooters, whistles and shouts, as though the crowd not merely beholds but, through its active participation, actually creates this cathartic experience of controlled, directed violence.

West Indian men, it seems to me, watch and play cricket with minds, hearts, values and expectations shaped by the street culture of boyhood, adolescence and early manhood. Concerned as they are with the enhancing of individual and group reputation, those values are potentially — though rarely in fact — at odds with the values of respectability, seriousness, moderation and obedience associated with the home, the church and the ethos of the dominant white and coloured élites. So long as the course of the cricket match is such that street values and emotions can be expressed and released through a cathartic identification with the West Indian cricketers and their deeds, areas of potential conflict are avoided. But should something 'go wrong' in the symbolic drama being acted out — should, for example, one of the crowd's heroes be dismissed in a manner the crowd finds unacceptable — then, as Orlando Patterson has argued,[34] the conflict of values symbolized in the cricket match abruptly ceases to be symbolic and becomes real. The crowd's passions are no longer channelled and sublimated through identification with its heroes. The imaginative spell is broken and, no longer able harmlessly to project its feelings into the match and on to the players, the crowd now directs them towards and against those embodiments of law and order, the umpires, or against whatever representatives of the established order present themselves to its fury: administrators, selectors, the police, dignitaries in the pavilion or the main stand, though rarely, if ever, it should be stressed, the opposition team itself. Bottles, seat cushions and other missiles rain forth: a riot has begun.

Cricket, Culture and Resistance

Before I discuss some of the cases of riots at cricket matches in the West Indies, it will be necessary to say something of the physical conditions in which cricket is played and watched in the region. In the first instance, all of the Test match grounds are extremely small, built as they were in the late nineteenth and early twentieth centuries before cricket became a mass spectator sport in the Caribbean; the crowd is literally on top of the players at Sabina Park (Kingston), Kensington Oval (Bridgetown) and elsewhere, and almost always there are many more spectators than the grounds can possibly accommodate with comfort. People watch from surrounding buildings, from trees, lamp-posts and telegraph-poles; at Sabina Park, and probably at other grounds, smart operators make holes in the perimeter fence and actually charge others for the privilege of entering the ground via these improvised entrances. There are almost no facilities and refreshments available in those parts of the ground where poorer spectators congregate. A vast amount of beer and rum is consumed and in the cheap uncovered seats known in the Caribbean as 'bleachers', the heat, at around three or four in the afternoon, can be incredible; the crowd's already passionate feelings about the game are commonly heightened still further by the large amount of betting on batsmen's scores that is a regular feature at Test match grounds in the West Indies. In addition, as Patterson has neatly shown,[35] the lay-out of a ground like Sabina Park represents an exact microcosm of the structure of West Indian society: the pavilion for whites and the wealthiest coloureds, the main stands for the black lower-middle class, the bleachers for the masses. The dichotomy of pavilion and main stand, on the one hand, and bleachers on the other comes over, in Patterson's description, as a modern equivalent of the dichotomy of Great House and barracoons on the slave plantation, an analogy that has been brought out still more in recent years by the presence at most Test matches in the West Indies of large numbers of police armed with nightsticks, riot shields, guns and tear-gas canisters. In such supercharged conditions, riot is an ever-present possibility, requiring only certain circumstances to actualize it.

In the last thirty years there have been four major instances of crowd disturbance at Test matches in the West Indies, plus a number of lesser incidents and four or five 'near misses', not least, I suspect, in England in 1976 when England captain Tony Greig — he of the Aryan good looks and unreconstructed South African accent — announced his intention not merely to defeat the West Indies but, in his singularly inept phrase, 'to make them grovel'.[36] Fortunately the West Indies overwhelmed England that year, and cricket-lovers will recall the endless chant of 'Grovel, Greig, grovel' that resounded across the Oval as Vivian Richards swept, drove and hooked his way to 291 and the West Indies reached 687 for eight declared in the fifth Test; to cap it all, the winning calypso at carnival in Richard's native Antigua the following February was entitled 'Who's grovelling now?' sung — or so I am told — to the tune of 'Who's sorry now?'!

The first major instance of crowd violence at a Test match in the West Indies occurred at Georgetown, British Guyana, during the unhappy MCC tour of the Caribbean in 1953–54. The Test match, it is relevant to note, took place against a background of political tension and crisis: just a few months previously, British troops had intervened directly in British Guyana to prevent the installation of an elected left-wing government under Cheddi Jagan, the constitution had been suspended and a number of local nationalist politicians interned.[37] The riot began when a partnership of ninety-nine between McWatt and Holt of the West Indies ended with McWatt, a local hero, being given out run out. There was, it seems, no doubt that the umpire's decision was correct, but it may be that the crowd was still upset by England's disputing of umpiring decisions during the previous match on the ground between MCC and British Guyana. A more likely cause is disappointment at the abrupt end of a partnership which seemed to be rescuing the West Indies from a calamitous first innings collapse; in addition, many members of the crowd are known to have placed bets on McWatt and Holt reaching a century partnership.[38] Whatever the cause, bottles and, according to Wisden, wooden packing cases were thrown on to the playing area, though there was no actual crowd 'invasion'. Despite urgent pleas from the President of the British Guyana Cricket Association, the England captain, Len Hutton, refused to lead his team off the field. Order was quickly restored, and England went on to win the match easily by nine wickets.

The second major incident again involved West Indies versus England, this time at Port of Spain in January–February 1960. Again a background of political tension may have had some bearing on events at Queen's Park Oval, though the links between politics and sport were far less clear-cut than in the earlier incident and in those that were to follow. It is more than likely, however, that the continuing controversy over the West Indian captaincy and its inevitable social and racial implications did have a considerable influence on events, since the 1959–60 series was the last occasion on which the West

Indies were led by a white captain, Gerry Alexander, who, in the eyes of Trinidadians, compounded the 'sin' of whiteness with being Jamaican as well. The immediate cause of the riot was, once more, a West Indian batting collapse: bottles were thrown on the third day when the home team had slumped to ninety-eight for eight in its first innings. No controversial umpiring decision was involved, though both umpires had previously cautioned the West Indian fast bowlers, Hall and Watson, for excessive bowling of bouncers; significantly, perhaps, one of the umpires, Lee Kow, was of Chinese origin and, as such, a representative not merely of 'authority' and 'law and order' but also of probably the most strongly disliked ethnic group in West Indian society. Whereas the first disturbance in British Guyana had been but a brief affair, in Trinidad six years later play was abandoned for the day. The England players were escorted from the field by the police though once again no animosity was shown towards them; as in the earlier match, England went on to win convincingly by 256 runs and, in so doing, won a Test series in the West Indies for the first time.

In the third major incident — that which occurred during the West Indies versus England Test match at Sabina Park in February 1968 — we can discern a clear link between the crowd's reaction and the general social and political climate in Jamaica towards the end of the 1960s. By 1968 it was apparent that the 'honeymoon period' that followed the gaining of political independence in 1962 had finally ended. There was widespread hostility to the Jamaica Labour Party government led by Hugh Shearer and a growing feeling throughout society that independence had changed little either in the island's internal social, economic and racial structure or in its relationship of dependence towards the outside world. Political and criminal violence was on the increase — it was often impossible to tell one form of violence from the other — and there was a growing receptiveness among young black Jamaicans both towards Rastafarianism and towards the Black Power ideas and attitudes that were beginning to reach the island from the United States, from West Indians living in Canada as well as from elsewhere in the Caribbean. It was surely no accident that, seven or eight months after the rioting at Sabina Park, downtown Kingston was to witness a far more serious and violent upsurge of popular protest in the wake of the government's decision to refuse the Guyanese Black Power leader Walter Rodney permission to re-enter the country where he was working as a university lecturer.[39] In early 1968, the authorities in general, and the police in particular, were undeniably nervous, and, in retrospect, it is hardly surprising that, yet again, a seemingly trivial incident at a cricket match should have sparked off such considerable violence.

The riot began in mid–afternoon on the third day of the Test match when England appeared to be well on the way to victory. The West Indies had been forced to follow on 233 runs behind and had reached 204 for four when Basil Butcher of Guyana was given out caught at the wicket; the decision was, by all accounts, perfectly correct,[40] though once again it is relevant to note that the umpire concerned, Donald Sang Hue, generally thought to be the best umpire in the Caribbean at the time, was a Jamaican of Chinese origin. As he walked off, Butcher slapped bat against pad in annoyance at getting out, a gesture which the crowd appears to have interpreted, quite wrongly, as meaning that he disagreed with the decision; as the batsman entered the pavilion, bottles and stones began to be thrown on to the playing area from the bleachers. Over-reacting in a manner that was becoming increasingly common in Jamaica at the time, the police duly released their tear-gas: unfortunately, the wind was in the wrong direction, and it was the players and the dignitaries (including the Governor-General and his wife) in the pavilion who suffered its effects! 'Order' was gradually restored, and after seventy-five minutes play was resumed though the England players, to say nothing of the hapless umpires, were clearly rattled. The West Indies recovered sufficiently to be able to declare at 391 for nine with Sobers making 113 not out, and by the end of the match England were struggling to survive at sixty-eight for eight. The last innings, says Wisden with some understatement, 'was played in a feverish atmosphere, which seemed to unsettle the umpires'.

Later in the same series versus England there was another incident which, though not a riot, is again highly indicative of West Indian attitudes towards cricket. The fourth Test at Port of Spain seemed to be heading for a peaceful draw when Sobers, the West Indies captain, abruptly and without justification declared at ninety-two for two, leaving England to score 215 in 165 minutes, a target they achieved without undue difficulty. The fury among Trinidadians and West Indians in general at Sobers's suicidal declaration knew no bounds. There was, Clive Lloyd writes in his autobiography, 'an eerie silence when we walked off the ground', and that evening, in a classically carnivalesque gesture, an effigy of Sobers was hanged and burned in Independence Square in the centre of Port of Spain; 'it was then that I really came to realize what losing meant to West Indians', is Lloyd's comment, 'a lesson I have never forgotten'.[41] Sobers's reputation both among the West Indian players and among West Indian cricket followers collapsed literally overnight. Previously he had been an almost God-like figure for many West Indians, especially in his native Barbados; now his authority over his players vanished and in the next few years, disintegrating once more into a collection of highly gifted but disunited individuals, the West Indians underwent the leanest period in their recent cricketing history, losing not only to Australia but also to India, and managing only to draw with New Zealand.[42]

This violent swing of public favour away from the charismatic cricket-hero Sobers may be set beside the fate that has commonly befallen erstwhile or would-be charismatic political leaders in the Caribbean such as Eric Williams of Trinidad or Michael Manley of Jamaica. West Indian politicians are often projected less as leaders than as potential Messiahs, as Moses-figures or — to invoke the name widely given to Michael Manley in the early 1970s — as political Joshuas who will shortly lead 'their' people into the Land of Milk and Honey. So long as these Joshua-figures succeed, they can, it is claimed, count on total devotion from their followers, but should they fail or be seen to fail, as Williams, Manley and, in his own field, Sobers were seen to have failed, they will be rejected with that same passionate uncritical completeness that they were but a short while ago revered. Nursing an almost unbearable sense of betrayal, the theory goes, the erstwhile followers will seek scapegoats on whom to vent their frustration: the saviour-traitor himself and/or a variety of outside forces, groups and individuals. Whether or not this theory of the relationship between leaders and led in West Indian politics is correct, it is surely significant that the only clear instance in West Indian cricket of violence being directed at the opposition players occurred during and immediately after the self-inflicted debacle at Port of Spain in 1968. The utterly blameless English captain Cowdrey was booed as he made the seventy-one that ensured England's victory and, after the final Test at Georgetown (a drawn match which gave England victory in the series), stones were thrown at the England team as it left the ground and poor Cowdrey was, it appears, virtually besieged in the pavilion until a police escort arrived to accompany him back to the team hotel.

The last 'incident' that I want to discuss, that which occurred on the last day of the Test match between the West Indies and Australia at Sabina Park in 1978, was in many ways the most serious, at least inasmuch as it led to the abandonment of a match which the West Indies were almost certain to lose. There can be no doubt that in 1978 the underlying cause of the riots lay in the widespread resentment throughout the West Indies concerning the organization of World Series Cricket by the Australian television magnate, Kerry Packer; characteristically, however, public resentment in the Caribbean was directed not at Packer himself, his organization or the players he had signed up — in the case of the West Indies, all the leading Test cricketers, minus Kallicharran — but above all against 'the authorities' as embodied in the West Indies Cricket Board of Control which, to a large extent, remained dominated by members of the old white and coloured West Indian élite.[43] After the West Indies had easily won the first two Tests with a team made up almost entirely of 'Packer players', a confrontation between the leading players and the Board was precipitated when three 'Packer players', Austin, Haynes and Deryck Murray, were dropped from the Test team. Clive Lloyd protested and resigned the captaincy, all the other 'Packer players' withdrew from the Test team, and the West Indies took the field for the third Test at Georgetown with an entirely new team composed of inexperienced but 'loyal' players captained by Kallicharran; not surprisingly, they lost by a considerable margin. Despite intense public feeling, there was, however, no crowd trouble either at Georgetown or during the fourth Test at Port of Spain compared with a normal Test attendance of 20,000 to 25,000 — and there was talk among cricket enthusiasts of boycotting the Tests completely until the Board agreed to reinstate the 'rebel' players. By the time of the final Test in Kingston some kind of crowd disturbance was likely, particularly given, once again, the highly charged political and social climate in Jamaica at the time: a crippling economic and financial crisis, endemic gang warfare, a widespread belief that the left-wing or left-inclined Manley government was being 'destabilized' by the CIA, increasingly violent confrontations between the governing People's National Party and the opposition Jamaica Labour Party, and so on.[44] The origins and nature of the riots follow a familiar pattern: a probable West Indian defeat (when the riots began, the West Indies were 258 for nine with six overs to go) combined with a controversial umpiring decision when Vanburn Holder was given out caught at the wicket — not, for once, by a Chinese umpire! — and lingered at the crease, apparently disagreeing with the decision. Almost on cue, stones and bottles began to be thrown, followed by predictably severe police intervention and the abandonment of the match. 'So a series bedevilled by rancour and controversy ended unhappily' is Wisden's dry comment.

Conclusions

What interpretation are we to put on such outbursts of rage and frustration which are now sufficiently commonplace to be regarded, as I say, as a permanent potentiality in West Indian cricket? It would, in the first instance, be simple-minded and misleading to view them as straightforward expressions of anti-English or anti-white hostility. With the one minor exception to which I have referred, the rioters' target — to the extent that they have identifiable targets — has been not the opposition team, whatever its colour, but the umpires or, more generally, 'the authorities' or, still more generally and, I suspect, most profoundly, 'the system'.

Orlando Patterson's explanation is more subtle. He argues that the West Indian attitude towards cricket is a deeply ambivalent one in which love and hate co-exist, but in which, contrary to appearances, it is actually the 'hate element' that predominates. Deep down, Patterson claims, West Indians hate cricket because it is the game of the colonizers and their local allies, the old white and coloured élites, and, to that extent, it embodies everything that the lower-class black West Indian is not; it functions as a constant reminder of his imposed economic, social, political, racial, cultural and personal inferiority. When black West Indians like himself triumph over the opposition — especially, obviously, when the opposition is white — his enthusiasm for the game knows no bounds. But should things go the other way, and the black heroes with whom he identifies be bested, or appear to be on the point of being bested, then his underlying hatred of the game — the game itself, not the players, the umpires or whatever — reasserts itself and in anger and frustration he destroys it with the most powerful and obvious, indeed the only, weapon at his disposal: violence.[45] Or, to use the cultural terms employed by Wilson and Abrahams, cricket, by dint of its English origins, embodies the established values of order and respectability from which the black West Indian male is alienated but, by dint of its subsequent creolization, has been, so to speak, turned against itself by black West Indians and made to embody the counter-values of aggression, reputation and individualism that govern street culture. All is well so long as the street ethic holds sway over the values of order and respectability but once order reasserts itself (that is, when the West Indies are defeated), the street culture of violence takes its revenge by stripping the whole affair of its symbolism and transforming it into an out-and-out physical confrontation of 'Us' and 'Them'.

This is all very well, but unfortunately for the theory there have been many occasions when West Indian crowds have peacefully and sportingly accepted the defeat of their team, even in such highly-charged and dramatic circumstances as the fifth Test versus England at Port of Spain in 1974 when England won by twenty-six runs with an hour to spare with Tony Greig — an archetypal 'hate figure' if ever there was one — taking thirteen wickets in the match. Patterson's theory also implies — and it is an implication which, one imagines, most West Indians would not accept — that the very success of West Indians at cricket is an expression not of achievement but of alienation and false consciousness. It could also be argued — and one can readily imagine certain Marxists taking this view — that cricket in the West Indies has the effect of neutralizing and defusing popular discontent and frustration by channelling them into an essentially harmless activity, an activity which, despite the violence it intermittently provokes, remains a play activity, a fiction, a lie. If this is so, then once again West Indian cricket closely resembles West Indian carnival whose long history, Michael Craton has written,

> shows how festival can actually be used as a safety valve or an anodyne by a ruling class, releasing harmlessly, or damping down, the energies of popular discontent so that actual revolution is averted or indefinitely postponed.[46]

Many questions remain: no doubt further research, less in libraries than at the Oval — Kennington or Kensington, it matters not — will help provide some answers.

Notes and References

The International Journal of Sports History are to be thanked for giving permission to reprint this article from their 1985 volume.

1 Among the mass of descriptive, historical and, above all, biographical and autobiographical material relating to West Indian cricket, three items, in addition to James, C.L.R. (1963) *Beyond a Boundary*, London, Stanley Paul, stand out. All have greatly contributed to the present study: Patterson, Orlando (1969) 'The Ritual of Cricket', *Jamaica Journal*, **III**, No. 1, reproduced in Salkey, Andrew (1973) (Ed.), *Caribbean Essays: An Anthology*, London, New Beacon Books, pp. 108–18; St. Pierre, Maurice (1973) 'West Indian Cricket: A Socio-Cultural Appraisal', *Caribbean Quarterly*, **XIX**, No. 2, pp. 7–27, and No. 3, pp. 20–35;

Thompson, L. O'Brien (1983) 'How Cricket is West Indian Cricket? Class, Racial and Colour Conflict', *Caribbean Review*, **XII**, No. 2, pp. 23–5 and pp. 50–53.

2 The reference is, of course, to Lord Kitchener's celebrated calypso 'Cricket, lovely cricket'.

3 See, in particular, Lamming, George (1960) *The Pleasures of Exile*, London, Joseph, especially pp. 15, 107 and 115.

4 For cultural pluralism in the Caribbean, see Smith, M.G. (1965) *The Plural Society in the British West Indies*, Berkeley, University of California Press.

5 For the theory of creolization, see Brathwaite, Edward (1971) *The Development of Creole Society in Jamaica 1770–1820*, Oxford, Oxford University Press, especially pp. 307–9, and Mintz, Sidney W. and Price, Richard (1976) *An Anthropological Approach to the Afro-American Past: A Caribbean Perspective*, Philadelphia.

6 Patterson, (1969), p. 109.

7 On the importance of the delimitation of space in play, see Huizinga, Johan (1970) *Homo Ludens, A Study of the Play Element in Culture*, London, Routledge and Kegan Paul, pp. 28–9.

8 On religion in the Caribbean, see Simpson, George Eaton (1978) *Black Religions in the New World*, New York.

9 See, among many other examples, the remarkable entry for April 1790 in *Souvenirs du Baron de Wimpffen, Saint-Domingue a la veille de la Revolution* (1911) Paris, p. 147.

10 For the whole of this question, see Brathwaite, Edward (1970) *Folk Culture of the Slaves of Jamaica*, Port of Spain, University of West Indies.

11 All quotations in Abrahams, Roger D. (1983) *The Man-of-Words in the West Indies, Performance and the Emergence of Creole Culture*, Baltimore, Johns Hopkins University Press, p. 52.

12 See Craton, Michael (1982) *Testing the Chains, Resistance to Slavery in the British West Indies*, Ithaca, pp. 235–6.

13 See Craton (1982), pp. 235–6 and pp. 299–316.

14 The following account is based on Hill, Errol (1972) *The Trinidad Carnival: Mandate for a National Theatre*, Austin, University of Texas Press, and Brereton, Bridget (1979) *Race Relations in Colonial Trinidad 1870–1900*, Cambridge, Cambridge University Press, especially Chapter 8, 'The souls of black folk', pp. 152–75.

15 See Brereton (1979), especially Chapter 8, 'The souls of black folk', pp. 152–75 and pp. 166–7.

16 See Hill (1972), pp. 21–4.

17 Brereton (1979), p. 162. On steel bands themselves, see Hill, (1972), pp. 48–51.

18 For the 'February Revolution' in Trinidad, see Oxaal, Ivar (1971) *Race and Revolutionary Consciousness*, Cambridge, MA, Shenkman Publishing.

19 See especially Abrahams, Roger D. (1976) *Talking Black*, Rowley, MA, Newbury House.

20 See Warner, Keith (1983) *The Trinidad Calypso*, London, Heinemann, pp. 11–20.

21 Hill (1972), pp. 24–7.

22 On jamet 'bands' in Trinidad, see Brereton (1979), p. 167.

23 Quoted in Hill (1972), p. 26.

24 See above all Ladurie, Emmanuel Le Roy (1980) *Carnival in Romans, A People's Uprising at Romans 1579–1580*, translated by Mary Feeney, London, Scolar, especially Chapter XII, 'The Winter Festival'.

25 Craton (1982), p. 235.

26 Warner (1983), pp. 15–16.

27 Brathwaite, Edward Kamau (1969) *Islands*, London, Oxford University Press, pp. 40–46, reprinted here by kind permission of Oxford University Press. This magnificent poem is essential reading for all who would understand the elaborate psychodrama of West Indian cricket.

28 Abrahams, Roger D. *The Man-of-Words in the West Indies*, pp. xv–xxxi.

29 Wilson, Peter J. *Crab Antics, The Social Anthropology of English-Speaking Negro Societies of the Caribbean*, New Haven, Yale University Press, especially Chapters 7 and 8.

30 Wilson (1973), pp. 165–8.

31 See especially Abrahams, *The Man-of-Words in the West Indies*, pp. 21–40.

32 See especially Abrahams, *The Man-of-Words in the West Indies*, pp. 21–40 and pp. 51–4.

33 Referring to the MCC tour of the West Indies in 1934–35, the 1936 edition of *Wisden* states (p. 617) that

> while the West Indians never resorted to the 'packed leg-side' and orthodox placing of the field was usual throughout the tour, some of the England players complained of occasional attempts at intimidation in the matter of short-pitched deliveries and full-tosses directed at the batsmen.

34 Patterson (1969), p. 117.

35 Patterson (1969), pp. 111–2.

36 The West Indians' reaction to Greig's 'grovel' remark is discussed in McDonald, Trevor (1984) *Viv Richards: The Authorised Biography*, London, Pelham, pp. 10–11.

37 On the 1953 constitutional crisis in British Guyiana, see Lewis, Gordon K. (1969) *The Growth of the Modern West Indies*, New York, Monthly Review Press, pp. 170–5.

38 See the account of the match given by the West Indies' captain at the time, Stollmeyer, Jeffrey (1983) *Everything Under the Sun, My Life in West Indies Cricket*, London, Stanley Paul, p. 148.

39 On Jamaica in the 1960s, see Lacey, Terry (1977) *Violence and Politics in Jamaica 1960–1970*, Manchester, Manchester University Press.

40 I have been told that, as the English wicket-keeper, Parks, took the catch

which dismissed Butcher, the back of his glove touched the ground. In the laws of cricket, so long as the ball does not touch the ground, this constitutes a perfectly legal catch, but my Jamaican interlocutor suggested that, according to the conventions of Jamaican street cricket, if the fielder's or wicket-keeper's hand touches the ground, as Parks's did, then the batsman is 'not out'. If this is so and I am right in attributing considerable importance to the formative influence of street cricket in the Caribbean, then the reactions of parts of the Sabina Park crowd become rather more comprehensible.

41 Lloyd, Clive (1983) *Living for Cricket*, London, W.H. Allen, pp. 45–6.
42 It is not always realized that between the third Test versus Australia in 1964–1965 and the first Test versus England in 1973–1974, the West Indies failed to record a single Test match victory in front of their own crowds in the Caribbean.
43 Many competing versions of the 'Packer intrusion' exist. The present account is based essentially on McDonald (1984), pp. 107–16 and Stollmeyer (1983), pp. 203–11.
44 For Jamaica in the 1970s, see Payne, Anthony J. and Sutton, Paul K. (Eds) (1984), *Dependency under Challenge: The Political Economy of the Commonwealth Caribbean*, Manchester, Manchester University Press, pp. 18–42.
45 Patterson (1969), pp. 113–14. See also St. Pierre, (1973), No. 3, pp. 27–35.
46 Craton (1982), p. 238.
47 *The International Journal of Sports' History* is to be thanked for giving permission to reprint this article from their 1985 volume.

Chapter 2

Sport, Schooling and Asian Male Youth Culture

Scott Fleming

Throughout the history of organized sport there have been numerous examples of the way that it has acted as a powerful vehicle for the development of ethnic identity and the expression of ethnic pride (Birbalsingh and Shiwcharan, 1988; Gorn, 1986; James, 1963; Shipley, 1989). For people from the Indian sub-continent, sport has been both emblematic of national aspiration (Miles and Khan, 1988, p. 7), and a divisive force fostering regional, ethnic and religious rivalries (Kureishi, 1989, p. 27). In the context of a hostile society, minority groups are using sport as an increasingly important means of establishing cultural identity and asserting independence (Hargreaves, 1986, p. 108). Roberts (1983, p. 154) elaborates: 'Some blacks see sport as an area for ethnic achievement where they can outplay whites at the latter's games, rules and grounds'. In the investigations of sport and 'race' or sport and ethnicity, however, there is a preoccupation with Afro/Caribbean sports stars — the various works of Ellis Cashmore (1981, 1982a, 1982b, 1983, 1986, 1990a, 1990b) are good illustrations; and as I have demonstrated elsewhere (Fleming, 1989, p. 95), the sporting participation, patterns, preferences and meanings of the Asian[1] communities in Britain are neglected and under-researched areas of investigation. The apparently 'exceptional' sporting exploits of some young Asians have been reported by the national press (Datar, 1989; Hopps, 1989; White, 1990), and a small number of studies have considered related topics (Carrington and Williams, 1988; Carrington, Chivers and Williams, 1987; Child, 1983; Lewis, 1979), but the significance and function of sport in Asian cultures is not yet adequately understood (Hargreaves, 1986, p. 108).

In view of the prevailing lack of understanding, the importance of school-based sporting activities should not be underestimated.

It is through frequent and regular exposure to formalized physical education lessons, organized extra-curricular clubs and teams, and informal 'play' that young Asians have the opportunity to formulate their own realities of sport and physical activity. It is also through these sources of social interaction that ethnic tension and racial conflict enter school sport (Hargreaves, 1986, p. 179).

This chapter provides an overview of a study of young Asian males in the highly influential environment of the secondary school. It deals with their daily lived experiences as expressed in their own words, and considers the implications for their perceptions of sport, and their participation in it. At the same time, it offers an analysis of the impact of personal racism on the role that sport plays in their leisure lifestyles, and presents a commentary on the masculinity of Asian male youth culture.

Data Collection

The following is one aspect of a larger project concerning sport and Asian youth cultures.[2] In the proven and well established case-study paradigm in the sociology of education (Ball, 1981; Burgess, 1983; Hargreaves, 1967; Lacey, 1970), the research was based at a single secondary school. A methodologically pluralist strategy was employed, but the focus of this analysis will be the ethnographic thrust of the research, drawing upon findings from participant observation and interview techniques of data collection.[3]

The approach adopted is necessarily interpretative, and seeks to describe and analyze the actors' interpretations of the social situations in which they find themselves. The main purpose, as Harris and Park (1983, p. 10) contend, 'is to communicate understandings about a culture which are held by the members of the culture themselves'. To this end, a theoretical framework based on an emergent typology provides a useful working model; not only as an organizing theme for this discussion, but more importantly, as a generalizable construct generated from the research. For though a single case-study is presented, its significance, as Lacey (1970, p. xi) explains of his own case-study analysis, 'is not confined to the particularistic concerns of one school. It extends to general problems in sociology and education'. Hence, an understanding derived from this specific situation increases the understanding of other such situations, and also informs wider debates.

The fieldwork was conducted during 1988 and 1989 at a large

mixed multi-ethnic inner-city secondary school. From the outset the study was concerned exclusively with Asian *male* youth, and as a physically large, white, adult researcher, I could not participate fully in the activities of that subject group. Thus the role I adopted was loosely and somewhat ambiguously couched in the dual role of researcher/writer and physical education teacher, but the image projected to informants was that of a sympathetic and approachable confidant.

The Setting

The Elm Park[4] estate is a sprawling residential area of north London. Streets of relatively modern, but otherwise unremarkable, terraced houses combine with a small number of drab multi-storey tenement blocks to create a sense of oppressive structural symmetry. The feeling of environmental claustrophobia, however, is eased by expanses of urban greenery, which also provide welcome splashes of colour.

At the heart of the estate are the two-storey buildings of Parkview School. Close by there is a large, modern 'show piece' sports centre, and a youth club that is popular with the Parkview pupils. The immediate scene is a mixture of breezeblock and green fields, fenced playgrounds and grassy verges, open spaces and quiet corners. Around the school there is evidence of use and of the users: an ice-cream van in the car park, discarded cigarette-ends behind the bike sheds, distorted wire fences, and the ubiquitous hieroglyphic 'tags'.[5]

The school caters for 1,000 pupils, including a small sixth form, with males and females represented in approximately equal numbers. The school population is drawn from a predominantly working-class catchment area that extends beyond the Elm Park estate, and is representative of the rich ethnic mix and cultural diversity of the borough in which it is located.

The Asian males at Parkview number fifty, and reflect the complexity of the multi-cultural and multi-religious heterogeneity of the Asian communities in Britain. They are influenced by national and religious variables — as well as more specific regional differences, language, class and 'caste', familiarity with culture of origin, and other differences associated with an urban or rural lifestyle.

In the context of the school, however, these characteristics of heterogeneity are not the only criteria upon which young Asian males structure their social interaction and behaviour. In an investigation of the meanings and values attached to sport, an analysis based on such criteria individually, or even collectively, has proved inconclusive (Fleming, 1990, p. 5). A more appropriate point of departure is a consideration of experiential commonalities, the social divisions that occur, and the type of interaction that takes place.

At Parkview there are four broad categories that can be easily identified. They are not strictly defined according to any specific cultural parameters; but most individuals, most of the time, can be identified as a member of one of them from his behaviour and general demeanour. Of the fifty male Asian pupils, sixteen are 'Victims', nineteen are 'Straights', six are 'Boffins' and nine are 'Street-kids'.

The Victims — 'Everyone picks on us, I think they hate us'

The Victims can be simply defined as persecuted migrants from Bangladesh. They are strict Muslims, and many of them have left a rural environment to settle in Britain. They are committed to their traditional religious and cultural way of life, and this influences their involvement in sport. They are invariably part of large, sometimes very large, working-class families, struggling against the multiple difficulties of poor housing and unemployment.

In the social environment of the school, the Victims perceive themselves to be 'picked on', and the evidence they cite supports that view. They are unpopular because they are 'different' in their culture, appearance and behaviour, and because they are often submissive in the face of undisguised hostility from the other pupils in the school.

> They [the other pupils][6] call me 'Paki' and 'faggot'. It's because they find me soft — they can pick on me. I don't talk a lot, so they think I can't fight. (Rashid)

Their unfashionable clothes and their unwillingness to communicate with each other in English, accentuate their 'differentness', and draw attention to it.

The Victims are subjected to verbal abuse and physical bullying on a regular basis, and this significantly shapes their day-to-day school life. They live in fear of it, and they feel the powerlessness of their situation very acutely. They refer to the other pupils, particularly those that deliver the abuse as 'them' and 'they':

We don't like them because they say things to us, 'Paki', 'smelly-face', 'fucking bastard'. If we say them back, they hit us. If we do anything, they are going to hit us. (Akram)

I am scared of them. Stewart started hitting me once, and everyone came and hit me. They don't like me. They hit me everyday, I don't know why. (Mukhtar)

I tell Miss, but she didn't do anything. (Massur)

Not surprisingly, they are reluctant to seek popularity outside their immediate group of Bangladeshi friends. They retreat to the security of kinship networks and public spaces of relative safety, which merely serves to alienate them further.

The Victims' experiences of sport are largely confined to what is done in school. Their opportunities to take part outside school are very limited, as they often have important family, religious and cultural commitments to attend to:

I can't stay after school, I have to go home with my sisters and read Koran. (Mukhtar)

If I don't read the Koran I get beaten. My dad says I have to pray. (Akram)

The Victims at Parkview are frequently excluded from any of the informal playground activities of other young males. They are not invited to take part in playground games of football, and any games that they do play are disrupted. Consequently, they are forced to seek the refuge of the relative safety of the lawn in front of the staff common room, associating proximity to staff with avoidance of danger. They use it to play the sorts of 'chasing' games more readily associated with much younger children.

They [the other boys] don't say 'Come and play football with us', so we play on our own. In the first year we had two footballs. We don't want to play with them because they push us, and they don't pass it [the football] to us. Boys stole one of them and kicked it on the roof of the hall, and we say we aren't playing there because they nick the ball and kick it away. So we play on our own on the grass. We like it there.

> We play 'He' games — if you go off the grass you're out.
> (Akram)

As a result, their involvement in all types of play suffers, they have a deficient vocabulary of basic motor skills, and their sporting competences are clearly underdeveloped.

Their opportunities for involvement in sport are therefore restricted to physical education lessons; but for the Victims, physical education is no different from any other aspect of their daily existence. Personal racist abuse — both verbal and physical — is as prevalent there as elsewhere.

> I was tackling Mark and he didn't want me to take the ball off him, and by mistake I just pushed him, so he started swearing at me, very rude — 'You "Paki", bastard, idiot, get back to your own country'. (Aslam)

Moreover, what they consider to be physical violence directed against them is often legitimized through sport.

> I like football, all the Bengalis do. But people think we are not good; we can't stop the ball. They have boots on and they kick us. (Akbar)

The harsh reality is that for the Victims, sport through physical education is not the 'great equalizer' that it is often claimed to be. On the contrary, the inequality is evident even before the lesson begins from the physical education kit that is worn.

> Those kids in the second year [a group of Victims], their parents are not rich, and they don't wear good trainers like 'Reebok', 'Nike' and so on. So the other kids, they say 'Oh look at him, he's got shit trainers' or 'they're crap trainers', and they take the Mick. (Rashid)

Thus by their appearance alone, the Victims are isolated, marginalized and ridiculed, and their experiences of participation reflect this. Further social stratification occurs as a result of apparent success or failure in sport. Low sporting ability is very visible and frequently results in rejection by peers, especially when it merely confirms some of the stereotypic assumptions that are made about Asians in sport.

Even within physical education lessons, therefore, some Victims are denied some of their opportunities to take a fully active part in sport. Football is a high-status activity among young working-class males, and could be the unique opportunity for contributing to 'multi-racial' understanding and harmony that Townsend and Brittan (1973, p. 32) suggest. Yet the Victims start with little emphasis placed on their 'play learning activities' (Coventry LEA, 1980, p. 43), they have little or no prestige in sport, and are invariably not permitted the opportunity to gain any. Far from breaking down cultural barriers and encouraging tolerance, sport serves to maintain and fortify ethnic boundaries (Allison, 1982, p. 166), and is a source of discord and conflict (Sargeant, 1972, p. 225).

In spite of this, the Victims' attitude to physical education is very positive: 'I love it. It keeps me fit and I enjoy it' (Rashid). This is all the more surprising in view of the religious and cultural considerations that undoubtedly influence their perceptions of physical education and sport, and their participation in it. The approach that recognizes the problems faced by Asians in relation to cultural diversity in physical education has caused concern (Bayliss, 1989, p. 19), but certain Asian lifestyles do mitigate against participation in sport (White, 1990, p. 29). The Victims are clearly affected by at least three of the so-called 'problems'. First, showering after physical education, often identified as an important issue for Asians (Coventry LEA, 1980, p. 35; Sarwar, 1983, p. 14), causes some of the Victims some genuine anxiety. On more than one occasion Akram (a younger Victim) chose not to take part in physical education lessons, and in so doing incurred the usual sanction imposed on non-participants, writing lines. To Akram and some of his Victim friends, writing lines was a preferable alternative to taking part in the lesson. Reluctantly, he explained:

> We don't like showers because it's cold and we are shy to take our clothes off. Muslims are supposed to be shy. That's why I don't do shower at school. (Akram)

Second, involvement in dance as part of the physical education curriculum poses another potential moral and cultural dilemma for some of the Victims. For though Lashley (1980b, p. 71) remarks on the cultural significance of dance to various groups of young Asians, and Kansara (1984, p. 22) describes the value of Indian dance for fostering respect for a variety of cultures, it can also cause a real moral and cultural predicament:

> Our religion [Islam] says you don't dance, to music and that
> ... Our holy book says if you dance, you get punishment.
> (Rafiq)

Third, the relative unimportance of sport for the Victims means
that it is often low on their list of priorities. Prayer is one important
aspect of Muslim lifestyle that many strict Muslims prioritize ahead of
sport. Rashid comments on the difficulty encountered if the pattern of
Muslim prayer is to be devoutly adhered to:

> It's quite difficult for me. I have to pray five times a day. If I
> have to pray at twelve o'clock, and there's a match, I can't
> play ... If it's a matter of 'life and death', you can pray
> afterwards. But sport doesn't count as a matter of 'life and
> death'. (Rashid)

The Victims are caught in a vicious circle where the difference in
sports skill level between them and their peers from other ethno-
cultural groups is constantly increasing. Sport is becoming less and
less attractive to them. They are suffering abuse in their sporting
experiences — sometimes for their lack of sporting ability, sometimes
taunts and bullying that are motivated by overt racism. They are
made 'uncomfortable' by the post-sport ritual of the communal shower, and for these reasons may choose not to take part in activities that
they actually enjoy. They have few opportunities to take part in sport,
and these are diminishing.

The Straights — 'Hindus aren't that good at football'

The Straights are basically conformers. Many are the British-born
sons of Asian parents, and do not belong to any particular religious
group. They are still committed to their religion and traditional culture, though for some, maintaining this is proving to be difficult as
they strive to assimilate into a predominantly Western culture. Rajesh
and his family, for example, are not strongly committed to the Hindu
faith. They adhere to certain Hindu codes of behaviour — those that
are easiest to observe, but there are many others that they choose to
ignore, especially for functional purposes:

> My dad does not believe a lot. He goes to the pub. He drinks
> alcohol and he smokes. And he once won £85 on the pools.

We speak Gujerati at home, but my dad sometimes makes us speak English at home, because it's necessary for jobs. (Rajesh)

Many of the Straights are caught 'between two cultures'. Neither totally Asian nor fully Westernized, they often express uncertainty about their individual cultural identity, though, interestingly, few expressed the inter-generational conflict that has been considered symptomatic of the difficulties facing young Asians in Britain (CRC, 1976, p. 7).

They are keen to achieve academically, and view education as their most accessible means of upward social mobility. Career aspirations are often directed toward the affluence, material rewards and status of the professions, and because professional sport is considered to require a negligible intellectual capacity, it is held in low esteem:

A lawyer, an accountant, or an engineer ... Sikhs take the attitude that a lawyer or an accountant is better than sport. Parents want their children to be fit, clever and everything. But the attitude is that you don't have to be clever to be a sportsman, you can be really stupid. They'd rather you be clever. (Ranjit)

Some, however, are realistic enough to appreciate that the academic success and qualifications required to enter the professions may be beyond them:

I have chosen to do electronics engineer. First of all I wanted to be policeman, but you don't get much money at it. Then I chose mechanic, but it's not for me. Then I chose electronics engineer. I'll see how physics goes, if I'm no good at it I'll be a mechanic. I want to work for someone then get my own business. (Ravi)

The Straights are also subjected to personal racist abuse, and while this angers many, they tend to succumb to the apparent futility of confrontation, and accept it with self-imposed tolerance:

I don't like it when people call me 'Paki' and so on. I feel like hitting them, but I don't like fighting, and you get into trouble. (Rajesh)

I get angry because I'm not really a 'Paki', but I still get called it ... If they're older than me I ignore them. If they're younger I tell them not to do it ... I don't get into fights, I don't like fighting. (Arun)

I hate the name — being called 'Paki' ... I'd just like to beat them up, but I just ignore them, 'cos they are bigger than me and they can beat me up. Even if they were weaker I wouldn't 'cos some of the weak boys have big brothers and sisters who might beat me up. I just wish I was big and strong. (Javinder)

As a consequence the Straights seem to avoid conflict situations, and are cautious about where they go, when, and with whom.

I'm careful, I don't go down alleyways and stuff, and I don't go to some places. If I go out in the night I just walk along the main roads. I don't live far from the tube station, so it doesn't matter, and I just walk home; no problem. (Farukh)

They modify their behaviour to avoid confrontation and abuse. This takes them away from a number of scenes of social interaction, and inevitably includes leisure and sporting venues.

Their experiences of sport at Parkview also reflect racial tension and acrimony.

If I am a goalkeeper and I let in a goal, people say 'Look you fucking "Paki", you can't do anything' — that happens even at school. (Naresh)

The Straights are, however, positively motivated towards physical education. They always take part, and wear the regulation kit; but seldom involve themselves in extra-curricular sports clubs and teams. Physical education is frequently seen as a welcome distraction from the classroom, and serves a number of functions:

It's good. You get to do some exercise, so you're more fit and healthy. And it's enjoyable. (Naresh)

It's not like other lessons because the time passes quicker, and it's not so long till going home. (Gurmit)

If I do lots of sport, it helps me to be skinny. (Ravi)

Overall, the general attitude to sport is also favourable. In addition to the health-related benefits, the Straights acknowledge the cognitive, social and enjoyable aspects of sport.

> Sport is good because it's a good way of keeping fit, because it's fun. Some people will do twenty press-ups for a good workout, but not everyone likes that. So you can run about in games like football. You're more active, and you use your brain more. You get to meet people as well. (Javinder)

The Straights tend to have a restricted range of leisure-time interests which are often home and/or family centred, but often include snooker as a sporting activity. A typical evening after school was described thus:

> In the evenings I do my homework for about an hour, and I watch television — I do a lot of that. Sometimes I go upstairs and play on my computer if there's nothing on television. And I don't have time for anything else. (Ranjit)

They tend not to participate in sports clubs outside school that require regular attendance. Some take part in recreational physical activities as part of their family's leisure, while others become involved in sport through religious and cultural commitments. The local Sikh Temple hosts a number of low-key and non-serious sports clubs.

> It was announced at the Temple, and mum said 'Why don't you go and see what it's like?' So I did. We play badminton, basketball and volleyball; and we're going to start playing hockey and football as well. (Javinder)

Some of the Straights are evidently affected by various, sometimes conflicting, perceptions of Asians in sport. Two seemingly contradictory views of Sikhs exist. On the one hand, there is an emphasis on musicality at the expense of sport in Sikh culture:

> Most of the Sikh people are into music not sport ... All sorts, pop and disco music. (Sanjit)

On the other, participation in sport may actually be valued by the Sikh religion:

If anything my religion probably encourages it. (Javinder)

The latter view is supported by some quasi-historical evidence:

> The last Guru was a fighter, and he used to race a lot and keep his body fit. The Sikhs were being terrorized by Muslims and people like that, so he fought them, and taught the other Sikhs to fight. And he said 'You've got to be fit, you can't be fat and podgy'. So he gave them exercises. (Javinder)

There is, understandably, a sense in which these views are somewhat self-serving. Javinder is very enthusiastic about sport, while Sanjit, by his own admission, would prefer not to do sport:

> It's tiring ... I don't like exercise, it pains me. (Sanjit)

For the Straights generally, more common perceptions are the prevalent stereotypes of Asians, especially those concerning football and cricket.

> Hindus aren't that good at football ... They don't know how to play football, they only know how to play cricket ... Cricket is a famous game in India. Their ancestors taught them how to play, so they still play. But they don't want to play football, they don't like it. (Rajesh)

An awareness of the absence of Asian footballers seems to confirm the suspicion about relative sporting abilities held by some of the Straights; and justified, in part, by success and preoccupation with games and activities more extensively practised on the Indian subcontinent.

> I had a football book and there was no Indian playing for any team. They're probably no good. Well, some of them might be good, but the people who are good, they will have other jobs or something like that ... They don't play football very much in India, they play loads of Indian games — marbles and Kabaddi.[8] (Arun)

This suspicion is reinforced by their own experiences of sport at the lowest level where Asians are proportionally under-represented in participation statistics.

> I went to [the sports centre] with my dad, and I looked very carefully, and I saw that there weren't any Indians there ... They must be scared of coming there as well ... I don't know why, but I kept looking to see any Indians there. I was wondering why there weren't any Indians. We were the only ones and I was a bit scared ... White people don't like us, and they might do something. I was embarrassed, I couldn't find any Indians doing anything. That's what my brother is scared of, no Indians there. (Rajesh)

The Straights are keen to assimilate into British society, and sport is one scene of social interaction that is perceived to be confrontational. Hence, they often choose to avoid it. Rajesh (a 14-year-old Straight) explained how he thought even his allegiance to Indian sporting teams could pose difficulties for him, should the Indian teams become successful:

> I'll give you an example. Brian is an Arsenal fan and Stefan is a West Ham fan. Once West Ham won against Arsenal, and Brian was so angry he started to beat him up. And if there was an Indian team against someone, and if the Indian one won, they would beat me up. (Rajesh)

Sport is not an important part of the Straight's lifestyles, and for families that are socially and economically disadvantaged in particular, sport and exercise do not rank as a priority (Malik, 1988, p. 4).

The Boffins — 'Maybe we're just not interested in sport'

As a sub-group of the Straights, the Boffins have much in common with them. They too are conformers, and very 'respectable'. Most are very aware of their religion and traditional culture, but are more strongly committed to it. Their fathers, who greatly influence the Boffins, aspire to the material rewards and comforts of the middle classes, and are ambitious for their sons. The Boffins are very sensitive to this ambition, and are highly motivated to achieve at school, reflecting the high esteem in which education is held by many Asian families (Dove, 1975, p. 65; Hiro, 1973, p. 178). Achievement is equated to examination qualifications, and for them, high educational achievement is a realistic expectation.

The Boffins encounter personal racist abuse in sport — particularly football — as in other spheres of life. The coping strategy is to question the appropriateness of the insults, and reason that if they do not apply, then they need not cause offence:

The sort of thing I get most often is 'Paki' or something like that. But I'm not really all that bothered because I'm not a Pakistani. (Suman)

Occasionally they call me 'Paki' and stuff . . . I just ignore it, I don't come from that country, don't come from that part of the world. I just ignore it. (Paramjit)

Minority ethnic groups at Parkview constitute the majority of the school population (about 55 per cent), and the school is seen as something of a cultural 'melting pot'. Different ethnic groups are striving to assert their cultural identity all the time, and occasionally this manifests itself as abuse of other groups. It is this that seems to cause the Boffins most unease and alarm.

I find that very offensive. They're attacking a whole country, a body of people. If someone says anything to me, 'Paki' or whatever, I don't take it personally. But if it's about my family, then that's when it hurts. (Suman)

Their leisure-time activities are all pursued with vigour and enthusiasm, and often include a wide range of interests:

Homework, television, reading adventure and science fiction stories, going to the shops, playing the piano, judo, and going to the cinema. (Suman)

These are pursued with parental encouragement, but on the condition that studies do not suffer as a result.

Boffins evidently enjoy physical education, but it can prove to be something of an inconvenience, as it is seen as an unnecessary and unwelcome distraction from the important business of being prepared for academic exams. Through physical education there is also the opportunity for 'differentness' to be highlighted and ridiculed. Sohan, for example, takes trouble to avoid drawing attention to the 'Kusti',[9] a religious adornment that he, as a Zoroastrian, is supposed to wear at all times. He removes it either at home before going to school, or when he goes home at lunchtime. The Kusti never actually poses a difficulty for him, he doesn't allow it to. What is important though, is that he thinks it might:

> I was concerned that other people might make fun of the cord when they see me get changed, because they might find it unusual. (Sohan)

The Boffins have a real sense of relevance of their qualifications, and GCSE physical education, though a qualification like any other, is deemed by some older Boffins less 'valuable' than other subject areas:

> If I choose physical education, I can't do one of the other more important subjects. (Sohan)

The Boffins appreciate the instrumental values of sport for maintaining physical and mental fitness, acquiring specific skills, encouraging team spirit and 'sporting' behaviour, and engendering strict discipline. They tend to see sport in these terms rather than for any of its intrinsic rewards. Many choose sporting activities that they consider will have a 'useful' purpose for them, with self-defence and the martial arts being especially popular. Indeed some of their sporting interests are pursued because of the threat of physical attacks.

> Doing Judo's good because I can defend myself if I ever get attacked ... That's why I started it, I haven't been attacked yet, but if I was I think I could look after myself better. (Sohan)

The Boffins have an interest in sport, and a favourable attitude towards it, but tend not to consider it as a possible career. Their analysis of the functions of sport is more concerned with its health-related outcome, and value to whole communities. Suman commented:

> Sport is important to the Zoroastrian community because it improves your health, body and mind.

Their perception is shaped further by their own understandings of Asian involvement in sport, and interestingly these understandings are expressed in the 'third person':

Not many Asian people go into sport. They don't get recognized too much, it's mostly white people ... There's hardly
any Asian players in the football world. In the Asians there's
less people going into football. They go on to other jobs, and
do other things. They're just as good at sport but they do
other things. (Paramjit)

An extended general knowledge that reflects their interest in sport,
gives the Boffins, especially those in the sixth form, a heightened
awareness of sportsmen (though not sportswomen) from the Indian
sub-continent.

I know [of] Vijay Amritraj, and there's Ramesh Krishnan; and
the squash players, they're Muslims, Jansher Khan, Jahangir
Khan. I know [of] some of the cricketers as well, Imran
Khan, Kapil Dev, Gavaskar ... As sportsmen I think they're
good, but I couldn't really say that they inspire me. (Suman)

Asians are disproportionately under-represented in the high-
profile media sports that influence working-class Asian youths —
athletics, boxing and football, though in Bradford, where cricket is
the central leisure-time pursuit of many young Asian boys, the Pakistani all-rounder Wasim Akram is one sportsman with whom many
of them do identify (White, 1990, p. 29). The Boffins identify the
absence of Asian sporting role-models as being of considerable
importance, and relate this to the effects of discrimination. In so
doing they acknowledge the stereotypic academic Asian:

English people see Asian doctors, and they just assume that all
Asians are going to become doctors. So I would be glad to see
some Asian people in football. (Paramjit)

The link between this perceived absence and the various mechanisms
of discrimination is cautiously hypothesized:

I've never seen any Indian footballers. I don't know if it's the
Indians being too shy to play football, or just being rejected —
perhaps because of their ability or the colour of their skin.
(Devendra)

The more forthright opinion of the powerful forces of discrimination against Asians is also expressed, and again Paramjit, a
14-year-old Boffin, speaks in the 'third person'.

Their colour doesn't change their ability does it? . . . But the
other people don't let them play. The black and whites don't
let them play, and won't allow them to play. (Paramjit)

For the Boffins, sport is only a very peripheral 'life interest'. It is
only one part of a very full programme of leisure-time activities.
Their experiences of personal racism in sport reflect their day-to-day
existence, but these do not deflect the Boffins from an interest in
sport. Paradoxically, they may even have stimulated the interest in a
functional sporting activity that some of the Boffins believe may be
used to combat racism.

The Street-Kids — 'If you're quiet and Asian, you're open to prejudism (sic)'

The youths in this group are very 'street-wise'. They are mostly
British-born Asians who have lost their strong commitment to traditional religious values and cultural mores; they are very aware of their
'colour', however, and they take great pride in it.

I can't get rid of my colour, I have to face up to my colour.
I'm proud of it. It depends how you take it. If you think your
colour's bad, then that's a bad thing. But if you think about
your colour — you have to put up with it. You have to like or
lump it, and I like it. (Dinesh)

They form part of a much larger multi-ethnic street gang that has
an integrated sub-culture that is heavily influenced by Caribbean
youth street culture. Occasional deviant behaviour, and a general
reluctance to accept the authority of the school establishment, has led
to some of them being viewed with suspicion by members of the
school's staff. Indeed, for Street-kids, there is a good deal of 'sport' to
be had in the high-status activity of giving the school's teachers a
'hard time' by being generally uncooperative and disruptive.

The clothes they wear constitute the 'uniform' of the street:
loose-fitting shirt; baggy jeans; a jacket of leather, pseudo-leather, or
denim, or a ski-jacket; running shoes or basketball boots (with laces
left untied); and personal stereo. All of it is fashionable, and there is
appreciable kudos to be gained by wearing new and expensive training shoes with a recognized brand name.

It's the way people dress. In this school there's Jayant in the fifth year, and the way he dresses, they all like him, he's trendy. So he doesn't have a problem. (Ranjit)

At Parkview they are respected, though not necessarily admired, by the other Asians, and enjoy high social status amongst their peers. They are hostile to any remarks made with racist intent, and used to get into numerous fights over this. They have all acquired a reputation as fighters, and hence do not get insulted with the frequency that they used to — thereby supporting the suggestion that attacks on Asians decrease as the ability to fight increases (CARF, 1981, p. 47). Within this street gang, the group members often address each other by terms of racist abuse,

Sometimes my friends — Tony, Virendra[10] — say stuff like 'Paki' or 'Nigger', and I suppose it's kind of racist, but they don't really mean it. It's a joke. (Ranjit)

If, however, the comment were not made as 'a joke', the reaction would be somewhat different:

Someone once called me 'Paki' in the street. He didn't know me, so me and my mates went and beat him up ... If I know someone says something as a joke, it'd be different. But if he was serious I'd go and kick his head in. (Dinesh)

At break-times during the school day the Street-kids can often be found kicking a football around, or playing either 'pool' or table-football at the local youth club with the gang. A good deal of time is also spent 'doing nothing' or 'hanging around', which was described as:

Going out with my mates, having a few laughs, walking around the streets, smoking a few fags, and having a couple of drinks. (Jitendra)

Generally the Street-kids are positively motivated towards physical education, but tend to 'vote with their feet' by excluding themselves from activities that they do not enjoy:

It depends what sport. I don't like things like badminton, it's boring. I don't like volleyball, it's boring too, and dance and gym ... I find football interesting, I like it, and play it a lot. I like hockey as well. (Ranjit)

They opt to continue with it beyond the Third Year when it ceases to be compulsory, seeing it as preferable to sitting in a class-room. Some take the GCSE physical education option,

I decided I was going to do physical education; it's better than proper lessons 'innit'! And I thought I might as well do the GCSE to get a qualification out of it. (Dinesh)

More opt to do recreation physical education,

GCSE wouldn't help me as a mechanic ... I wanted one lesson when I didn't have to think about school, and I could mess about. And I like physical education, it keeps you fit. (Suresh)

For those not engaged on the GCSE option, physical education also enables them to express their dissatisfaction with the authority structure of the school. By not wearing correct physical education kit, or even bothering to change out of their 'everyday' clothes, they are able, in a very clear and visible way, to 'buck the system', thereby causing members of the Parkview staff substantial irritation.

I just can't be bothered to bring all the kit. And if Mr Taylor [physical education teacher] is saying that we've got to bring all our kit, we'll leave it in the classroom. Never wash it, just bring it out, and never have a shower. Or most probably, we'll go in the shower and use the same smelly towel every week. It's a waste of time really. But it's Mr Taylor's new rules, and we're laying down a new way to get out of it. (Suresh)

Sport, or more specifically football, plays an important part in the lifestyle of Asian Street-kids, though they are seldom sufficiently motivated or committed to join and remain a member of a sports club or team.

If they wanted me to play for the school team, I would; but I'm not interested in all the training and going to away games and that. (Salim)

They play a lot of informal, non-serious 'pick-up' games in parks, in playgrounds, or on the streets. Football is characterized not by eleven-a-side teams, goal posts, nets, corner flags, and referees, but by a non-competitive informal 'kick-about' that enables them to show off their skills — many of which would have little value in the full game, but which look impressive. They describe themselves as supporters of one of the local First Division football teams, but this seldom extends to attending live games. For this, they are often accused, in a good-humoured way, of being 'armchair supporters' by other members of the street gang.

Despite their interest in football, though, the Street-kids do not dream of becoming professional players, and have more realistic and attainable career goals:

I'm only interested in it [football] as a hobby. I want to be an electrician. (Dinesh)

The implication is that football and paid employment are perceived as mutually exclusive:

Asians aren't really interested as much in football as getting a job. (Salim)

Thus, while there may be unrestricted and multiple avenues for a young Asian to achieve wealth, status and a feeling of self-adequacy (Cashmore, 1982a, p. 63), sport is not seen as one of them.

I never thought of doing it [sport] and earning money ... They [Asians] see it like me. They don't see it as a money-making prospect. (Jitendra)

The processes identified by Cashmore (1990b, pp. 79–93) that make sport seem like an attractive 'way out' for young blacks (by which he means Afro/Caribbeans), do not, therefore, apply to the Street-kids and to young Asians in general. The attitudes of the Street-kids shed some light on this. Unlike the Afro/Caribbeans to whom Cashmore (1990b, p. 70) refers, the Street-kids do not see sport as a mechanism through which they can escape the limits imposed on them because of their 'race' and because of racism.

Perceived parental attitudes also reflect the esteem in which sport is held by older Asians:

> I doubt my dad wants me to take up sports. He says 'Try to get a good job, and don't waste your time on sport'. Dad would rather I got a real job. (Suresh)

Such attitudes are strengthened by the absence of sporting role-models which confirm the marginal status of sport as a career outlet:

> They don't really see Indian people doing sports, they think no one does it really. (Salim)

Yet somewhat incongruously, the Street-kids are aware of the stereotypical view of Asians' involvement in sport, and curiously Jitendra, a Street-kid, also talks of this view of Asians in the 'third person':

> They only play certain types of sport. There's cricket, badminton, squash ... Hmm, I think that's it. They're the most publicized with Asians in it. They don't play the others. (Jitendra)

Their experiences of sport have not been without personal racist abuse being directed at them, but this is accepted as part of their normal existence.

> Now and then when I go down the park to play football, they [people at the park] say things like 'Get back to your own country "Paki", What are you doing here? Your lot can't play football'. At the time you just swear back: 'Fuck off! You don't know what you're talking about'. Or sometimes I just lose my temper and say 'OK, if you want to fight, let's fight now'. Sometimes they back off, but sometimes they start fighting; I've had lots of fights. I used to get called a lot — a couple of years ago — but not so much now. (Dinesh)

Despite this coping strategy, the influence of personal racism is an important factor in an analysis of Asians' sports participation.

> Asians can't be bothered. Either that or they're scared. If they get called racist names and that, they'll lose confidence. (Jayant)

Concluding Comments

The young Asian males at Parkview School are a heterogeneous population. They come from a range of ethno-cultural backgrounds, and their lifestyles are clearly affected by a myriad of complex inter-related variables. Yet their shared perceptions and experiences of daily life generally, and sport in particular, enable them to be identified in terms of a four-category typology. The Victims, Straights, Boffins and Street-kids all respond differently to their experiences, but there are certain common themes that apply to them all.

The common denominator across all categories is pervasive personal racism. It includes a whole range of phenomena from verbal abuse, through offensive graffiti, to physical violence; and is the most prominent single factor in shaping attitudes to sport and physical activity. This finding confirms the centrality of racism as a crucial component in understanding the leisure relations of Asians throughout Britain (Bradford YRT, 1988, p. 57; Carrington, Chivers and Williams, 1987, p. 274). There are different reactions to it. The Victims suffer most, but then so, it seems, do Bangladeshis generally (Coleman, 1990, p. 23; Kerridge, 1989, p. 12). They submissively retreat, and consequently they are denied opportunities to participate in sport. The Straights are both cautious and tolerant, and try to avoid the conflict of sport and the hostility — either real or imagined — of sporting venues. Boffins respond by rationalizing the nature of the abuse, and develop a coping strategy that in some instances includes the pursuit of sporting activities that are considered valuable for self-defence. The Street-kids confront racism directly, and it would appear that their sporting behaviour is not significantly altered by it. However, membership of the street gang is almost incompatible with the acquiescence to authority that representing school teams implies, and a rejection of the work-ethic associated with committed sport participation. Thus peer group pressure indirectly restricts involvement in a number of sporting activities.

There are other spheres of influence that seem to be common across all categories. The absence of Asians in certain sports, especially the high-status activity of football, is identified by them all. Coakley (1986, p. 149) suggests that interest and motivation to participate in sport is determined, at least in part, by how chances for involvement and success are defined; and in this regard role-models are of critical importance. In spite of the international achievements of some Asian sportsmen and sportswomen from the Indian sub-continent in cricket, hockey, squash, tennis and weight-lifting, and the success of Asian cricketers and hockey players in Britain, the young Asians at Parkview are largely unaware of them. This is perhaps not too surprising, for as Cashmore (1990a, p. 11) observes, cricket in particular is 'organised along stubborn traditional elitist lines', and so too are the other sports in which Asians have been seen to be successful. The traditional élitism inherent in these sports makes them seen unlikely avenues for young Asians to succeed in sport. In addition, these sports tend to be accessible only to the middle class (Cashmore, 1990b, p. 86), and with limited disposable income and access to sporting facilities being significant constraining factors, these sports are not those with which the young Asian males at Parkview associate themselves. For whilst some have heard, for example, of Imran Khan, they identify more readily with non-Asian sports stars from athletics and football, but they do so without ever expressing a desire to become a professional footballer. As Datar (1989, p. 20) comments,

> What [one 12-year-old Bengali] and his soccer-mad mates do not have, by way of encouragement or role model, is a single player from Britain's various Asian communities in a professional league side.

The absence of role-models serves to confirm the view apparently held by many Asian parents, that sport and physical education is 'just playing around' (Carrington and Williams, 1988, p. 88), and therefore, at best, less valuable than academic subjects (Coventry LEA, 1980, p. 29), and at worst, a waste of time (White, 1990, p. 29). Furthermore, without any evidence to the contrary, the predominant perception of Asians in sport has progressed little beyond gross stereotypes (Kew, 1979, p. 31). There is still a view that Asian pupils are below par in physical education (Craft and Klein, 1986, p. 70), and are therefore not expected to succeed at sport (Lashley, 1980a, p. 5). School sport reinforces and perpetuates such stereotypes; and others of a more specific nature, often based on physiological and anatomical prejudices,[11] remain unchallenged.

It is clear that for the Asian males at Parkview, sport is not high on their list of priorities, and as Javinder (a Straight) commented:

> I play for fun. I don't want to be really serious about it.

Herein, however, lies the essence of a problem for the understanding of the role that sport plays in Asian lifestyles, for the meanings attached to sport are not easy to establish. Roberts (1983, p. 153) acknowledges this, but suggests 'quantifying participation rates and levels of achievement poses few methodological problems'. Such statistical analyses do not, though, accommodate the Street-kids' informal kick-abouts and the Straights' home-based snooker. Both are meaningful sporting experiences for the people concerned, but both would be neglected by 'official' participation figures.

Formal organized sport is only a peripheral life interest for the Asian youths at Parkview, and as Roberts (1983, p. 149) observes:

> We cannot assume that the minorities would wish to emulate middle-class whites' leisure habits if granted equal opportunities.

The reality is, though, that sport, popularly conceived of as providing minority groups with equal opportunity, is not only failing to integrate them, but is a vehicle for the expression of ethnic antagonism and racial tension, and is consolidating and even exacerbating social division.

Cashmore, in the television documentary *The Race Game* (BBC, 1990) remarks that the sporting success of blacks (Afro/Caribbeans) is a 'litmus test' of a racist society. Yet sporting success is not a 'universal indicator' for all minority groups. Asians in Britain are affected by societal racism at least as much as other minorities, but sport is not perceived by them as the only route to fame and material rewards. It is seen as just the same as any other social institution. Consequently it is not a hollow and unrealistic source of hope, and it is not pursued with the conviction that:

> ... While society is mired in racism, sport remains one islet in which young blacks can discover themselves in a land of equal opportunity (Cashmore, 1990a, p. 10).

While the findings of *The Race Game* (BBC, 1990) indicate that the success of Afro/Caribbeans in sport is proof of a racist society, the conclusion from studying the sporting experiences of these young Asian males is that sport is as riddled with discrimination, prejudice and racism as the rest of society.

Notes

1 'Asian', in this context, is a cultural rather than a geographical term, and refers to a traditional culture and lifestyle that originates from the Indian sub-continent.
2 This study has been undertaken with the assistance and collaboration of Jim Atkinson and the Greater London and South East Regional Sports Council.
3 For a further description of the methodology, see Fleming and Lawrence (1990).
4 In the interests of protecting the identity of those concerned, pseudonyms have been used throughout the text.
5 'Tags' are a form of graffiti, and are the personalized insignia of an individual or group.
6 'They' refers to the other pupils, and includes other Asians that abuse the Victims in this way.
7 For example, a list of demands that the Muslim community of different areas may submit to their Local Education Authority for necessary action, includes the following:

> Head teachers should allow Muslim pupils to be excluded from *dance*, drama, music, sex education lessons when a request is made to them by the Muslim parents (Sarwar, 1983, p. 19, emphasis added).

8 For a description of 'Kabaddi' and other Asian cultural and traditional games and sporting activities — 'Guli-Danda', 'Daria Bandha', 'Kho Kho' — see James (1974, p. 28) and Coventry LEA (1980, p. 23).
9 The Kusti is:

> The sacred cord which all initiated Zoroastrians wear at all times around the waist. It is untied and retied several times a day to the accompanyment of prayers (Hinnells, 1981, p. 77).

10 Tony and Virendra are two of Ranjit's closest friends. Tony is of Caribbean origin, and Virendra is a British-born Sikh, whose parents were born in the Indian Punjab.
11 For example: 'Asians are too frail for contact sports' (cited in Bayliss, 1989, p. 20), 'Asian girls have difficulty reproducing certain body postures' (cited in Cherrington, 1974, p. 41), 'Sikh children not liking rugby' (cited in Coventry LEA, 1980, p. 28).

I would like to thank Dr Alan Tomlinson and Lesley Lawrence for their constructive comments on an earlier draft. The final product is, of course, entirely my own responsibility.

References

ALLISON, T.T. (1982) 'Sport, Ethnicity and Assimilation', *Quest*, **34** (2), pp. 165–75.

BALL, S.J. (1981) *Beachside Comprehensive: A Case-Study of Secondary Schooling*, Cambridge, Cambridge University Press.

BAYLISS, T. (1989) 'PE and Racism: Making Changes', *Multicultural Teaching*, **7** (5), pp. 18–22.

BBC TELEVISION (1990) *Inside Story — The Race Game*, BBC1, produced by TERRILL, C., 2.5.1990.

BIRBALSINGH, F. and SHIWCHARAN, C. (1988) *Indo-Westindian Cricket*, London, Hansib Publishing.

BRADFORD YOUTH RESEARCH TEAM (1988) *Young People in Bradford Survey 1987*, Department of Applied and Community Studies, Bradford and Ilkley Community College, Ilkley, West Yorkshire.

BURGESS, R.G. (1983) *Experiencing Comprehensive Education: A Study of Bishop McGregor School*, London, Methuen.

CAMPAIGN AGAINST RACISM AND FACISM (CARF) (1981) *Southall: The Birth of a Black Community*, London, Institute of Race Relations and Southall Rights.

CARRINGTON, B. and WILLIAMS, T. (1988) 'Patriarchy and Ethnicity: The Link between School Physical Education and Community Leisure Activities', in EVANS, J. (Ed.) *Teachers, Teaching and Control in Physical Education*, London, Falmer Press, pp. 83–96.

CARRINGTON, B., CHIVERS, T. and WILLIAMS, T. (1987) 'Gender, Leisure and Sport: A Case-Study of Young People of South Asian Descent', *Leisure Studies*, **6**, pp. 265–79.

CASHMORE, E. (1981) 'The Black British Sporting Life', *New Society*, 6 August, pp. 215–7.

CASHMORE, E. (1982a) *Black Sportsmen*, London, Routledge and Kegan Paul.

CASHMORE, E. (1982b) 'Black Youth, Sport and Education', *New Community*, **10**, pp. 213–21.

CASHMORE, E. (1983) 'The Champions of Failure: Black Sportsmen', *Ethnic and Racial Studies*, **6**, pp. 90–102.

CASHMORE, E. (1986) 'Glove Puppets', *New Socialist*, **40**, pp. 24–5.

CASHMORE, E. (1990a) 'The Race Season', *New Statesman and Society*, 1 June, pp. 10–11.

CASHMORE, E. (1990b) *Making Sense of Sport*, London, Routledge.

CHERRINGTON, D. (1974) 'Physical Education and the Immigrant Child', in GLAISTER, I.K. (Ed.) *Physical Education — An Integrating Force?*, London, ATCDE, pp. 33–45.

CHILD, E. (1983) 'Play and Culture: A Study of English and Asian Children', *Leisure Studies*, **2**, pp. 169–86.

COAKLEY, J.J. (1986) *Sport in Society: Issues and Controversies* (3rd Ed.) St. Louis, MO, Times Mirror/Mosby Publishing.

COLEMAN, P.K. (1990) 'Giving Hope to Brick Lane Youth', *Asian Times*, 13 March, pp. 22–3.

COMMUNITY RELATIONS COMMISSION (CRC) (1976) *Between Two Cultures: A Study of Relationships between Generations in the Asian Community in Britain*, London, Community Relations Commission.

COVENTRY LOCAL EDUCATION AUTHORITY (1980) *Physical Education in a Multi-Cultural Society*, Coventry, Elm Bank Teachers' Centre.

CRAFT, A. and KLEIN, G. (1986) *Agenda for Multi-Cultural Teaching*, York, School Curriculum Development Committee Publications, Longman.

DATAR, R. (1989) 'An Elusive Goal for the East-end Pele', *The Guardian*, 28 June, **20**.

DOVE, L. (1975) 'The Hopes of Immigrant Children', *New Society*, 10 April, pp. 63–5.

FLEMING, S. (1989) 'Asian Lifestyles and Sports Participation', in TOMLINSON, A. (Ed.) *Youth Cultures and the Domain of Leisure*, Leisure Studies Association Conference Papers No. 35, Eastbourne, Leisure Studies Association, pp. 82–98.

FLEMING, S. (1990) 'Sport and Social Division: The Heterogeneity of South Asian Male Youth', paper presented at the British Sociological Association Annual Conference — 'Social Divisions and Social Change', University of Surrey.

FLEMING, S. and LAWRENCE, L. (1990) 'Methodological Pluralism: A Case for a Multi-Method Approach to Social Research', paper presented at the British Sociological Association Annual Conference — 'Social Divisions and Social Change', University of Surrey.

GORN, E.J. (1986) *The Manly Art*, Ithaca, Cornell University Press.

HARGREAVES, D. (1967) *Social Relations in a Secondary School*, London, Routledge and Kegan Paul.

HARGREAVES, J. (1986) *Sport, Power and Culture*, Cambridge, Polity Press.

HARRIS, J.C. and PARK, R.J. (1983) *Play, Games and Sports in Cultural Contexts*, Champaign, IL, Human Kinetics Publishers.

HINNELLS, J.R. (1981) *Zoroastrianism and the Parsis*, London, Ward Lock Educational.

HIRO, D. (1973) *Black British, White British*, rev. ed., London, Review Press.

HOPPS, D. (1989) 'Black Yorkshiremen Crossing the Boundary', *The Guardian*, 13 October, p. 21.

JAMES, A.G. (1974) *Sikh Children in Britain*, Oxford, Oxford University Press.

JAMES, C.L.R. (1963) 'Cricket in West Indian Culture', *New Society*, **36**, pp. 8–9.

KANSARA, B. (1984) 'Indian Dance in London Schools', *Impulse*, Summer, pp. 22–4.

KERRIDGE, R. (1989) 'Oy! For England ...', *Midweek*, 5 January, pp. 10–13.

KEW, F. (1979) *Ethnic Groups and Leisure*, Review for the Joint Panel on

Leisure and Recreation Research, London, Sports Council and Social Science Research Council.

KUREISHI, O. (1989) 'The Patriot Game', *Cricket Life International*, August, pp. 27–8.

LACEY, C. (1970) *Hightown Grammar*, Manchester, Manchester University Press.

LASHLEY, H. (1980a) 'The New Black Magic', *British Journal of Physical Education*, **11**, pp. 5–6.

LASHLEY, H. (1980b) 'Rhythms of Life', *British Journal of Physical Education*, **11**, pp. 72–3.

LEWIS, T. (1979) 'Ethnic Influences on Girls' PE', *British Journal of Physical Education*, **10**, p. 32.

MALIK, R. (1988) 'Exercise', in *Heart-Health and Asians in Britain*, Health Education Authority and Coronary Prevention Group, London, pp. 4–5.

MILES, K. and KHAN, R. (1988) *Jahangir and the Khan Dynasty*, London, Pelham Books.

ROBERTS, K. (1983) *Youth and Leisure*, London, George Allen and Unwin.

SARGEANT, A.J. (1972) 'Participation of West Indian Boys in English Schools' Sports Teams', *Educational Research*, **14** (3), pp. 225–30.

SARWAR, G. (1983) *Muslim and Education in the UK*, London, The Muslim Educational Trust.

SHIPLEY, S. (1989) 'Boxing', in MASON, T. (Ed.) *Sport in Britain, A Social History*, Cambridge, Cambridge University Press, pp. 78–115.

TOWNSEND, H.E.R. and BRITTAN, E.M. (1973) *Multi-Racial Education: Need and Innovation*, Schools Council Working Paper 50, London, Evans/Methuen Educational.

WHITE, J. (1990) 'Yorkshire's Biggest Test', *The Independent*, 26 May, p. 29.

Chapter 3

Sport, Racism and Young Women

Tessa Lovell

Sport is often perceived as having less relevance for women. However, the role which sport plays within women's lives is gradually being documented. This is, in part, reflected by the growing body of feminist literature on women and leisure, which has considered the sporting experience of women (Deem, 1986; Hargreaves, 1989; Talbot, 1979). The social and economic constraints affecting women's leisure experiences have been the focus of much feminist writing on sport and leisure. Yet the ethnocentralistic nature of this work has meant that little research has been undertaken which examines the role of sport for women from ethnic minority backgrounds, or the way in which women's sporting experiences are mediated by racism. What work has been done has tended to take a liberal discrimination approach, looking at ways of establishing equality of opportunity. One of the problems with this type of analysis is that it does not take account of cultural variations and the ways in which people are channelled into different sporting avenues.

Women are obviously not an homogenous group, but are divided by race and class, and as such there is not a uniform set of constraints which equally affect all women. Racism is an obvious illustration of this, adding another dimension to sexism, for ethnic minority women. The effects of racism are diverse and vary between different ethnic groups. This is depicted by certain racist stereotypes; Asian women are often considered weak and passive, while Afro/Caribbean women are often depicted as aggressive and dominating. Racism can also take on different forms within similar cultures; Indian cultures illustrate this point. Southern Asian peoples do not have a single, uniform culture, which is in part reflected by religions, of which there are many, Muslim and Hindu being the central ones. Since there are many Muslims outside India, this gives a different quality and distinct identity to Indian Muslims. This may also mean the nature of racism varies between these two groups.

The ways in which culture, racism and gender operate for various groups of women, therefore, alters the relationship between freedoms and constraints. Sport, because of the nature of racism, is a more accessible leisure activity for Afro/Caribbean women than Southern Asian women. This tendency, however, gives Afro/Caribbean women more scope for expressing themselves physically, often allowing them to show abilities and attributes often quite alien to the concept of femininity. Thus the complexity of racism may provide a means of challenging traditional ideals of womanhood.

In analyzing race and gender, it is also necessary to recognize that women are not simply oppressed but do have, to some extent, control over their own lives. This is especially relevant with regard to ethnic minority women. It is argued by Bryan, Dadzie and Scafe (1985) that the image of 'black women as long suffering, heroic and passive victims of the triple oppression of class, race and gender, is a romantic myth'. These women are active in challenging their situations and circumstances. Indeed they participate in the making of their own life histories but not always under circumstances of their own choosing.

This chapter shall specifically explore the role of sport in the lives of some Southern Asian and Afro/Caribbean women, and how racism impinges upon that experience. The role of sport within the lives of Southern Asian women is of particular interest, since this is a sub-culture which participates least within traditional British sports (The Sports Council, 1988). Given the scope of the research and the lack of analysis and information within this area, this piece of work is necessarily exploratory, and as such is not definitive. Consequently, the main objective is primarily to raise questions and awareness. The main sources drawn upon emanate from black feminist work and the literature on women and leisure. The ethnography attempts to highlight the stories and experiences of women themselves.

Women's Sporting Experience

The leisure literature in the 1970s (Parker, 1971, 1983; Roberts, 1978, 1983) has been criticized for its failure to take account of the position of women. This led to the emergence of a debate around women's experiences of leisure. Part of this debate revolved around the fact that the leisure-work dichotomy made little sense of the lives of many women. This is fundamentally because many women usually take responsibility for the home and family and consequently do not have time which is totally uncommitted. Behind this model of work and leisure is the ideology that free time has be to earned, and that paid employment provides the right to leisure. This notion inevitably excludes large numbers of women who are housewives (Green, Hebron and Woodward, 1987). Furthermore, the world of sport and leisure is often premised upon the power of consumption at the point of production and not all people can buy into this world on an equal basis.

The boundary between work and leisure is usually hazy for women; leisure is not associated with free time in the same way that it is for men. The difficulty for many women in finding space for regular leisure activities is well documented (Deem, 1986; Wimbush and Talbot, 1988). This situation inevitably means that within Western societies a greater importance is often placed upon male leisure. The significance of this gap is accentuated when looking at sport. With some exceptions, such as tennis and athletics, sport is rarely an avenue whereby women can gain financial independence. At a more recreative level, less than 14 per cent of women regularly watch sport while participation rates for women in 1988 were only 24 per cent for indoor sport and 24.3 per cent for outdoor sports (The Sports Council, 1988). It is necessary to establish just exactly how sport fits into the overall leisure patterns of women.

Despite the barriers, many women at some stage in their lives participate in sport, yet ideals of femininity have perpetuated and restricted the form and nature of this involvement. Traditional qualities considered as 'natural' female attributes include grace and agility, not strength, power and aggression, thus placing certain limitations on women and the sports they are involved in. 'Female' sports, such as netball, are often non-contact, which is supposed to reflect lack of aggression. It is therefore not surprising that activities such as aerobics and Callanetics are popular, since they are perceived as an avenue for achieving the 'perfect', slim feminine physique. When female athletes transcend concepts of femininity, they are often considered 'freakish and unnatural'. This concept is perfectly illustrated in attitudes towards Jarmilla Kratochvilova and Martina Navratilova, who are often perceived as 'butch' and unnaturally masculine (Hargreaves, 1989).

Nevertheless, sport does have significance for many women, despite being a predominantly male domain. It is argued by Hargreaves (1989) that regardless of the subordinate position of women, sport does have the potential to be a 'liberating experience'. One of the main benefits of sport is the potential it has for giving women control over their own bodies. It can also give women the opportunity to participate in activities which require competitiveness and aggression. Sport, in a similar vein to other leisure activities, may also provide a means of gaining access to female companionship in a relatively safe environment.

Black and Asian Feminist Critiques

Having looked briefly at women's experience of sport, it is necessary to analyze the role of sport for ethnic minority women and the effects of racism. Mainstream feminism has been criticized by many Asian and black feminists not only for its silences on racism, but also for being dominated by white, middle-class women (Amos and Parmar, 1984; Davis, 1982; Hooks, 1982). It is argued by Amos and Parmar that there is not enough research on the ways in which 'white women have benefited fundamentally from the oppression of Black women' (Amos and Parmar, 1984, p. 8). The 'Reclaim The Night Marches' through black areas of London in the early 1980s, protesting against sexual harassment and attacks against women, is but one instance of this insensitivity to racism. These marches perpetuated stereotypes of black male sexuality, reinforcing the idea that women are most threatened sexually by black men.

The social, political and economic deprivation, produced by racism, it is suggested, has also meant that issues of race for black and Asian women have at times superseded debates over gender (Amos and Parmar, 1984, p. 12):

> Our very position as Black women in a racist society has meant we have been forced to organize around issues relating to our survival. The struggle for independence and self determination and against imperialism has meant that for Black and Third World women in Britain and internationally, sexuality as an issue has often taken a secondary role and at times not been considered at all.

Although this debate has now become to some extent sterile, much interesting analysis and discussion has subsequently emerged. For instance, much has been written about the role of women within Afro/Caribbean families. It is argued by many black feminists (Davis, 1982; Phoenix, 1987) that theories based around white families and patriarchy are taken as the norm: the dominant father, who provides economically, and the submissive, caring mother, who provides emotionally. This, it is claimed, does not give an accurate picture of women's position within Afro/Caribbean families. Women from this cultural background, according to Phoenix (1987) often have quite different roles within the family than white women. For a number of economic and social reasons, children from Afro/Caribbean backgrounds are more likely to come from families where the mother is more in control economically, than within the equivalent white family. Historically, Afro/Caribbean women did the same work as Afro/Caribbean men during the slave era, which it is claimed, has lead to greater equality for black women within the family. In 1982, 41 per cent of Afro/Caribbean women were in full-time paid employment, compared to 21 per cent of Asian and 21 per cent of white women (Phoenix, 1987).

Aspects of Southern Asian family culture, such as arranged marriages, are also often considered abnormal and viewed as detrimental, because they conflict with western values. Many Southern Asian feminists have argued that this represents an insensitivity and misunderstanding of Indian culture (Amos and Parmar, 1984; Trivedi, 1984). Furthermore, it should be recognized that Afro/Caribbean men are often viewed as being subordinate to white men. This distinction is important, because this affects the relationship between Afro/Caribbean men and women. Afro/Caribbean women are less able to rely on Afro/Caribbean men financially. Afro/Caribbean men are more vulnerable to imprisonment, poor pay or unemployment. As a consequence of this Afro/Caribean women are often forced to become more independent.

These factors have implications for Afro/Caribbean women's experience of leisure. Perhaps Afro/Caribbean women have relatively more autonomy in determining their leisure patterns than white or Asian women. According to Phoenix, Afro/Caribbean women are less likely to be constrained by the culture of femininity. This lack of constraint, argues Phoenix, affects the way in which daughters are brought up; they are likely to be more independent. In terms of sport, Afro/Caribbean women, because of the nature of racism and their historical and cultural development, may be more assertive physically.

In saying that Afro/Caribbean women have economic independence, it would be incorrect to assume that this means that Afro/Caribbean women have equality with Afro/Caribbean men. According to Hooks (1982), Afro/Caribbean men and women are just as susceptible to gender socialization.

Writers such as, Bryan, Dadzie and Scafe (1985), Davis (1982), Hooks (1982), and Phoenix (1987) have considered attitudes towards sexuality, and how race and gender influence these images. It is argued by Davis (1982) that the threat of rape may be more evident for Afro/Caribbean women than Southern Asian women because they are more likely to be viewed as sexually available. The image of Afro/Caribbean women as more sexually assertive may contribute to the belief of athletic prowess of this group of women. This situation serves to point out some of the paradoxes of racism. The myth of the over-dominant Afro/Caribbean woman has some advantages: the space and scope for greater independence, and the greater acceptance of power and strength. However, these positives come at the expense of being perceived as lacking certain fundamental western feminine graces.

Southern Asian women, on the other hand, are very often perceived as passive and frail. It is suggested by Trivedi (1984) that the stereotype of female Asian passivity, reflects the institutionalization of racism within British society. The 'myth of passivity' is challenged by Trivedi, who points to struggles in India in which women have been involved. These images can restrict the involvement of Southern Asian women within sport, since these qualities are not associated with athleticism and sporting ability. Southern Asian girls are not usually encouraged to become athletes, and therefore interested in sports. Often teachers automatically assume Asian girls will lack sporting ability and commitment. Lewis (1979) in her analysis of ethnic influences on girls' physical education claims that Afro/Caribbean girls are the most gifted at sports, with white girls falling in the middle, and Asians coming last. She goes on:

When they arrive West Indian and Asian girls are poles apart in terms of games skills, due to different cultural backgrounds ... where stamina is required, Asian girls are often at a disadvantage as they are usually small and quite frail (Lewis, 1979, p. 1).

This quotation illustrates the power and complexity of racist attitudes. For while sport may not have a lot of significance within Southern Asian culture for women, racist attitudes and images perpetuate this belief. Consequently Southern Asian girls are not encouraged at an early age to become involved within sports. This may be to such an extent that many Southern Asian girls themselves start to believe that they lack sporting ability, and to some extent begin to internalize a self image of passivity and frailty.

The Ethnography

Looking at women, racism and leisure, the ethnographic setting of the research was located around a community college of a comprehensive school. The school is situated within a predominantly Southern Asian, Afro/Caribbean working class area of Coventry. Afro/Caribbean and Asian people constitute 42 per cent of the population in this area while 57 per cent of the population work within the skilled, semi-skilled or unskilled manual sector (Community Education Team Report, 1990).

The researcher was a former pupil of this school, which gave improved access to the community college and familiarity with the area. The study was based around the community college evening classes, consisting of interviews, questionnaires, documentary sources and participant observation. In addition the study also included the in-depth interviewing of ten women who were contemporaries at the school. The age range of all the women involved in the research was between 17 and 30.

Initially the researcher informally interviewed the community education team, which consisted of a female Muslim and two white males. The objective of these interviews was to gain overall impressions of the aims of the community college. The first community worker interviewed was mainly interested in the daytime classes, either 'Second Chance to Learn' or 'Infill'. These classes try to give working-class people some further access to education. White working-class women were the main users of this provision. Traditional night classes, therefore, for this community worker were limited: they were mostly recreational and not always reflective of the area. The Muslim worker, on the other hand, seemed more interested in developing traditional classes. She was obviously involved in encouraging Asian use of the community college facilities. Since she had been appointed to the community team, several classes, based around religion, had been established for Muslim women, and these apparently were very successful.

In this study, the researcher found that different groups of women are attracted to different sports, although there were also several similarities; for instance all the women seemed to have been at some stage involved in 'keep fit' or aerobics, while very few women expressed any interest in watching sport. Afro/Caribbean women seemed more integrated into British sporting culture than Southern Asian women. An illustration of this was the community netball team, the main female sports club, which was dominated by Afro/ Caribbean and white women.

Southern Asian Women

Leisure, for women within the Southern Asian community in Britain, centres around the family and religion. There are many religious events, weddings and community gatherings, which mean that Southern Asian women often have, on one level, a full and varied social life (Gahir, 1984). However, this type of social life does not leave much scope for participation in sport, compounded by the fact that the Southern Asian community lacks many role models of sportsmen and women in the main British sports. This situation contrasts sharply with the Afro/Caribbean community, who are disproportionately represented within certain élite level sports, such as athletics, although having very little presence in others such as tennis and swimming.

It would, however, be a distortion to suggest that Southern Asian women have no involvement within sport. Many Southern Asian women were involved in community classes generally, but also in sports classes, for instance, badminton. This was partly due to the appointment of the female Muslim community worker, who was well respected within the Southern Asian community. Dance is an obvious example of Southern Asian women's involvement in a leisure activity which is in some respects similar to sport. The Asian Dance competition, attended while completing the research, was enormously successful and created a lively and stimulating atmosphere. All of the competitors were girls and young women, who appeared at ease performing in front of a large audience. Dance competitions are held regularly at the community college.

It was noticeable that, although Southern Asian women were involved in the community college evening classes, they tended to congregate in classes such as Urdu and Punjabi, to do with Indian culture, or educational classes, mainly learning to speak better English. Very few Southern Asian women took part in the daytime English classes. No Asian women attended the art, pottery or ceramic classes. The Punjabi class, at the beginning of term, was supposed to be cancelled due to a misunderstanding over deposits. This class consisted of four women and one man. The women in the group were keen to continue the class and seemed genuinely interested in improving their Punjabi. The class did not appear to be simply a vehicle for escaping the home for a few hours.

Many of the Southern Asian women who filled in questionnaires or were interviewed expressed some interest in sport. The most popular activity was 'keep fit' or aerobics. This activity was associated with slimming, health and increased attractiveness. Aerobics and its association with slender, attractive women seemed to be as popular amongst women from different ethnic backgrounds as it is for white women. This can be seen, in part, as an example of the westernization of Afro/Caribbean and Southern Asian women, in terms of what constitutes the ideal female physique. The Western ideal of slim females contrasts sharply with subsistence economies, in which fat is symbolic of wealth. It also suggests that one of the overriding factors behind all of women's involvement within sport is to do with improving personal appearance.

What then are the main factors behind Southern Asian women's experience of sport and how do race and gender affect leisure patterns? One reaction to racism has been for Southern Asian communities to become very close knit, maintaining a distinct identity, focusing upon the Hindu or Muslim religions. There is enormous pressure put upon Southern Asian women to conform to traditional values of womanhood. Arranged marriages and traditional Indian dress are but two examples of this pressure.

These attitudes were expressed vehemently by the Southern Asian community worker. Throughout the interview she expressed her concern that Southern Asian girls within the school had acquired too much freedom in terms of the way they behaved and dressed. Although Southern Asian males face the same culture conflict, it is not to the same degree. At no time in the interview was a similar view expressed towards Asian boys.

One of the women interviewed depicted the existing conflict between two cultures. At the age of 24, she lived at home with her parents and was employed as a sales representative. She felt that her job required her to dress in a traditional western way, despite the hostility of her parents. She resolved this dilemma by changing into western clothes when she arrived at work. In talking of her relationship with her parents, it became apparent that the main opposition came from her father, although she seemed to have established a compromise. She felt her relationship with her father had altered; 'I don't get so angry with him any more'. The implication was that she had learnt to negotiate the limits and scope of her life outside the family and community.

This retreat into Southern Asian culture has its advantages and disadvantages. As stated earlier, Southern Asian women often have lively social lives. However, sport is an example of some of the disadvantages. It is often very difficult for Southern Asian women to become involved or heavily committed in regular sporting activities, which are not part of Southern Asian female culture, for instance, team games such as netball or hockey.

Most of the Southern Asian women interviewed felt they had enough leisure time, but that this time was not totally uncommitted. In other words, they could do as they wished within the home, but were not free to leave the house because of responsibilities such as child care, looking after sick or elderly relatives, or simply providing company for husbands or fathers. Although these constraints are common to many women, cutting across race and class, it can be argued that they are more accentuated for Southern Asian women. The extended family gives women support but also can mean much responsibility and commitment.

One 19-year-old Muslim woman found it difficult to say whether she had enough free time. She had enough time which she considered to be essentially her own, yet this time was not completely uncommitted. Her words were, 'I find it hard to get away from things'. It seems therefore to be more a question of degrees of freedom. This problem of quality of leisure time was also expressed by another Southern Asian woman interviewed. Although this 21-year-old woman was unemployed, establishing time which was solely for herself was awkward, since she was expected to take some responsibility for the family shop, alongside domestic duties.

Racism can also operate to accentuate, for Afro/Caribbean and Southern Asian women, other constraints which face women generally. Afro/Caribbean and Southern Asian women are likely to live in the most deprived and run-down areas. The school on which the research is based is situated in one of the most deprived areas of Coventry. In the questionnaires and interviews, many women drew attention to the fact that the school was situated within a 'red light' area. This, many felt, created a hostile, unfriendly environment.

This area of Coventry is also perceived as being the main 'drug' area. During the time I was completing my research there was a drugs raid. The headline in the local paper read as follows: 'Drug Busters In Huge Swoop' (*Coventry Evening Telegraph*, 25.5.90). Some women also referred to this reputation for drugs and violence as a problem in terms of going out to classes and other leisure time activities. One woman, who attended a pottery evening class, claimed that she had been offered drugs on the way to attending a class. Whether or not this reputation for being a drug area has been exaggerated by the police and media, this association puts a brake on leisure involvement.

In talking to Action Sport employees working in this area of Coventry, the difficulties of involving Asian women in sport were very apparent. There was a sense of imposing sport on Southern Asian women, instead of looking more closely at the reasons behind the lack of interest. Further, there is often a tendency to assume that because Southern Asian women participate least in sporting activities, that they are automatically deprived. Hence the emergence of studies which try to find ways of increasing the participation rate of this group of women. It is not the case that these women simply lead deprived and oppressed lives. It is the case, however, that sport often does not play an important role within leisure as a whole for Southern Asian women.

It would be interesting to determine what the role of sport is for women in India, compared with Southern Asian women living in Britain. For instance, there is a national female Indian Cricket team. There does not appear to be much interest in cricket amongst this group of women in Britain, although cricket is very popular amongst Southern Asian males in Britain.

Afro/Caribbean Women

Within the case study, it was found that fewer Afro/Caribbean women were involved within the community evening classes, generally and yet they were much more evident within the sports classes. The community college netball club is a good example, having many Afro/Caribbean players. Sport seemed to play an important part in the culture of Afro/Caribbean women.

Why then is sport a significant factor within Afro/Caribbean women's leisure? Racism is a crucial factor in looking at Afro/Caribbean people's experience of sport. As stated earlier, there are many Afro/Caribbean sportsmen and women at the top level. Afro-Caribbean people are often perceived as automatically good at sports, because the Afro/Caribbean stereotype is that of natural athlete. Underlying this assumption is the racism that Afro/Caribbean people are closer to the animal kingdom, and therefore naturally faster and stronger (see Chapter 5, this volume, for a discussion of how these preconceptions affect opportunities for black males in sport). Sport is also, obviously, a way out economically for many Afro/Caribbean people. All these factors reinforce the significance of sport for many Afro/Caribbean people. Yet it is a double edged sword in the sense that it is often racism that leads Afro/Caribbean people into sport and racism which stops representation from this group within the sporting power structure. Racism also alters Afro/Caribbean people's experience of sport. The increase of all-black teams is an example of this. It is argued by Parry (1989) that there is increasing evidence of the 'West Indian Community organizing itself autonomously'. In his article 'A Prejudice For Fairness' (*The Independent*, 6 February 1987), Foster cites examples of autonomous Afro/Caribbean sports teams. The Sheffield-based Caribbean Sports Club, which has separate netball and cricket teams, is an illustration of this phenomenon.

This trend was also evident within the community college. In 1984, many of the Afro/Caribbean players in the community college netball team decided to form an autonomous club. This decision was partly due to the experience of racism. The netball first team, of which four were Afro/Caribbean women, had established a reputation for aggressive behaviour within the netball league. They felt this reputation made many of the netball officials, all of whom were white, biased against them.

As stated at the beginning, a disparity of sporting interests was found between Asian and Afro/Caribbean women. Again, it is difficult here to determine the extent to which racism affects sporting choices. Badminton and squash classes were predominantly attended by Southern Asian and white men and women. This may be because of the belief that these are traditional Asian sports. However, there is often a lack of understanding of the causes behind the various cultural sporting patterns. The factors behind these cultural choices are complex. It is easy to establish reasons why there is a lack of involvement of Afro/Caribbean and other ethnic groups in a sport such as tennis. Factors such as expense, racism and the élite nature of tennis mitigate against the involvement of these groups. However, class does not easily explain the low participation rate of these groups in an activity such as swimming. It would seem that it is the combination of the relationship between cultural identity and racism which produce certain sporting patterns.

In general, the case study found that there was a distinct difference in leisure and sporting patterns between Southern Asian and white women. Only three white women did not express interest in going to wine bars, pubs or discos. None of the Asian women stated that these were significant or regular pastimes. Afro/Caribbean women, on the other hand, appeared closer to white leisure patterns, although there were fewer Afro/Caribbean women involved within the community classes. I was therefore less able to gain an accurate picture of this group of women's leisure patterns.

In terms of sport, Southern Asian women's involvement in sport seemed to be more recreational. That is to say, sport did not appear to be a central part of Southern Asian women's leisure culture. However, it is also the case that participating in sport did not appear to be a central leisure interest for white women either. Again aerobics or 'keep fit' appeared to be the most popular sporting activity. More white women than Southern Asian women were involved in the community sports evening classes.

The similarities between the groups of women examined were most striking in terms of constraints. Transport was a considerable problem for many of the women, especially at night. Fear of attack was also considerable, given the nature and reputation of the area. In their study of women and leisure in Sheffield, Green, Hebron and Woodward (1987), suggest lack of companionship as a constraint; this was mentioned by several of the women who filled in questionnaires. Family responsibilities, such as caring for old and sick relatives, or young children, also restricted women's leisure and sporting involvements. Increased economic power was seen by many of the women as the central factor restricting their leisure.

Several questions and issues seem to emerge from the research. Whether or not Southern Asian women are significantly deprived by their low participation in sport would seem to be a central point. If this lack of participation is considered detrimental, then it appears very difficult to alter, for it is only by confronting the barriers of racism that any significant changes would occur. By eradicating racism, Southern Asian communities would not feel so threatened, which may result in producing a more racially integrated society. Southern Asian peoples may then become more involved within mainstream British leisure culture. However, it would also be necessary to remove many of the constraints which restrict women's leisure participation. Since Southern Asian women usually live in areas which are the most deprived and have reputations for violence, this is especially problematic.

This viewpoint, to some extent, takes for granted that a more homogenous British culture would be advantageous. Perhaps the extent to which Southern Asian women choose not to become involved in sport should be recognized more. Being sensitive to cultural varia-tions, however, should not be at the expense of being critical of the ways in which women are oppressed. It is easy in recognizing the role of culture to condone the position of women.

Conversely, with Afro/Caribbean women, the extent to which sport is made popular by racism should not be overlooked. As Cashmore argued in a recent British television documentary, reduced interest in sport within the Afro/Caribbean community may be a sign of a more egalitarian society, although as stated earlier, the nature of Afro/Caribbean women's involvement in sport can be very positive.

Conclusions

While the analysis presented in this chapter has been at a relatively concrete level, I should like to finish by highlighting a few important points. First, there is the issue of existing feminist writings on sport and leisure. While the challenge of Afro/Caribbean and Southern Asian feminists has occasioned some rethinking in the 1980s, the feminist writings on sport and leisure remain relatively silent concern-ing the specific experiences of Afro/Caribbean and Southern Asian women. There is a need for more specific research on the meaning of leisure and sport in the lives of such women.

Second, while this chapter has largely concerned itself with sport-ing participation of Afro/Caribbean and Southern Asian women, the issue of racism relates to the organization of power. Who allocates sporting resources? Who makes decisions about sport and recreation in Britain? Who runs the facilities? Who has access to power? As such it is important to highlight two interrelated points: 1) that arguments which relate to rates of participation and resource distribution are of secondary importance to those arguments which raise questions of levels of control, access to power and the hierarchical arrangements concerning the organization of sport and leisure within any society, and 2) it is unlikely that many young Afro/Caribbean or Southern Asian women will experience equality of opportunity in sport as long as well-placed families are able to confer differential advantages upon their children. This area is ripe for action research on a larger scale than has been possible here.

Finally, it is also necessary to recognize the ways in which sport is tied up with concepts of gender and culture. A redistribution of power, with equality of access is obviously essential. However, this would not automatically alter sporting and leisure patterns of inequality. The main objectives of this chapter have been to illustrate ways in which gender and racism influence sporting and leisure choices, but also to recognize different cultures and their perceptions and experiences of sport.

References

AMOS, V. and PARMAR, P. (1984) 'Challenging Imperial Feminism', *Feminist Review* (17) Autumn, pp. 3–21.

BHAVNANI, K. (1989) 'Complexity, Activism, Optimism: An Interview with Angela Y. Davis', *Feminist Review* (31) Spring.

BIRRELL, S. (1989) 'Racial Relations Theories and Sport: Suggestions for a More Critical Analysis', *Sociology of Sport Journal*, **6**, pp. 212–7.

BRYAN, B., DADZIE, S. and SCAFE, S. (1985) *The Heart of the Race — Black Women's Lives in Britain*, London, Virago Press.

CLARKE, J. and CRITCHER, C. (1985) *The Devil Makes Work: Leisure in Capitalist Britain*, London, Macmillan.

COMMUNITY EDUCATION TEAM REPORT (1990) *Towards An Area Profile of Hillfields*, Coventry, Coventry City Council.

DAVIS, A. (1982) *Women, Race and Class*, London, The Women's Press.

DEEM, R. (1986) *All Work and No Play? The Sociology of Women's Leisure*, Milton Keynes, Open University Press.

DIXEY, R. (1982) 'Asian Women and Sport — The Bradford Experience', *The British Journal of Physical Education*, **13** (4) July, pp. 108–14.

FOSTER, J. (1987) 'A Prejudice for Fairness', *The Independent*, 6 February, p. 24.

GAHIR, N. (1984) 'Gone West' in *Sport and Leisure*, January.

GREEN, E., HEBRON, S. and WOODWARD, D. (1987) *Leisure and Gender: A Study of Sheffield Women's Leisure Experiences*, London, The Sports Council, ESRC.

GRUNEAU, R. (1983) *Class, Sports and Social Development*, Amherst, Massachusetts University Press.

HARGREAVES, J. (1989) 'The Promise and Problems of Women's Leisure and Sport', in ROJEK, J. (Ed.), *Leisure For Leisure*, London, Macmillan.

HOOKS, B. (1982) *'Ain't I A Woman', Black Women and Feminism*, London, Pluto Press.

LEWIS, T. (1979) 'Ethnic Influences on Girls' Physical Education', *The British Journal of Physical Education*, **10** (5) September, p. 113.

PARKER, S. (1971) *The Future of Work and Leisure*, London, Paladin.

PARKER, S. (1983) *Leisure and Work*, London, Allen and Unwin.

PARRY, J. (1989) *Participation by Black and Ethnic Minorities in Sport and Recreation: A Review of Literature*, London, London Research Centre.

PHOENIX, A. (1987) 'Theories of Gender and Black Families', in *Gender Under Scrutiny*, London, Allen and Unwin.

ROBERTS, K. (1978) *Contemporary Society and the Growth of Leisure*, London, Longman.

ROBERTS, K. (1983) *Youth and Leisure*, London, Allen and Unwin.

SPORTS COUNCIL (1988) *Women and Sport: A Regional Strategy*, Birmingham, West Midlands.

STOCKDALE, J. (1985) *What is Leisure? An Empirical Analysis of the Concept of Leisure in People's Lives*, London, The Sports Council.

TALBOT, M. (1979) *Women and Leisure*, London, The Sports Council.

TRIVEDI, P. (1984) 'To Deny Our Fullness: Asian Women in the Making of History', *Feminist Review* (17), pp. 37–55.

WIMBUSH, E. and TALBOT, M. (1988) *Relative Freedoms — Women and Leisure*, Milton Keynes, Open University Press.

Chapter 4

Sport Festivals and Race Relations in the Northwest Territories of Canada

Vicky Paraschak

Two festivals have existed in the Northwest Territories (NWT) of Canada since 1970, the dominant Arctic Winter Games, and the emergent Northern Games. In 1970, ten Eurocanadian sports comprised the schedule of events for the Arctic Winter Games. In contrast, the Northern Games schedule offered traditional Inuit (Eskimo) games, the good woman contest, fiddling and dancing. Twenty years later, these festivals appear, on the surface, to have remained fairly stable. In 1990, the Arctic Winter Games had some 'uniquely northern' events, such as Arctic Sports and Snowshoe Biathlon, but the majority of events can still be found in multi-sport festivals in southern Canada. Meanwhile, the various Northern Games held in 1989 included activities similar to 1970: Inuit games, the good woman contest, fiddling and dancing competitions.

Upon reading this snapshot description, one might superficially label the Northern Games as a festival projecting a native 'traditional games' ethnic identity, and the Arctic Winter Games as a very different type of festival projecting a Eurocanadian, northern 'sport' ethnic identity. The Government of the Northwest Territories (GNWT) reinforces this interpretation, which suggests that these are two unique and separate festivals. The Government administers the Arctic Winter Games within its sport programme area, while the Northern Games are part of the Traditional Games Programme located within the community recreation programme area.

The policy guiding the Government of the Northwest Territories' financial support to the Sport and Recreation Division also clearly delineates between the objectives to be achieved by 'sport' and 'traditional games'. The principles underlining this policy are essentially two-fold (GNWT, 1989):

1 Sport and recreation activity ... enhances the image of the Northwest Territories [in sport] nationally and internationally.

2 Traditional native sport and recreation activity preserves and strengthens the traditional ways of life of native peoples and contributes to a pride in our northern culture.

However, these festivals have not existed in completely independent social contexts. Since their inception, several 'ethnic' characteristics of both festivals have been subject to challenge, negotiation and occasionally alteration. A deconstruction of the history of these festivals demonstrates clearly that they have been a site where race relations have been both contested and reproduced in the North.[1] An examination of their history thus illuminates not only the contested nature of 'legitimate sport' in the North, but also the nature of ongoing race relations within this social formation.

This study is premised upon the assumption that there is a 'power-bloc' which reproduces relations of privilege and oppression in northern society and which, in part, is relatively structured along racial lines.[2] This 'power-bloc' has been defined by Hall (1981, p. 238) as 'the side with the cultural power to decide what belongs and what does not' — in other words, the monopolistic capacity to define what sport is and what sport should be. This group would thus, for example, have the power to define the range of legitimate practices associated with sport and consequently structure them in preferred ways. In the North, this power-bloc has been comprised of, until recently, non-native Eurocanadians who have operated with a colonial framework: government workers, teachers, missionaries, owners of businesses, and sportspeople alike who have all brought their southern-based skills, values, and expectations to the North. The resultant ethnocentric services have remained largely unaltered by native people, who have lacked the economic and political power to seriously challenge the colonial mediation of southern institutions.

The 'culture of the excluded' during this time included those groups of northerners, primarily native, in the smaller communities who sat outside the decision-making structures when it came to defining and structuring 'legitimate' sporting opportunities. However, this did not mean that they were passive recipients of the dominant culture. As active creators of their own social world, they have at times adopted, and occasionally resisted dominant cultural forms and practices.

The power-bloc began to transform as non-natives ceased to

monopolize northern political processes (Dacks, 1981). Native political groups, which were started in the 1970s, had gathered support from both native and non-native southern organizations by the end of the decade. These native political groups promoted candidates for the ninth Legislative Assembly in 1979, and the elected, pro-native voices on the Assembly linked, for the first time, the 'legitimate' government system with native political organizations.

The power gap between natives and non-natives has continued to close since 1979, as the two groups have been forced to acknowledge one another and combine forces to achieve 'northern', rather than just 'colonial' or 'native' goals. The placing of native leaders within the power-bloc was further facilitated in 1979 when elected politicians on the Executive Committee were put in charge of government departments (Dacks, 1981). This development placed native politicians in the position of being able to direct government employees for the first time. Under the leadership of native politicians, the specific concerns of northerners increasingly became the focal point of government services during the 1980s.

Race relations in the North can thus be broken into two phases. Phase one includes the period up until 1979, when native people remained outside the 'culture of the power-bloc'. Thus the period around 1979 might be termed a dominant moment in Northern race relations. The entrance of native politicians into the power-bloc enabled some native leaders to define and relatively control what they considered to be 'legitimate' activities and structures for the North. It also marked the point after which 'northern' ethnic festivals were challenged to include a genuine, rather than a token consideration of native needs and traditions. It is within this context of racism and changing power relations that the Northern Games and the Arctic Winter Games may be examined. The two festivals will be discussed individually within the context of the two periods of race relations.

Inception and Initial Operation of the Arctic Winter Games

Considering the colonial sporting context of the Northwest Territories in the late 1960s, one might easily have predicted the inception of the Arctic Winter Games (AWG). The Northwest Territories and the Yukon Territory athletes performed poorly, in relation to athletes from other provinces, at the first national, multi-sport Canada Games of 1967. Politicians from these Territories subsequently pushed for a

'Canada Games' type of festival north of the sixtieth parallel, the rationale being to arrange a more equitable competition for northern athletes which would in turn lead to the development of competent national and international calibre competitors. These Games thus fitted comfortably within the dominant system of sporting practices in Canada during this epoch.

The Arctic Winter Games were firmly ensconced within the culture of the power-bloc in the North. These Games were conceived of by non-native politicians, and remained a creation of government without native representation. Structurally, these Games were developed to operate at three separate organizational levels, all of which liaised closely with, and were relatively shaped by, the pertinent government departments. On the Arctic Winter Games Corporation, which serves as the permanent governing body, each director must be acceptable to the government of the participating unit. The second administrative structure, the Arctic Winter Games Society, was created anew by the host community for each separate Games. It functioned as a coordinating agency for the organization and administration of the event. Government officials in various capacities were required to become involved with the Society, so that the coordination of all parties was ensured. The final structure looked after the identification and transportation of athletes from each 'unit' to the Games — the original 'units' being the Northwest Territories, Yukon Territory and Alaska. In the Northwest Territories, this duty was transferred to Sport North, an organization founded in 1976 and funded in large part by the Northwest Territories government. Sport North served as the agency responsible for the delivery of the sports programmes. Thus, within each Arctic Winter Games administrative structure, government input was present at both the conceptual stage and funding stage.

The Arctic Winter Games has been perceived as a sports competition since its inception. It was immediately viewed as a 'sports' festival, and thus received ongoing funding from both the federal and territorial government departments. At the federal level, bureaucrats, although having documented the low level of competitive skill in the Games, nevertheless continued to refer to the Games as an 'international sports competition ... intended (in part) to be common ground for developing northern athletes in Olympic sports ...' (FAS, 1976).

Ongoing funding, linked to an established government programme, has been provided by the Government of the Northwest Territories Recreation Division (later known as the Sport and

Recreation Division), which has similarly viewed the Arctic Winter Games as a sports competition. The responsibility for the Games has thus remained in the hands of the Manager of Sport Programmes within of the Government of the Northwest Territories. The Sport North Federation, which administers several government sports programmes in the Northwest Territories, also received funding from the Recreation Division to select the Northwest Territories contingent. In addition, the Recreation Division has consistently supported the Games financially as being the major opportunity for sport competition in the Territories. Thus, although the amount of funding for each Games had to be negotiated, the assurance that funding would be forthcoming was always there.

Range of 'Legitimate' Activities for the Arctic Winter Games

The range of 'legitimate' activities for the Arctic Winter Games fluctuated somewhat during its first decade, but it still primarily reflected the sporting traditions of southern Canada. These activities were further sanctioned by sportspeople from the South, who in the early years attended the Games in order to provide needed technical expertise.

A few events which have been more representative of northern culture have been gradually introduced. Traditional Arctic games and dance were first included as demonstration activities in 1970 and 1972. 'Arctic sports' were installed as an official event in 1974, and have since remained the primary focus of the media as well as the major attraction for spectators. Snowshoeing, which was introduced in 1974, and the snowshoe biathlon, which was introduced in 1978, were also considered to be 'unique northern sports' which were appropriate to the Arctic Winter Games.

A concern over the limited, Eurocanadian range of 'legitimate' activities was raised immediately by elected members of the Territorial Government, although such an intervention did not alter the nature of Games events. As early as 1968, a member of the Assembly suggested that a large number of traditional native games should be included in the Arctic Winter Games (*Debates*, 1968). The Commissioner for the Northwest Territories made it clear that although these activities could be demonstrated, they could not be incorporated as an integral event (*Debates*, 1969). This position was supported by other members of the Assembly which suggested in one instance that the traditional games '. . . had no common rules or regulations to form a unit through which these people could compete against one another' (*Debates*, 1970). One politician argued that the traditional games, if kept solely as a demonstration event, might be exploited as a product for consumption by the public by 'adding ... an Arctic and Northern flavour to the Games and draw[ing] interested people from the South' (*Debates*, 1970). An examination of media coverage today would substantiate this point, since coverage focuses overwhelmingly on the 'unique' Arctic sports event, despite the fact that it was only one of seventeen sports represented in the 1990 Arctic Winter Games.

'Legitimate' Structuring of the Arctic Winter Games

The 'legitimate structuring' of the Arctic Winter Games was initially a fairly uncontentious issue. The organizational structure, which has already been discussed, was modelled on the Canada Games structure, and fused to government at all levels. In keeping with the nature of the dominant system of Eurocanadian sport, the festival operated as a meritocracy based on skill (Birrell, 1989). Territorial 'unit' teams were identified by a process of preliminary trials with each 'unit' contingent member then being outfitted with an identifiable uniform.

Arctic Winter Games events also experienced a process of standardization. Most events were broken down into junior and senior age categories, and separated by gender. The inclusion of adults, while different from the Canada Games, was justified because it was felt that the '... adults in the North often [had] limited opportunities to engage in meaningful competition, or even recreational activity' (Arctic Winter Games Corporation, 1974, p. 10). Event schedules were established and adhered to, in keeping with the expectations of the spectators who attended in order to see a performance. Thus, spectators from southern Canada who were familiar with the Canada Games would feel at home if they were to attend the Arctic Winter Games.

The initial emphasis of the Games was placed on excellence, as evidenced by the presentation of the Games flag to the unit achieving the largest number of points from all events (FAS, 1975). By 1978, this practice had been replaced by the presentation of the Stuart Hodgson Award to the most sportsmanlike team. The Games flag was then presented to the host of the next Arctic Winter Games. Although this transformation marked a shift towards participation rather than excellence, it did not change the unofficial medal count which was tabulated daily for the units and reported in the official Games newspaper.

A few concerns over the low number of native people involved in the Arctic Winter Games were raised by members of the legislature in the early years, although no actions were taken subsequent to these comments. A politician from the Central Arctic, for example, read a telegram in the Assembly before the first Games, which stated that if Central Arctic athletes were not acceptable for the Games, then the name of the Games should be changed to the Western Arctic Winter Games (*Debates*; 272, 1970).

Members of the Legislative Assembly occasionally raised concerns about the underlying structure. One member asked if the Arctic Winter Games personnel had examined '. . . the [traditional Eskimo Olympics] programme and the way in which these events are organised' in order to incorporate an approach more in keeping with native cultural practices (*Debates*; 272, 1970). The response given reflected the wide gulf in perspectives existing between natives and Arctic Winter Games organizers at that time. The Games representative, who had just attended the festival under discussion, claimed that it was 'the poorest organised event I have ever attended' (*Debates*; 272, 1970). What his comment really reflected was his inability to appreciate a festival which was more in tune with native, rather than Eurocanadian values.

Inception and Initial Operation of the Northern Games

The concept of the Northern Games originated in Inuvik in opposition to the proposed structure of the Arctic Winter Games, which was to include only Eurocanadian sports primarily for younger participants (Dittrich, 1976). The Inuvik committee proposed an alternative festival — a weekend of native games and activities in Inuvik as a Northwest Territories Centennial project. A special grant was made to the organizing committee in early 1970 from the Government of the Northwest Territories Centennial fund. Several local communities also donated funds towards the project. The first Northern Games, held in July 1970, brought together 175 people from twelve communities in the Western Arctic, Yukon Territory and Alaska.

This festival did not develop within the sporting context of the Northwest Territories but rather in opposition to perceived inadequacies in the current sport system. It was thus an 'emergent' festival Williams, 1977), conceived of and developed by native people outside of government, in opposition to what was considered a 'legitimate festival' by the power-bloc. Aspects of the 'residual' system of traditional games, which were played informally in the native communities, were incorporated into the Eurocanadian concept of a trans-Arctic festival in order to create this emergent festival. Williams (1977, p. 124) notes that

> To the degree that a new practice emerges, and especially to the degree that it is oppositional rather than alternative, the process of attempted incorporation significantly begins.

This festival, which was definitely oppositional rather than just alternative to existing sporting traditions was initially incorporated to some degree by numerous federal and territorial sport departments.

From 1972, funding was consistently provided by the territorial Recreation Division although monies at the territorial level were also attained directly from the Northwest Territories Commissioner's special projects fund. Federal funding was provided by four different departments beginning in 1973, including Fitness and Amateur Sport (FAS), Secretary of State, Indian Affairs and Northern Development, and Loto Canada.

There has been an ongoing debate about whether or not this festival was to be considered 'sport', and funding sources throughout the 1970s tended to reflect this ambiguity. Several sources were tapped in the first decade, under a variety of labels including 'recreation', 'sport' and 'culture'. Many of these departments have subsequently ceased to fund the Northern Games using the rationale that the Games no longer fell within their mandate.

The funding relationship between the Northern Games and the Fitness and Amateur Sport Branch exemplified this dilemma. Fitness and Amateur Sport did, at one point, consider the Northern Games to be 'sport', describing it as a '... competition in traditional native sports as well as cultural and social activities' (Government of Canada, 1976). The Games, however, were apparently not enough of a 'sports competition' to remain funded under Fitness and Amateur Sport. In 1978, this federal department began to reduce its funding to the Northern Games, with plans to phase out all funding by 1980. In a letter to the Northern Games Association, they explained this decision by claiming that the Arctic Winter Games were seen to be more suited to the Fitness and Amateur Sport mandate than the Northern Games. Thus, the Arctic Winter Games were placed in direct competition with the Northern Games for federal sport dollars. The former festival was not surprisingly perceived to be more legitimate within federal 'sport' circles.

In contrast to the federal government's view of the Games as being non-sport, the Northern Games Association did see a sports and games thrust to the festival. By 1977 in reply to the federal Fitness and Amateur Sport Green Paper on Sport, the Association had disputed the claim that their festival was merely cultural in nature (Northern Games Association, 1977):

> It seems that some outsiders view Northern Games only as a cultural organization. It is a cultural event of the best kind, but its focus is on games and sport. Sports in the south are also cultural events with a different purpose (i.e., a winning purpose in a win-orientated culture). Must we buy that ethic to be funded?

Government funding was provided on an annual basis by all funding departments, which led to a lot of energy going into annual applications, and ongoing uncertainty over funding from year to year. The Government of the Northwest Territitories Recreation Division was the only department to provide an ongoing programme specifically linked to the Northern Games. Grants from other departments were provided out of general programmes, within which some aspects of the Northern Games were considered to fit. Without an identified programme specific to the Northern Games, annual funding could never be ensured, a situation all too familiar to activities which fell outside the dominant southern culture of the power-bloc.

Range of 'Legitimate' Activities for the Northern Games

The Northern Games provided participants with a traditional range of physical activities. Women competed in the Good Woman Contest. This event included a variety of activities which simulated traditional living skills, such as bannock making, tea boiling, seal skinning, muskrat skinning, and fish cutting. Men's events include various sports, such as one- and two-foot high kick, ear pull, knuckle hop, rope gymnastics, musk-ox push, and head pull. Although these contests were primarily Inuit games, various Indian events such as stick gambling, mooseskin handball, and Indian blanket toss, were also included on occasion. There has never been an attempt by government to modify and/or limit the range of 'legitimate' activities for this festival. That right has been left to the organizers of the Northern Games, who are seen to be the 'experts' on this matter.

'Legitimate' Structuring of the Northern Games

While the traditional practices inherent in the Games were not questioned by the territorial government, the structure of the festival was an ongoing concern of the Recreation Division, which primarily raised questions relating to accountability. However, the Northern Games Association remained autonomous from the government in its first decade of operation, and its structure thus reflected a freedom from the 'legitimate' structure preferred in government programmes.

The Northern Games Association never developed a well-defined structure. A steering committee, called the Board of Directors on paper, was identified from among the native membership. They have monitored the Games, with the assistance of a paid coordinator, since 1973. Although there were never any formal terms of reference for this position, the coordinator's duties included obtaining funds for, and administering each Northern Games, as well as the coordination of all auxiliary services. The coordinator's salary was usually paid with project funding earmarked for administrative services. The coordinator often set the direction for the Association, usually with no formal direction from the Board of Directors. This situation was understandable in light of the fact that the Board of Directors existed in name only. No regular meetings were held prior to the greater formalization and bureaucratization of the Association in 1980. By the end of the 1970s, the Western Arctic Association, based in Inuvik, was still viewed as an unofficial parent body, although in reality there were three associations each functioning as independent regional associations.

The government did not initially concern itself with the fact that the Northern Games operated according to a traditional, rather than a Eurocanadian, meritocratic concept of sport. Participants for the annual Games were not selected through a regional playdown. Instead, a number of seats on a chartered airplane were delegated to each community. When the plane arrived in the community, interested people would 'hop on' and attend the Games. This pattern reflected the more informal Games ideology which encouraged participation over excellence, and an atmosphere of socialism and self-testing rather than competitive inequality.

At the Northern Games, competing contingents were recognized by settlement, including communities from Alaska, Northwest Territories, Yukon Territory, Arctic Quebec and Labrador. The teams were chosen by the community, although no particular uniform was used to identify allegiance. It thus became a 'gathering' of people, rather than a competition among adversaries. This environment lends itself to competing with others against oneself, rather than the Euro-canadian 'us against them' approach.

Although the Northern Games published a list of daily events and daily starting times, these only served as rough guidelines. Despite their large size, the Games continued to be a flow of experiences — a 'happening'. Events started and finished when people and the natural realities of sun and season suggested. Since people came to visit and participate, there were few true spectators; hence, no one expected a spectacle to start 'on time'. People, equipment and food converged harmoniously, and flowed apart just as naturally when the experience ended.

There were initially no age categories used in the Northern Games. Participation came from all ages, and individuals were often recruited just prior to the event. These activities also fell in line with traditional lifestyle patterns in terms of gender roles, as evidenced by the differentiation in, and nature of men's and women's events.

The development of standardized rules for the events was never a priority for the Northern Games Association. They did, however, eventually acknowledge a need to formalize their event rules, due to the sporting variations existent within their wide participation base. In 1978, a workshop was held at the University of Alberta in order to identify and formalize rules for Inuit games across the Arctic. While the rules for a variety of traditional contests were documented, the application of these rules at subsequent Northern Games remained flexible.

Race Relations Since 1979

Race relations in the North have been in a state of flux over the last decade. The government is still largely premised on a principle of 'guided democracy', a colonial value which borrows heavily from southern Canada, and stresses equality of opportunity. There has also, however, been a growing political movement for native rights, which has entered into the forum of the Legislative Assembly and placed native leaders in a position where they have become members of the power-bloc, and thus 'definers' of what is legitimate. These native leaders have been supported to various degrees by Eurocanadians who desire independence for the Northwest Territories, and realize that they need a united, clearly articulated 'northern identity' if they are to be successful.

It is now accepted within northern race relations that native people have a right to the privileged benefits formerly accruing only to Eurocanadians in the North. The operationalization of that recognition, however, is still in its infancy. Northerners face a difficulty in this task because they have no model to look to for direction, since the colonial model, their only choice, is deemed to be inadequate. Race relations in the North have thus shifted over the past twenty years. They were initially framed within a colonial mentality, which believed that Eurocanadian institutions were the best and only acceptable model. They have now shifted, however, to an acceptance of traditional native activities and involvement as 'legitimate', necessary parts of any institution, demanding concomitant adjustments to Eurocanadian structures as necessary.

This change in race relations has been evident in the ongoing, contested realm of sport. This chapter will continue by examining the ways in which the 'legitimate' activities and structures of these festivals were further shaped in light of changing race relations.

The Operation of the Arctic Winter Games Since 1979

Range of 'Legitimate' Activities for the Arctic Winter Games

The emphasis on creating 'unique northern events' has continued throughout the 1980s. In the 1986 Games, for example, the sixteen events included ski biathlon, snowshoe biathlon, and silhouette shooting along with the longstanding events of Arctic sports, and snowshoeing. Events more suited to native participants from the smaller communities have also been slowly introduced, beginning with indoor soccer in 1980. Most recently, a Dene Games category was incorporated into the 1990 Arctic Sports event, by adding five Dene games to the nine Inuit contests already included in this event. Each of these events are considered by those involved in the Games as contributing towards a northern cultural identity.

Nevertheless, there still have been concerns that traditional games and cultural events in particular lack recognition within the Arctic Winter Games. At a meeting of the Board of Directors of the Arctic Winter Games and the Ministers from the different government units, it was noted that less emphasis has been placed recently on the cultural component of the Games. The Minister from the Northwest Territories (AWG Corporation, 1988) commented:

> that the Arctic Sports were being relegated to a lower priority and [that] the conventional sports were taking over. If this occurs then the Games could lose their special appeal and become just another regular Games session.

He further noted that to get support from southern media, they must stand out as being uniquely northern. This statement reflects the dependency which the Arctic Winter Games have on maintaining a 'unique northern identity', both for promoting the North elsewhere, and for securing ongoing funding from the federal government.

Concern has also been voiced by the smaller communities in the Northwest Territories that the events do not reflect their interests or expertise. The government has responded to these requests by providing recreation facilities which make southern sports activities possible, increasing the developmental opportunities for sport to the smaller communities, and slowly introducing the occasional activity to the Arctic Winter Games, such as indoor soccer, a popular activity within the smaller communities.

'Legitimate' Structuring of the Arctic Winter Games

Challenges to the 'legitimate' structure of the Arctic Winter Games have not focused on the meritocratic process inherent within the Games. Instead, concerns have surfaced around the lack of native participants at the Games, as well as the more élite Canada Games. The percentage of native people in the Northwest Territories contingent has been fairly small, ranging between 22 per cent and 33 per cent of the Northwest Territories 'unit' in any one Games (Kyllo, 1987). The government has accordingly been pressured to ensure more involvement from the smaller communities, by recruiting a more representative sample of athletes from throughout the Northwest Territories, rather than just in the Western Arctic (and more specifically from Yellowknife).

In 1983, this concern was voiced in the Legislative Assembly when sport executives were criticized over the social and racial composition of the Canada Games contingent. They were instructed to send athletes from all ethnic backgrounds and all parts of the North rather than just send an exclusive Yellowknife contingent composed only of white people (*Debates*, 1983). The accompanying rationale pointed out that there were important social and educational benefits which would be valuable for all northerners even though this idea was contradictory to the Games tradition, whereby only the best were chosen to attend.

Funding for travel to regional trials, along with the creation of a new region, have both been seen as steps which have been taken aimed at resolving this problem. There had been some resistance to the 'legitimate structure' of the Games, due to the procedure in place in the Northwest Territories in order to qualify for the Arctic Winter Games. Until 1982, communities had to pay for their regional travel costs. The regional winners would then be assisted financially to attend the Territorial championships, where the Games athletes were selected. Small communities, which have a very small economic base, would thus be expected to raise the large costs to fly athletes out of their community to the regional trials. Financial pressures therefore impinged upon representation at those trials. The larger communities, which most often held the regional trials, would not face the same financial demands.

Beginning in 1982, the Sport North Federation has tried to respond to this pressure by the native communities, through the provision of travel money for regional as well as territorial trials. Unfortunately, Arctic Winter Games athletes continue to originate primarily from the larger Northwest Territories communities where large numbers of people, better facilities, and coaching and player clinics are more readily available. The major benefactors of the Arctic Winter Games experience thus continue to be non-native individuals who have been previously trained in southern Canada.

Sport North took a further step aimed at increasing the number of native participants involved in the Games. In 1986 a new, seventh region was created for regional trials. This Mackenzie Region was composed of the small communities which had formerly competed against Yellowknife at the regional level. Since Yellowknife athletes consistently dominated the Games, few athletes from these smaller communities would be represented at the Territorial trials. Both the funding of regional travel costs, and the creation of a seventh region did not actually increase the number of native people attending the Games — the percentage of native people within the Northwest Territories contingent has never risen above 33 per cent. However, the number of native athletes involved in the overall Arctic Winter Games process, which includes the regional participation statistics, has continued to rise each Games since these changes were implemented.

Despite these changes, questions about the 'legitimate structure' of the Games continue. A member of the Legislative Assembly, for example, challenged Sport North officials in 1987 to restructure their Board to include regional community representatives along with representatives from the Sport Governing Bodies (*Debates*; 386, 1987). This would effectively alter the power-bloc to include more native people with a small community focus, rather than just individuals espousing the Eurocanadian perspective fostered through sport associations.

The Range of 'Legitimate' Activities within the Northern Games

In 1988, the Government of the Northwest Territories further incorporated the 'emergent' Northern Games festival, by creating a traditional games programme which provided ongoing funding to both the Northern Games, and the Dene Games (a similar style of festival held by Dene people in the Western Arctic). For the first time, the government specified what were to be considered 'legitimate' traditional sporting events. Two of the four principles in the programme guidelines outlined both why the traditional games were 'legitimate', and what these 'legitimate' activities would include (GNWT, 1988):

1   Traditional native sport and recreation activity contributes to the well being and quality of life of residents of the Northwest Territories, preserves and strengthens the traditional ways of life of native peoples and contributes to a pride in our northern culture.
2   The fabric and foundation of traditional games is native recreation and life style demonstrations, competitions and celebrations. While non-traditional activities may contribute to the participation of all communities and their residents, the primary focus of the games remains traditional native games and recreation activity.

These principles reinforced the fact that the traditional games had a different purpose from sporting activities, and that the activities held at such Games should reflect a more traditional focus. This approach differed from the initial treatment of the Dene Games of the 1970s, which were funded as a traditional festival because it was a gathering of native people, even although the central event of the festival was a baseball tournament. This change reflects very clearly the government's intent to separate the programme and delivery system related to traditional games from those of sport activities in the North.

'Legitimate' Structuring of the Northern Games

Initially, the Games existed independently of any specific government influence. However, in 1981, when the Government of the Northwest Territories agreed to accept funding responsibility for the Games, the government also stipulated that the Association must become more community-orientated, and strengthen its organizational structures.

Continued problems with accountability further shaped the organizational structure of these Associations. Regional associations, rather than a territorial association became the rule, so that associations were not saddled with the debts of another group. This also meant, however, that 'official' participants could only come from the region where the Games were being held, thus contradicting the initial, trans-Arctic nature of the Games. Members of the Recreation Division provided ongoing consultation to these organizations, and thus the government became more involved at both the conceptual level as well as the operational level of the Games.

While specific expectations were outlined by the government as criteria for funding, such as the incorporation of the regional association, there was also informal encouragement to structure the Games along the Eurocanadian, meritocratic model of sport. Several changes were recommended, including the division of events by age and gender, the development of community trials to choose participants, the standardization of rules, and the improved scheduling of events.

A review of Northern Games programmes over the past few years would demonstrate that many of these suggestions have been incorporated, although they often reflect a native perspective. All of the programmes have Inuit games events for both men and women, and most Associations have the contests broken down into junior and senior categories. Interesting developments related to these changes can be seen in the good woman contest, which now has categories for both men and women. Another deviation, related to the categorization of sport by age, occurred at the Keewatin Summer Games of 1989. Their age categories included 'old person' (48 years of age and over), 'middle age' (35 to 45 years old) and young person (34 years and under). They carried this categorization one step further by stipulating that a coach had to be a minimum of 25 years of age.

The development of regional trials have not as yet been

incorporated into the Northern Games. Most of the Games have stipu-lated that a number of members would be financed from each commun-ity to attend the Games thus leaving the choice of actual participation up to the community. It appears that the idea of 'hopping' on the plane still occurs on occasion. A Recreation Development Officer report of the 1988 Baffin Games noted that athletes from all over the Baffin region except for Broughton Island had been able to attend. Her explanation concluded by noting that 'the plane was too full for them to get on' (Kadlutsiak, 1988).

This same report highlighted the fact that the standardized rules for the Northern Games were not necessarily enforced. She was recruited, while at the Games, to provide a variety of services includ-ing the judging of some events, although she had no previous experi-ence with these events. She went on to note the assistance of other community members with this task, and even the recruitment of competing athletes who served as judges while waiting for their next event. Clearly the camaraderie and friendliness of the traditional Games is an integral part of these Baffin Summer Games.

The Western Arctic Northern Games, held in Holman Island in 1988, provided a detailed schedule of events. An interesting aspect of their schedule was the timing of events. The first night, after a midnight feast at 12.00 midnight, they had a square dance scheduled 'outside on the platform till around 4.00 a.m.' (Western Arctic North-ern Games Association, 1988). Two days later, the junior events were scheduled at the school from midnight until 3.00 a.m. Each of these examples demonstrates that while the meritocratic principles inherent in Eurocanadian sporting practices may have been adopted to some extent in the Northern Games, the Games organizers seem able to use these principles in a way which does not constrain their traditional structure.

Perhaps the greatest threat to the ultimate incorporation of the Northern Games stems from a new group in the North, who are entering into the power-bloc of the Northern Games Association. In 1986, the Government of the Northwest Territories began a recreation leaders training programme, a two-year college programme which primarily trains aboriginal leaders who are sponsored by their home community. The government estimated that they would have forty new recreation leaders in Northwest Territories communities by 1993 (Sport and Recreation Division, 1986).

These long standing members of northern communities will have been trained in a programme which by necessity will have drawn extensively from similar programmes in southern Canada. These recreation trainees while being relatively familiar with their community, are not necessarily familiar with traditional games and practices. Possible problems which might arise when these leaders take over the organization of the Northern Games were reported in the minutes of a Western Arctic meeting in May 1988. These minutes noted unanimous concern that no one present had actually been involved with previous Northern Games. They thus found it difficult to make any decision on the future of the Association and/or the Games. All the community representatives at this meeting were recreation leaders or coordinators. The only positive aspect of this account is that at least the members recognized their lack of expertise, and therefore refused to act out of ignorance.

The Recreation Division has consistently encouraged members of the Northern Games not to join the Sport North Federation, because they felt that the Associations, while gaining a small amount of funding, would more importantly have to relinquish much of their autonomy in order to match the Sport North criteria. The government has thus consistently viewed Northern Games activities as unique cultural forms deserving of a separate programme delivery system within government.

Conclusion

While the Arctic Winter Games are essentially a 'northern' Eurocanadian ethnic festival, and the Northern Games are essentially an emergent, traditional ethnic festival, the changing race relations in the North have mediated both their social structure and content. An examination of specific ethnic characteristics demonstrates the types of changes which have occurred within each festival. Clearly the Northern Games have experienced the majority of changes. However, the resistance they have shown to the imposition of the Eurocanadian structure, and the 'legitimation' they have received through the formalization of a government programme, serve as indicators of the ongoing ability of native people to shape their own future. Meanwhile, the Arctic Winter Games have, on the surface, not changed dramatically but the process underlying the Games, and the attention given within the Games to native activities have remained ongoing issues which must be resolved if these Games expect to maintain a 'legitimate' status within the North.

Notes

1 The phrase 'northern frontier, northern homeland', coined by Justice Thomas Berger in his 1976 Mackenzie Valley Pipeline Inquiry (Berger, 1976), captures the general nature of ongoing race relations present in northern society. Southern Canadians see themselves as settling Canada's last frontier — the North. This vision of the North is contested by native people — both Dene and Inuit have called the North their homeland for thousands of years. Dene communities exist south of the treeline, while Inuit people inhabit communities to the north and east of the treeline. Together, native people outnumber Eurocanadians in the Northwest Territories, with approximately 13,000 Dene and Metis (28 per cent), 15,500 Inuit (33 per cent), and 17,500 Others (38.3 per cent) (Devine, 1981, p. 21). While Eurocanadian 'frontierspeople' have maintained control largely through the ongoing imposition of southern institutions, native people have increasingly contested colonial control over economic, political and cultural institutions in the North.

2 While 'race' is popularly viewed as a static biological trait, it has far more explanatory power when seen as a socially constructed 'category of experience marked by exclusionary practices and economic and cultural oppression' (Birrell, 1989, p. 214). In the Northwest Territories, 'race' has been socially constructed through the process of colonization. This process has oppressed the original inhabitants of the North, by devaluing and/or suppressing traditional economic, social, political and cultural institutions, and replacing them with Eurocanadian alternatives. This process has been fueled by an ethnocentric attitude on the part of the colonizers, who assumed that their way of life was 'the' way of life for the North.

References

ARCTIC WINTER GAMES CORPORATION (1974) *Historical Report of the Arctic Winter Games.*

ARCTIC WINTER GAMES CORPORATION (1988) *Minutes of the Board of Directors of Arctic Winter Games Corporation and Ministers*, **26**, August.

BERGER, T. (1976) 'North of 60: Mackenzie Valley Pipeline Inquiry', *Summaries of Proceedings, Volume 4: Community Hearings*, Ottawa, DINA.

BIRRELL, S. (1989) 'Racial Relations Theories and Sport: Suggestions for a More Critical Analysis', *Sociology of Sport*, **VI** (3), pp. 212–7.

DACKS, G. (1981) *A Choice of Futures: Politics in the Canadian North*, Toronto, Methuen.

Debates (1968) 36th Session, 6th Council, 51, 8 February.

Debates (1969) 36th Session, 6th Council, 7, 13 January.

Debates (1970) 41st Session, 6th Council, 272, 19 January.

Debates (1970) 41st Session, 6th Council, 518, 21 January.

Debates (1970) 41st Session, 6th Council, 526, 21 January.

Debates (1977) 41st Session, 6th Council, 526, 21 January.

Debates (1983) 10th Session, 9th Assembly, 829, 7 March.

Debates (1987) 9th Session, 10th Assembly, 386–7, 25 February.

Debates (1987) 9th Session, 10th Assembly, 346–87, 25 February.

DITTRICH, D. (1976) 'Cultural and Recreational Aspects of Northern Society and Life', paper presented to Mackenzie Valley Pipeline Inquiry, June.

DEVINE, A. (1981) *Northwest Territories Data Book 1981*, Yellowknife, Outcrop Ltd.

FITNESS AND AMATEUR SPORT BRANCH (1975) *Letter to the Northern Games Association*, May.

GOVERNMENT OF CANADA (1976) 'Fitness and Amateur Sport', *Annual Report 1975–76*, Fitness and Amateur Sport Branch.

GOVERNMENT OF NORTHWEST TERRITORIES (GNWT) (1988) *Traditional Games: Programme Guidelines and Funding Application*, November.

GOVERNMENT OF NORTHWEST TERRITORIES (GNWT) (1989) *Sport and Recreation Grants and Contribution Policy*, Sport and Recreation Division, File No. 25–500–040.

HALL, S. (1981) 'Notes on Deconstructing "the popular"', in SAMUEL, R. (Ed.) *People's History and Socialist Theory*, London, Routledge and Kegan Paul, pp. 12–24.

KADLUTSIAK, R. (Recreation Development Officer) (1988) *Cape Dorset Trip Report*, September.

NORTHERN GAMES ASSOCIATION (1977) *Reply to Green Paper on Fitness and Amateur Sport*.

KYLLO, L. (1987) *Arctic Winter Games 1982–1986 Analysis*, Calgary, Urban Systems Limited.

SPORT AND RECREATION DIVISION (1986) 'Community Recreation Training Course Update' Briefing Notes, *Minutes of Local Government for Legislative Assembly*, February.

WESTERN ARCTIC NORTHERN GAMES ASSOCIATION (1988) 'Cultural Programmes/Projects: Northern Games, Western Arctic', *Sport and Recreation File*, May.

WILLIAMS, R. (1977) *Marxism and Literature*, Oxford, Oxford University Press.

Chapter 5

Sport, Racism and British Society: A Sociological Study of England's Élite Male Afro/Caribbean Soccer and Rugby Union Players

Joe Maguire

Sport has long been associated with a myth that it offers an avenue of social mobility for socio-economically deprived groups. Social mobility of this kind seemingly results from either 'contest' or 'sponsored' mobility. That is, either from an individual's own endeavours and ability or that granted to an individual by those already in positions of greater power, status and influence (Loy, McPherson and Kenyon, 1978, p. 350). Such mythological thinking has also informed people's understanding of the role that sport performs in British society. While this theory has traditionally been related to the involvement of white working-class males in sport, more recently it has been suggested that sport can also serve a similar function for Afro/Caribbean black Britons.

From both existing British research and anecdotal evidence, it is clear that 'black' Britons, especially Afro/Caribbean males, have made significant inroads as participants in a number of sports, particularly boxing, soccer and athletics and, to a lesser extent, rugby union. Research has found that some Afro/Caribbean males place a high value on achievement in sport, view sport as a central life interest and regard sport as an avenue for social mobility (Bale, 1982). In addition, the Sports Council, a quasi-state body, is intent on promoting greater ethnic participation in sport (Carrington and Leaman, 1983). This trend has not gone unnoticed by English newspapers. *The Sunday Times*, in an article entitled 'How sport helps blacks clear the high hurdles', suggested that 'young blacks have discovered that athletics can be the quick way to fame and money and also the quick way to clear social barriers in this country too' (*The Sunday Times*, 14 September 1986).

Clearly, some Afro/Caribbean black Britons can and have become more socially mobile as a result of either contest or sponsored mobility processes evident in sports such as professional soccer and 'amateur' rugby union. What needs to be grasped, however, is that it is perfectly possible to have individual mobility within a rigid stratification structure. Indeed, the social mobility so far achieved by specific individuals also needs some qualification. Is such mobility transitory, lasting only while these individuals remain at the top level within that sport? Furthermore, an unquestioned assumption underpinning these developments is that involvement is good in itself and that when Afro/Caribbean black Britons have entered a sport they are subject to fair and equal treatment. Indeed, even if successful in sport, such success may be paradoxically reproducing more general inequalities. That is, success in sport perpetuates the myth of the racially superior athlete (Edwards, 1974). In raising these issues, this study is in keeping with one of the hallmarks which Elias regards as characteristic of the sociological perspective: the sociologist as a destroyer of myths (Elias, 1978, pp. 50–70).

As with other areas of sociological enquiry, competing perspectives are evident (Banton, 1972; Moore, 1975; Rex, 1982). While it is not appropriate to articulate, in detail, the adequacy of these perspectives in this context, some elaboration is required. Two issues stand out. First, how appropriate is it to use the term 'race'? As used in this context, it has been employed not as a simple analytical category but rather in terms of the 'social construction of race'. This generation and reproduction of 'race' and 'racism' is seen to reflect the interwoven active role of people in creating and sustaining meanings and the structured nature of social life (Elias, 1978).

Attention must focus on both the 'folk' perceptions of 'race' and on the structural features of society. This relates to the second issue. There has been a tendency for analyses to compartmentalize social processes and to focus on either the 'cultural' or the 'structural' dimensions. It is argued here that the sociology of 'race' needs to synthesize an analysis of the cultural allegiances and traditions of British society with a recognition that racism is locked into broader structural dimensions of inequality; reference must therefore be made to the power discrepancies which mark all levels of social relations. Reference to either folklore or class struggle alone does not capture the emergence of the present pattern of ethnic relations (Dunning, 1972; Rex, 1982).

The intention here is therefore to critically consider the involvement of Afro/Caribbean black Britons in soccer and rugby union. These sports lend themselves to study as they arguably represent examples of the contest and sponsored social mobility processes referred to above. Professional soccer has been seen to provide a ladder of opportunity in which the most skilled of the working classes could, in contest with others, 'make the grade' and achieve financial security. But over the last 100 years professional soccer has arguably provided, at best, a transitory, and more usually an illusory form of social mobility for the majority of working–class males (Houlston, 1982). Since the late 1960s, white working-class males have been joined by their Afro/Caribbean counterparts. Nevertheless, specific individuals have 'made the grade' and by 1985–1986 Afro/Caribbean Britons made up 7.7 per cent of first team squads of the English Football League (Maguire, 1988).

Although the involvement of Afro/Caribbean black Britons in rugby union occurred later, it has not reached the same extent, and indeed, appears to involve middle-class as well as working-class black players. Their involvement has also been seen as indicative of a more general process of social mobility, that is, while rugby union has remained officially amateur, involvement with the 'old boy' network has ensured that access to higher status individuals and thereby superior employment positions are possible. It maybe, however, that black working-class rugby players 'need' sponsored mobility to a greater extent than their middle- or upper-class counterparts.

Such thoughts, however, may be based on a misperception of what the situation of Afro/Caribbean black soccer and rugby union players is really like. This study examines whether the perceived 'race' of individuals influences how players are assigned to particular positions in soccer and rugby union and how they themselves perceive their experience of playing at the élite level in these sports. In doing so, the present study seeks to challenge the idea that soccer, or indeed rugby union, provide any real, long-lasting chance for social mobility.

In tackling this issue the present study will initially review the merits of research conducted both in North America and Britain. On this basis, the substantive section will seek to provide both quantitative and qualitative data on the issues raised so far. By combining insights from these research traditions, guidelines will be offered on both the further exploration of specific issues raised by this research and on a systematic analysis of sport and Afro/Caribbean British males.

The Land of the Free and the Home of the Brave:
Racism and American Sport

Examination of North American textbooks in the sociology of sport reveals that considerable attention has been paid to the relationship between race and sport. As Birrell has recently pointed out, the dominant research tradition has employed 'bias' models of one form or another but has failed to adequately engage in debate with materialist and culturalist conceptions of racial relations and sport (Birrell, 1989). Empirical in orientation, such studies have tended to neglect theoretical discussion, especially concerning the need to synthesize analysis of the cultural traditions of a society with a recognition that racism is locked into broader structural dimensions of inequality (Maguire, 1988, p. 267).

One of the more favoured issues examined by this research tradition has been the allocation of positions by race in American football, basketball and baseball. Sociologists have emphasized that this allocation has nothing to do with physiological or psychological differences between races and more to do with socially constructed racial discrimination. Research to date has convincingly demonstrated the latter link (Chu and Segrave, 1983; Coakley, 1986; Curtis and Loy, 1978; Edwards, 1973; Loy and McElvogue, 1970; Yetman and Eitzen, 1972).

North American research initially examined the possibility that there was both over-representation and under-representation of blacks and whites in certain positions in major team sports. The research strategy adopted was to examine yearbooks which classified all starting players and their positions, and contained team photographs. In addition, an hypothesis was constructed which proposed that 'stacking', i.e., racial discrimination in team sports, was positively related to 'centrality'. In order to test this hypothesis, those researchers involved had both to define 'centrality' and 'non-centrality' and allocate specific positions to those categories.

'Centrality' was seen to designate how close a member is to the centre of the group's interaction, how frequently that member interacts with a greater or lesser range of other team-mates, and the degree to which the team member must coordinate tasks and activities with other members (Grusky, 1963). Viewed as an ideal-type, 'central' positions are those where high levels of interaction occur with the maximum number of team-mates; 'non-central' positions are those where a relatively low level of interaction takes place with few team-mates. Examining American football, basketball and baseball, researchers found it relatively easy to apply the idea of centrality to those sports and to assigning actual positions accordingly.

A significant feature of stacking in North America is that blacks have traditionally been over-represented in the non-central positions within the organizational structures of teams and under-represented in central positions; for whites, the patterns are reversed. These findings were common to the sports examined and have been replicated by a range of studies which have been usefully summarized by Curtis and Loy (1978). More recently, Chu and Segrave (1983) have moved away from using the centrality hypothesis in terms of rigid organizational structure towards using it in terms of the attributes which coaches associate with particular positions. They have been more concerned to correlate specific positions with access to future coaching appointments and whether there is a disproportionate number of whites occupying these positions.

Echoing the work of Curtis and Loy, Medoff cites four main hypotheses which have been offered to explain the phenomenon of stacking (Medoff, 1986). These include:

1 the 'role-modelling' hypothesis — based on the possibility that blacks emulate highly successful black athletes;
2 the 'differential attractiveness of positions' hypothesis — based on the possibility that blacks either select or avoid positions that offer maximum opportunities;
3 the 'outcome-control' hypothesis — based on the possibility that blacks are excluded from positions having the greatest opportunity for influencing game outcomes; and
4 the 'interaction and discrimination' hypothesis — based on the possibility that blacks are assigned to positions by white coaches using racial stereotypes of abilities.

The concern here is less with the possible significance that socialization experiences of blacks and whites may have, and more with the contention that blacks and whites are recruited and assigned their positions by people who mistakenly believe that there are crucial ability differences between the races.

According to North American research, black athletes seldom play central positions because coaches, managers and team-owners do not think they are capable or that it is not desirable for them to handle leadership and decision-making tasks associated with specific positions. The more 'central' the position, the greater the likelihood that it would be held by a white rather than a black (Eitzen and Tessendorf, 1978; Loy and McElvogue, 1970).

There have been two qualifications to this basic centrality argument. First, blacks have traditionally been excluded from roles in sport through which outcomes directly depend on their decisions and self-initiated actions. Second, coaches have been found to assign positions on the basis of general stereotypical beliefs about blacks and whites. Questionnaires were usually used to substantiate the latter. Attention focused on how coaches defined the qualities needed to play particular positions and what they saw as the characteristics of their black and white athletes (Edwards, 1973; Eitzen and Tessendorf, 1978; Williams and Youssef, 1979). In addition, Brower has noted that when coaches were asked to list the qualities needed to play the positions in which whites were over-represented they referred to leadership, intelligence, emotional control and the ability to make decisions under pressure (Brower, 1972). The qualities associated with those positions where blacks were over-represented involved strength, speed, quickness, high emotion and good 'instincts'. Before attention is paid to how this North American research strategy relates to the present study, however, consideration must also be given to the British research findings.

The Land of Hope and Glory: Racism and British Sport

In sociology and physical education in Britain, less attention has been paid to the experience of Afro/Caribbean Britons at élite level but has, in some ways, been more in keeping with the research model which Birrell has advocated. Existing research has examined the function sport serves for black Afro/Caribbean males and the role physical education plays in the establishment of sport as a central life interest in the culture of particular ethnic groups (Carrington and Wood, 1983; Cashmore, 1982; Sargeant, 1972). Unfortunately, some analyses have tended to be speculative and anecdotal rather than based on systematic substantive enquiry. This is surprising given the quality of work being produced in the sociology of race more generally (Rex, 1983; Troyna and Smith, 1983).

From both existing British research and anecdotal evidence, it is clear that Afro/Caribbean men have made significant inroads as participants in a number of sports, particularly as noted, boxing, soccer and athletics, whereas Afro/Caribbean women are more usually found in athletics and basketball. Though, according to the 1981 Census, black Britons born both in the Caribbean and in the United Kingdom amount to only 1.4 per cent of the total population (Official Census, 1981) they make up, for example, a third of the teams in athletics. Afro/Caribbean men place a high value on achievement in sport, view sport as a central life interest and regard sport as an avenue for social mobility (Bale, 1982). Work undertaken by Cashmore (1982) has questioned the assumptions on which such involvement is based. While his approach is not without value, its main weakness lies in its reliance on anecdotal data. He deliberately eschews the adoption of the research strategy employed by North Americans (Cashmore, 1982, pp. 177–80). In doing so, he goes some way towards the research strategy but not the theoretical position which Birrell (1989) favours.

Although he argues that there is no precise way of analyzing whether blacks have to outperform whites or whether they are stacked in specific positions in British sports, Cashmore argues that the real issue is whether blacks believe that discrimination exists. The emphasis is on the cultural experience of those involved. As such, one cannot argue with this assertion. However, Cashmore's work is ambiguous in a number of respects. Although he stresses the scope that sport offers blacks for self-actualization, he also acknowledges that a process of stacking similar to that in the United States exists in British sport. Despite this, he argues that such a process is 'by no means an inexorable one' and that 'black kids will vary their appetites in sport and officials will realize that the scope for potential is far wider than presently realized' (Cashmore, 1982, pp. 177–8).

At first sight these remarks seem rather naïve. The problem that one is faced with is how to judge the adequacy of such assertions. In contrast to Cashmore, this study is based on the assumption that both quantitative and qualitative data regarding the involvement of Afro/ Caribbean black Britons in sport is required, and that existing American research provides some useful lines of enquiry but that this needs to be combined with a theorizing of the experience of racism in British society.

Adoption of this approach does not blind the present study to reservations regarding quantitative measures of complex social processes in general nor to the specific problems associated with applying the research strategy dominant in North America to the British context. As a first step, however, such an approach seems both appropriate and sorely needed as a countermeasure to anecdotal evidence. By combining this data with qualitative evidence, one hopes that a more 'rounded' picture may be produced. In addition, without the necessary theorizing of such data, the research concluded would be necessarily limited.

Blending Research Traditions: Methodological Issues

While both North American and British approaches have provided specific insights, there has been little or no cross-fertilization of ideas. What is intended here is to utilize one of the more favoured research approaches employed by North Americans, i.e., the analysis of ascription and position along racial lines, in the study of English professional soccer and 'amateur' rugby union. Attention will focus on three questions: is there stacking in English soccer and rugby union? Does this relate to the concept of centrality? How do Afro/Caribbean Britons perceive their lived experience of these sports? The first step is to probe the relationship between position, ethnic group and centrality with reference to record book data.

The main problem in focusing on soccer lies in the applicability of the concept of centrality. In comparison to American sports, especially American football and baseball, the group-dynamics of soccer are arguably different in two respects (Dunning, 1970). First, the functions of the playing positions in soccer are less clearly demarcated. Second, the game form is marked by a greater degree of interdependence. Interaction between and within positions occurs more frequently across a greater range of positions. As a consequence, it is more difficult to allocate positions along the centrality, non-centrality axis.

A similar problem was noted by Edwards (1973) with reference to basketball. Edwards argued that 'there is no positional centrality' in basketball because 'there are no fixed zones of role responsibility attached to specific positions' (p. 213). The present study acknowledges the issue but argues that it is not one of either/or. That is, the differences between sports regarding zones of role responsibility are of a relative, not an absolute, nature and relate both to spatial location and the types of tasks, rates of interaction and qualities associated with particular playing positions. A preliminary investigation of English soccer managers' perceptions of those positions which they regard as crucial for decision-making, leadership and control of the pattern and interaction of the team's play, bears out the application of centrality utilized by the present study (Hawes, 1987). Whereas there is no rigid zone of role responsibility, coaches do associate specific positions as more 'central' than others.

With regard to rugby union, the problems are arguably less

evident. It appears that this sport form has greater similarity with the organizational dimension and role prescription of American football than other sports have. Given that American football developed out of rugby union, this is less surprising than perhaps it first appears. The functions of the playing positions in rugby union are more clearly demarcated. Second, interaction between and within positions occurs less frequently across a narrower range of positions. As a consequence, it is arguably less difficult to allocate positions along the centrality, non-centrality axis. Certainly coaches and players appear to have little difficulty in assigning positions to central or non-central categories (Wedderburn, 1989).

While the task set is not without its difficulties, the present study, however, is more optimistic in this regard than Cashmore when he argues that 'given the structure of British sport' it is 'virtually impossible to nail down' whether stacking, or the more subtle process of blacks having to outperform whites, is occurring (Cashmore, 1982, p. 178). While Cashmore suggests that attention should therefore focus on blacks' perceptions, it is argued here that a more adequate strategy would probe both dimensions. Hence, consideration of the issue of stacking will be combined with data drawn from indepth interviews with Afro/Caribbean Britons.

Afro/Caribbean Britons and English Soccer

This ethnic grouping first began to play soccer at Football League level during the late 1960s and early 1970s. It was not until the late 1970s, however, that they began to be present in first team squads in significant numbers. Those involved were often the sons of Afro/Caribbeans who had come to Britain during the late 1950s. In 1979, amid great publicity, Viv Anderson became the first Afro/Caribbean Briton to play for England at full international level. Others have followed him in to the team, so much so that Cashmore, writing in 1982, predicted that by 1990, half of the national team would be black.

Judging by the accounts of Afro/Caribbean players, their entry into soccer has not been an easy passage. Take the comments of Garth Crooks, then a first division player, when he reflected on his experiences for Cashmore (1982, p. xiii):

When I became a professional footballer at Stoke I had to do that little better than the equivalent White kid ... I have experienced racialism in football from other players and from crowds and in society generally. But I was prepared for it and like other Black sportsmen, I've had to prove myself.

Racist chants and the hurling of bananas have also greeted players (*The Independent*, 2 January 1987). In January 1988, Mark Walters became the first Afro/Caribbean Briton to be transferred from an English club to a club in the Scottish Football League, and only the second currently playing at the senior level in Scotland. While playing for the Glasgow Rangers, Walters so far has experienced racist abuse and has been struck by bananas thrown at him (*The People*, 17 January 1988).

Such conduct continues to be a feature of spectating at some grounds. The situation was sufficiently extreme at Leeds United soccer club, that the local Labour-controlled council sought to ban anyone convicted of racist offences at the ground from all city council facilities (*The Guardian*, 29 March 1988). The involvement of the National Front, an extreme right-wing organization noted for its racist policies, is also not unknown. Such episodes are the more public experiences which Afro/Caribbean players have had to endure. More subtle stereotyping also exists in English soccer. This can be highlighted by reference to the comments made by soccer managers.

From existing evidence, it would appear that both managers and players associate 'black' players with particular attributes. For example, according to Jim Smith, then manager of Queens Park Rangers, 'black' players 'use very little intelligence; they get by on sheer natural ability' (Cashmore, 1982, p. 45). In addition, John Sillet, manager of Coventry City, noted that 'black people have been known more for their speed, grace or flair' (*The People*, 23 August 1987). The importance of managers' perceptions is underlined by the fact that of the ninety-two managers in the English Football League, none are Afro/Caribbean. The same position holds with respect to assistant-managers. Such observations begin to map out the context in which the findings of the present study need to be understood.

Is there stacking in soccer? And, if so, does it relate to centrality? Relevant data were obtained from a systematic analysis of the Football League club directory for the 1985–86 and 1989–90 seasons. By examining two seasons over a five-year period, consideration could be given to observing similarities and differences over time.

Every club in each division of the English Football League was considered. Data were available from team lists and photographs on playing position and race for each player. Only those who had

Table 5.1: A comparison of race and position occupancy in the English Football League 1985–1986 and 1989–1990

Position	1985–1986			1989–1990		
	White	Afro/ Caribbean	Total	White	Afro/ Caribbean	Total
Goalkeeper	130 (99%)	1 (1%)	131	141 (100%)	0 (0%)	141
Fullback	249 (92%)	22 (8%)	271	243 (91%)	24 (9%)	267
Centre-back	238 (94%)	14 (6%)	252	227 (91%)	23 (9%)	250
Mid-field	354 (95%)	17 (5%)	371	361 (95%)	19 (5%)	380
Forwards	363 (86%)	57 (14%)	420	330 (79%)	86 (21%)	416
Total	1332 (92.3%)	111 (7.7%)	1445	1302 (89.5%)	152 (11.5%)	1454

played in the first team during the season were included. To establish whether stacking exists, 'race' and position categories were drawn up and the data handled in these terms. This initial step presented no significant problems.

Table 5.1 presents the number of Afro/Caribbean and white players occupying specific positions in the Football League during the 1985–86 and 1989–90 seasons. It is clear that there is an over-representation and an under-representation of Afro/Caribbeans in specific positions across all four divisions.

A number of features of this data deserve elaboration. On the basis, as already noted, that Afro/Carribean Britons make up 1.4 per cent of the population, one can conclude on this evidence that they are over-represented in soccer. Over the five-year period under considera-tion, this over-representation has increased even further. In the 1985–1986 season, Afro/Caribbean Britons made up 7.7 per cent of the total number of players: by 1989–90 this had increased to 11.5 per cent. The actual number of Afro/Caribbean players also increased by forty-one, this representing a 37 per cent increase. One can speculate that this increase may be due to a number of factors: the greater attractive-ness of the game to Afro/Caribbean Britons, a change in recruitment policies of the clubs and/or a trend towards Afro/Caribbeans out-performing their white counterparts in trials and training in a manner similar to that which Lapchick describes with regard to American sports (Lapchick, 1984).

However, whatever the explanation, what is also evident is that this involvement of Afro/Caribbean Britons is unevenly distributed across positions. That is, there is both positional under- and over-representation. This is clearly evident when goalkeepers are con-sidered. Despite the presence of 111 Afro/Caribbean players, during

Table 5.2: *Distribution of position occupancy among Afro/Caribbean Football League Players 1985–1986 and 1989–1990*

Position	Percentage	
	1985–1986	1989–1990
Goalkeeper	0.9% (1)	0% (0)
Fullback	19.8% (22)	15.8% (24)
Centre-back	12.6% (14)	15.2% (23)
Midfield	15.3% (17)	12.5% (19)
Forwards	51.3% (57)	56.5% (86)
	N = 111	N = 152

the 1985–86 season, there was only one black goalkeeper. By 1989–90, even with the 37 per cent increase referred to, none were located in the goalkeeper position. In addition, Afro/Caribbeans appear to be over-represented in forward positions. Although respectively making up 7.7 per cent and 11.5 per cent of the total number of players during the seasons under consideration, they account for 14 per cent and 21 per cent of forwards. This latter finding highlights that the increase in Afro/Caribbean involvement in soccer is disproportionately occurring in forward positions. For the other positions there is either little or no change in the relative percentage of their involvement.

Further support for the idea that stacking exists in soccer can be drawn from an analysis of the playing positions occupied by Afro/Carribean Britons alone. Table 5.2 examines this issue. Though there are slight changes in position occupancy, in general a remarkably similar positional distribution is evident for the two seasons under consideration.

From the data in Tables 5.1 and 5.2 it would appear therefore that some form of stacking does exist in soccer. But if the data contained in these Tables are sub-divided, then the general proposition can be further supported. Thus as is shown in Table 5.3, Afro/Caribbean Britons are unevenly distributed across divisions.

By 1989–90 each division shows an increase in the percentage of Afro/Caribbean Britons playing first team football relative to 1985–86. But what is also evident is that the actual proportion of Afro/Caribbean players — relative to the overall total of players for each division — decreases as one moves from the First to Fourth division. This pattern holds for both the 1985–86 and the 1989–90 seasons. Indeed, in both cases, there were over 50 per cent less Afro/Caribbean Britons playing in the Fourth than in the First division.

Such a finding is arguably not inconsistent with the 'unequal

Table 5.3: Afro/Caribbean involvement in the English Football League Division 1–4 1985–1986 and 1989–1990

	Percentage	
	1985–1986	1989–1990
Division 1	9.8%	15.4%
Division 2	8.7%	10.9%
Division 3	7.3%	8.1%
Division 4	4.8%	7.2%

Table 5.4: Afro/Caribbean involvement in selected European soccer leagues, élite divisions 1988–1989

Country	White		Afro/Caribbean		Total
Belgium	346	(95.6%)	16	(4.4%)	362
France	352	(88%)	48	(12%)	400
Holland	334	(93.3%)	24	(6.7%)	358
Portugal	271	(83.4%)	54	(16.6%)	325

(*Source*: Data drawn from Hammond, (1988) *The European Football Yearbook*)

access for equal ability' hypothesis proposed by Yetman and Eitzen (1972) with regard to American sport: Afro/Caribbeans have to be not only as good as their white counterparts, but that they have to clearly outperform whites. In this connection, one can speculate that 'mediocre' Afro/Caribbeans may be either overlooked, rejected or subsequently 'cut', while whites of a similar standard are scouted, recruited and/or kept on the team roster for longer. In addition, it may be that prejudice and discrimination are more evident in the arguably less cosmopolitan lower divisions.

The situation may be similar with regard to mainland European soccer leagues. Table 5.4 highlights the involvement of Afro/Caribbeans in a number of leagues. Afro/Caribbean involvement in the élite divisions of other leagues, such as the Danish, Spanish, West German and Italian, is negligible or non-existent. Their involvement in the leagues cited in Table 5.4 is less surprising, however, if one notes that all four countries have had, until recently, colonial 'possessions' in Africa and or the Carribbean. The Portuguese first division has the highest level of Afro/Caribbean involvement, both in terms of percentage (16.6 per cent) and actual number of players (fifty-four). Belgium has the smallest level, this despite also having overseas 'possessions' in Africa. The French league draws players from a range of African countries including Senegal, the Camaroons and Gabon.

French society itself is experiencing an increase in racism and far-right involvement in mainstream politics. At this stage, however, we cannot be sure of either the processes which give rise to this fluctuating level of participation or to the detailed experiences of Afro/Caribbean players in these leagues. However, the situation in France has prompted attention and some research (Beaud and Noiriel, 1990).

What is clear, is that racist abuse of players from the terraces of European stadia does occur. During the 1990 European Cup Semi-final between Bayern Munich and A.C. Milan, Frank Rijkaard, one of A.C. Milan's Dutch internationals was subject to racist chants by what was described as 'a hard-right section of the Bayern crowd' (*The Times*, 20 April 1990). Overt racism of this kind has, as noted, its parallel in English soccer. It would appear, however, that the covert racism highlighted in this paper also is evident in European soccer. During the qualifying tournament for the 1990 World Cup, the then Dutch manager, Thijis Libregts suggested that 'coloured players were lazy, especially in Winter' (*The Times*, 20 April 1990). Apparently these comments were directed at Ruud Gullit and Frank Rijkaard. A dressing room revolt ensued which led to Libregts' dismissal. Clearly a more detailed study of this aspect of European soccer is required.

Another way in which to demonstrate that some form of stacking does exist in English soccer is to consider dividing the broad categories of midfield and forwards. That is, while Afro/Caribbean representation in midfield appears to match their overall percentage in the league, when this broad category is considered in terms of wide/support midfielders and central midfielders then their absence in the latter position is marked. During the two seasons under consideration, out of the thirty-six players located in midfield, only six play in a central position. The same pattern is even more evident if the forward category is sub-divided into central strikers and wide/support strikers. For the same seasons, out of a total of 143 Afro/Caribbeans playing as forwards, only 30 per cent were in the central striker position. This compares with 41 per cent for their white counterparts. This disparity, however, relates to the concept of centrality and it is to this topic that we must now turn.

Having established that 'stacking' exists in English soccer, the next stage was to probe the possible link this might have with centrality. Some of the difficulties involved in applying centrality to soccer have already been noted. Soccer, relative to American football and baseball, is a more fluid game, is less role prescriptive in terms of specific positions, and has a number of different tactical formations within which players can be assigned specific roles. As a consequence, the designation of a position as central or non-central presents certain problems. The application of centrality in this context refers to both the spatial location of positions and to the types of task, the rate and range of interaction and the qualities associated with specific positions. In order to overcome this problem, reference was made both to coaching reports of the official governing body of the sport — FIFA — and work investigating English managers' perceptions of playing positions (Hawes, 1987).

A report, prepared by the coaching and technical committee of FIFA following the 1974 World Cup, examined the qualities required in order to be successful and is helpful in this regard. It concluded:

> A modern team has a 'backbone' of competence — that is, a sound goalkeeper, an active defensive libero, two skilful midfield players and two thrusty forwards. Other players fit around this spine responding to the promptings and interplay (FIFA, 1974, p. 70).

This 'backbone' of competence, it can be suggested, corresponds to the idea of centrality as utilized in the American context. On this basis, goalkeepers, centrebacks, central midfield players and central 'strikers' were assigned to the central category. Non-central positions were viewed as fullbacks, 'wide'/support midfield players and 'wide'/ support forwards. Support for this categorization comes from the perceptions of football managers. In justifying the selection of striker, centre half and goalkeeper as central positions, one first division manager remarked:[1]

> Well being forward oriented, you've got to have someone who can put the ball in the back of the net . . . centre half, if you're going to compete against another team that wants to win, er . . . you've got to have someone to be a stopper, and the goalkeeper can win you the game, like Peter Shilton, I think so far to date he's conceded about eighteen goals in league match- es and Derby haven't scored that many yet they're still in the top ten in the league . . .

This categorization was also supported by the findings of Hawes (1987) who found that English soccer managers tended to allocate similar importance and qualities of high and low interaction and decision-making to the central and non-central positions determined

Table 5.5: *A comparison of race and occupancy of central and non-central positions in the English Football League 1985–1986*

	Central				Non-Central			
	White		Afro/Caribbean			White		Afro/Caribbean	
GK	130	(99.2%)	1	(0.8%)	FB	249	(91.9%)	22	(8.1%)
CB	238	(94.4%)	14	(5.6%)	WSM	222	(93.3%)	16	(6.7%)
CM	132	(99.2%)	1	(0.8%)	WSF	211	(83.4%)	42	(16.6%)
CS	152	(91%)	15	(9%)					
Totals	652	(95.5%)	31	(4.5%)	Totals	682	(89.5%)	80	(10.5%)

Key: GK: Goalkeeper   FB: Full-back
CB: Centreback   WSM: Wide/support midfield
CM: Central-midfield   WSF: Wide/support forwards
CS: Central-strikers

by the present study. Asked about these qualities, another first division manager commented:

> I think central defenders need to be intelligent, often you find they are the best readers of the game. Most of them tend to be the most aware players or a central midfield player, wide players much more need pace to beat a player, central strikers are usually signified by goal scoring ... central midfield and centre halves probably, I think they are the main two ...

Table 5.5 reflects this classification outlined and addresses the issue of whether racial segregation in soccer is linked to centrality. Thus 28 per cent of Afro/Caribbean players in 1985–86 occupied central positions and 72 per cent played in non-central positions. When whites are considered, 49 per cent played in central positions and 51 per cent occupied non-central positions. Only a 2 per cent difference between occupancy of positions among whites is thereby evident. In addition, while Afro/Caribbeans make up 7.7 per cent of the total number of players, they compose 4.5 per cent and 10.5 per cent of central and non-central positions respectively. Significantly, they are under-represented in both the goalkeeping and the central midfield positions. In order to provide some comparative benchmark, the same exercise was conducted for the 1989–90 season. The results are shown in Table 5.6.

If the total number of white players is considered there is little difference (3.6 per cent), in their occupancy of the central (51.8 per cent) and non-central positions (48.2 per cent). For Afro/Caribbean

Table 5.6: *A comparison of race and occupancy of central and non-central positions in the English Football League 1989–1990*

	Central				Non-Central			
	White		Afro/ Caribbean			White		Afro/ Caribbean	
GK	141	(100%)	0	(0%)	FB	243	(91%)	24	(9%)
CB	227	(91%)	23	(9%)	WSM	194	(93.2%)	14	(6.8%)
CM	167	(97%)	5	(3%)	WSF	191	(77%)	57	(23%)
CS	139	(82.7%)	29	(17.3%)					
Totals	674	(92.2%)	57	(7.8%)	Totals	628	(86.9%)	95	(13.1%)

Key:	GK:	Goalkeeper		FB:	Full-back
	CB:	Centreback		WSM:	Wide/support midfield
	CM:	Central-midfield		WSM:	Wide/support forwards
	CS:	Central-strikers			

Britons, though the gap between occupancy of central and non-central positions had narrowed, the difference was still some 25 per cent. That is, of all Afro/Caribbean Briton first team footballers, 37.5 per cent occupy central and 62.5 per cent non-central positions.

In addition, while Afro/Caribbeans make up 11.5 per cent of the total number of players for the 1989–90 season, they comprise 7.8 per cent and 13.1 per cent of central and non-central positions respectively. In comparison with 1985–86, where Afro/Caribbeans comprised 4.5 per cent and 10.5 per cent of central and non-central positions, only a small shift towards narrowing this difference is evident. While this shift may be the product of variations in recording of the occupancy by players of specific playing positions, it is also possible that a significant shift in the relative balance of position occupancy is beginning. Clearly, further investigation is required. Chi square analysis further supports the contention that there is a connection between race and occupancy of central positions in English soccer.

If racial segregation does exist in soccer, then what does it entail? American researchers found that segregation consisted of the exclusion of 'blacks' from positions requiring relatively greater qualities of judgment and decision-making, from positions of responsibility and from positions which have the greatest opportunity for influencing the flow and pattern of the game (Loy and McElvogue, 1970). Analysis of the findings presented here suggests that similar processes are at work in English soccer. For the 1985–86 season, of the ninety-two clubs examined, there was not one Afro/Caribbean player listed as team

Table 5.7: *Chi square test of race and occupancy of position in the English Football League 1985–1986 and 1989–1990*

Position	White	Afro/ Caribbean	Total	White	Afro/ Caribbean	Total
Central	652 (95.5%)	31 (4.5%)	683 (100%)	674 (92.2%)	57 (7.8%)	731 (100%)
Non-central	682 (89.5%)	80 (10.5%)	762 (100%)	628 (86.8%)	95 (13.2%)	723 (100%)
Total	1334 (92.3%)	111 (7.7%)	1445 (100%)	1302 (89.5%)	152 (11.5%)	1454 (100%)
	2			2		

$$X = 18.02. \; (df = 1) \; P - < .001. \qquad X = 11.08. \; (df = 1) \; P - < .001.$$

captain, a role in soccer which is associated with qualities of leadership and good decision-making. During the 1989–90 season, only one black player is known to have captained his side.

In addition, as has been observed, Afro/Caribbeans are under-represented in the central midfield position. In soccer it is this position, above all others, which is associated with the capacity to influence the pattern, flow and outcome of the game and which is invested with qualities of good decision-making and intelligence. The observations made by two current first division managers noted earlier bear this point out. Their relative absence from this position may in part be better understood if considered in the light of the comments made by one London manager when he remarked that 'black players' need to develop 'their footballing brain and their passion for hard work' (cited in Wolff, 1989, appendix). What is evident in these comments are the stereotypes of stupidity and laziness which American research has highlighted.

Afro/Caribbean Britons, however, are also over-represented in positions which stress speed and quickness, i.e., fullbacks and 'wide' forwards. American research has shown that associating blacks with these qualities is also part of a more general stereotyping process (Edwards, 1973). This process also appears to be the case with English soccer. Take the comments made by the manager of another London first division club:

> I think that you find that, you know, black players are often quicker, therefore, that's why they're in attacking positions you know, they do better when they can like get on the end of things ...

When the same London first division manager who felt that black players were 'lazy', was asked why Afro/Caribbeans were found in forward positions he responded that it was 'their pace' and the fact that they wanted to be 'glory hunters' which stood out. Interestingly, this manager felt that they did not make 'natural goalscorers'. He remarked that they were:

> Not as natural as a white lad, because it's not something that's been orientated as a white lad, it's been there ... for a natural goalscorer you look at your Tony Cottees, Linekers and that's an instinct ... I think that the Danny Wallaces are the closest to it, but he's not a natural goalscorer.

Crucially, though Afro/Caribbeans are increasingly occupying forward positions, they tend to do so as wide/support forwards. As noted earlier, of those who play in forward positions, 30 per cent were central strikers, while some 70 per cent were in wide/support positions. White players tend to be associated with the key goal-scoring role. Support for such an observation can be drawn from an analysis of goalscoring records in the English league for the 1988–89 season. Out of the top ten scorers in each division of the Football League, only 2.4 per cent were Afro/Caribbean, yet this group make up 17.3 per cent of the total number of central strikers for the 1989–90 season. If the stereotype highlighted by the managers' comments cited above are widespread, then this may, in part, help to explain such features of Afro/Caribbean involvement in English soccer. The players themselves appear to believe that this is the case. Take the remarks made by a player of the club managed by one of the managers cited above:

> The stereotype is an attacking role, whether it be a winger, a striker or an attacking midfield player who has limited responsibilities but has flair, imagination and ability ... even if black players have such qualities as excellent tacklers and not particularly quick, it seems to go against them as opposed to them having the qualities to make the grade in that particular position in that area ...

The cumulative evidence does suggest that stacking exists in English soccer, that further qualitative data from interviews with players and managers supports the notion that this is related to centrality and that this pattern appears to be closely connected to

stereotypes held within the game by those making the key recruitment, selection and retention decision-making. Having considered
the situation with regard to English soccer, it is appropriate to turn
attention to English rugby union.

Afro/Caribbean Britons and English Rugby Union

Although the involvement of Afro/Caribbean Britons in English rugby union is relatively recent, and the data available are rather limited
in nature, they do shed light on some of the issues raised by the
soccer case study. Table 5.8 contains a breakdown of the data so far
accumulated.

*Table 5.8: Afro/Caribbean involvement in the English Rugby Union Courage Clubs
Championship Division 1–3, 1988–1989*

	Total	Percentage
White	527	97.6%
Afro/Caribbean	13	2.4%
Total	540	

Source: Data drawn from Wedderburn, 1989

The actual number of Afro/Caribbean players involved in these
leagues is relatively small. Of these thirteen players, eight are wingers.
This situation is not dissimilar to the situation in English rugby
league. Data based on an analysis of thirteen of the sixteen clubs
playing in the premier division of the English rugby league in 1986–
87 reveal that, of the 169 first team players listed in club photographs, nine were Afro/Caribbean. Comprising just over 5 per cent of
the total number of players, Afro/Caribbeans were again over-
represented in the wing position. Of the twenty-six wingers, seven or
27 per cent were Afro/Caribbean Britons (Maguire, 1988, p. 265). In
addition, the experience of Australian Aborigines playing rugby
league is very similar. Australian Aborigines are over-represented in
the wing position and the qualities coaches associate with that position
correspond to the dominant societal stereotypes of Aborigines
(Hallinan, 1991).

While such findings are suggestive of a pattern of position occupancy similar to that in soccer, in themselves they do not provide the
complete picture and should be viewed as a preliminary stage in the
analysis. Although it is arguably the case that the 'central' positions

within rugby union are hooker, scrum-half, number eight, fly-half and fullback, given the small numbers of Afro/Caribbean Britons currently playing at élite level, it is not possible, at this stage, to repeat the exercise conducted with regard to soccer and probe the issue of under-representation in such positions. However, evidence drawn from interviews with players currently involved at the élite level in English rugby union, does reveal aspects of stereotyping and racism in recruitment, selection and retention procedures which does parallel the situation revealed with regard to English soccer.[2]

Given that the majority of the thirteen Afro/Caribbean players are from middle or upper classes, (unlike the majority of Afro/Caribbean soccer players who arguably come from working-class backgrounds), and that they attended either public or grammar schools, it is no surprise that it is in the latter context that they were introduced to rugby union. Such schools have long been the recruiting grounds for English rugby union (Dunning and Sheard, 1979). Although rugby union players do not, officially, get paid to play the game, clubs keen to recruit and retain players are widely reported to secure employment positions for them. As such, for those rugby players from working-class backgrounds, opportunities of this nature do provide for social mobility of a 'sponsored' kind. Referring to the unofficial payment of players, one player also highlighted this 'sponsored mobility' process:

> I do think that it happens. I don't think it happens blatantly in London. I think there are other rewards. We know what they are, in terms of 'OK you want a job? We'll get you a job. You want a flat? We'll help you get a flat', and so on and so on. You want expenses, the expenses will be inflated ...

Of more significance, in this connection, is not simply that it was in the public school context that a number of them were introduced to the game, but that, at this early stage, their involvement was connected to specific positions. Take the comments made by one of the élite players interviewed regarding his involvement as a winger:

> I think that's the only position where we would have stood a chance initially to shine, you know a lot of us being graced with the gift of pace and all the rest of it ... People just wouldn't look on it as a black player in the centre or fly-half or whatever ...

When another of these élite players was asked whose decision it was that he first began playing as a winger, he replied,

> ... our coach at school, our master at school. Because like you said, you're black, you're quick, you're on the wing.

This stereotyping of Afro/Caribbean players has at least two main dimensions: what qualities they are assumed to possess and what qualities they are assumed to lack. In this connection, a player involved with one of the leading London clubs noted:

> ... I would think that from a very early age black people have been labelled as very fast but not with the best hands in the world. Safest to put them on the wing where the intricate moves have been completed and they just finish off with their natural speed ...

At the very least, such comments are suggestive of a pattern whereby Afro/Caribbean players are screened out of the key decision-making positions. In a similar vein, another player noted that black players were associated with specific attributes and weaknesses. He commented:

> Everyone seems to stereotype black people as just fast, they like the ball, they love to run at people. The other thing they say against black people is that they don't like being tackled, they don't like tackling, they haven't got good hands.

As in soccer, emphasis is placed on speed and quickness. In rugby league, a similar stereotype appears to exist. Martin Offiah, an Afro/Caribbean winger currently playing for Widnes, a rugby league side, has suffered racial abuse and has encountered the myth that 'black' players lack 'bottle', that is, they lack psychological toughness. Offiah recently remarked that he felt the situation was worse in his former game, rugby union:

> I'm not sure that union circles are so progressive. There are some who still like to believe that although the black man may run like the wind, he'll crack under a bit of pressure. (Maguire, 1988, p. 264).

The élite Afro/Caribbean players of rugby union are only too aware that stereotypes of this nature affect the selection process. One player interviewed remarked that people react with 'mild amazement' when they discover that he plays scrum-half, a position which is associated with cognitive qualities and an ability to 'control the game'. Commenting on the racism involved in the selection process, this player remarked:

> Oh yes, it upsets me a lot, but the unfortunate thing is that there's not much we can do ... you just have to accept it, very, very reluctantly ... But I am convinced I would at least have had an England trial if I'd been a white scrum-half ...

The fact this player believes that he was not selected because of his colour is apparently not unique. Another player who had been overlooked at English schoolboy level recalled that his father had said to him that

> in a situation like this, when its for England ... the coloured chap's got to play 200 per cent better than the white guy. You can't just play a sound game and expect to get through. You've got to play 200 per cent better and really shine ...

Remarks of this nature parallel those made with regard to soccer, that is, in 'making the grade', the Afro/Caribbean Briton not only had to be as good as his white counterparts, he had to be significantly better.

Covert racism of this type is matched by overt racism. Again, this can take several forms. Recalling a specific incident, one player remarked:

> I remember when I was in the England squad. One Christmas an envelope came through which just said 'Player X, care of [First Division] Rugby club. I opened it, all it had was a letter and it said 'Niggers out', that was it. I've kept it in my scrapbook and look back on it from time to time ...

Racist abuse of this nature is not confined to pre-match intimidation. Take the following example of a player encountering a range of racism during one particular match:

> ... The worst incident I've had with any of the away supporters has got to be at Gloucester ... The first time I ran out

there, there was probably about 7,000 in the ground, and as I've said there were the two wingers and myself, and as I ran out I heard someone say 'Good God, there's three of them', and the chants as soon as I touched the ball, you know the chants would come out, and if the Gloucester forwards managed to get hold of me there was a big cheer . . .

In a well publicized case, one Afro/Caribbean player, Gerald Cordle, then playing for Cardiff, clashed with a spectator who had repeatedly taunted him with racist remarks (*The Times*, 21 December 1987).

From the available evidence therefore, it appears that, in particular ways, the experience of Afro/Caribbeans in soccer and rugby is similar. In fact, rugby union players are not themselves unaware of this. In discussing the assignment of Afro/Carribeans to the wing position one player observed:

We've still got a long way to go to break that stereotype but as you see more and more black faces in the game, hopefully there'll be a few more in other positions. It's very much like soccer. I mean they had a stereotype that black players were skilful on the ball, but they couldn't take the knocks, you know and they had to live that down for ages. They'd play them on the flanks, on the wings to sprint down the touchline and cross the ball with the odd fancy footwork, but they'd never play them in the middle anywhere, you know, infield or whatever . . .

While this player correctly identifies the stereotyping and pattern of position occupancy which exists in soccer, he appears to believe that it has broken or is breaking down. The evidence presented earlier suggests otherwise. Indeed, despite having significantly greater numbers playing soccer, especially in the English first division, strikingly similar stereotypes exist in both sports. At this stage, it is perhaps best to attempt to place such findings within the broader context of racism, sport and British society.

Racism, Sport and British Society

In seeking to understand the processes at work in English soccer and rugby union, attention must focus on the specific relations at work in sport and in the wider context. The parents of the majority of those Afro/Caribbean Britons currently playing in soccer were invited and encouraged to enter Britain in the 1950s and 1960s. Crucially, these immigrants were recruited to fill lower-class occupational positions and have subsequently suffered low status and economic disadvantages. While this observation may not relate to the parents of some élite rugby union players or indeed to soccer players such as John Barnes, they appear to have experienced forms of racism. Cultural as well as structural dimensions need consideration.

While it lies outside the scope of the present study to detail its emergence, racism in British society is a product of long-standing, cultural, economic and political processes. It is important to stress its deep cultural roots in a society which once held colonial possessions all round the globe. In fact, as early as the eighteenth century the British had formed discrediting and patronizing views of the African (Walvin, 1984). Such racism, both in the past and in the present day, tends to be self-confirming: through discrimination Afro/Caribbeans are forced into subordinate positions which are then taken as 'proof' of their inferiority (Rex, 1983). The degree of significance which such ideologies have in British society appears therefore to be a function of the power discrepancies which exist (Dunning, 1972). 'Insider' groups with a great deal of power impose their definition of a situation upon the less powerful 'outsider' groups. Stereotypes suggesting stupidity, indolence, untrustworthiness and physical prowess have thus arisen about Afro/Caribbeans.

This situation may be even more evident in sport: given the powerful position which managers and coaches enjoy, players in general are subject to processes which they have few resources to control. One can speculate that the position of Afro/Caribbean players would appear to be even more problematic. Given these twin inter-woven processes, it is hardly surprising that they are significantly under-represented in specific sports in Britain, e.g., golf and tennis, and in soccer and rugby, where access has been gained, they are assigned to positions reflecting dominant stereotypes. Indeed, the locating of Afro/Caribbeans in positions which stress speed (wingers) also finds expression in other sports. In athletics, Afro/Caribbeans who make up to a third of the Great Britain team, are overwhelmingly found in sprint and explosive events (*Running Magazine*, September 1983).

The socialization of Afro/Caribbean males into sport in Britain has received a fair degree of attention, but more work needs to be done. Some members of this group appear to be highly motivated to participate in sport at all levels and, possibly as a consequence of role-modelling of sucessful black American as well as British sportsmen, perceive sport as a way of achieving status and social mobility. The evidence produced by the present case-studies would suggest that this perception may well need to be revised.

While Afro/Caribbean Britons such as Viv Anderson, Cyrille Regis and John Barnes in soccer (Hill, 1989) and Chris Oti, Andrew Harriman and Jeremy Guscott in rugby union have played at the highest level, those who wish to emulate them also share a problem which white working-class, and indeed middle-class males experience — not all of them make it!

Individuals who have devoted themselves to the prospect of a career in professional soccer leave school with little or no qualifications. This has, of course, always been a feature of soccer, but given the recession which the sport is currently experiencing, the opportunities open to new players appear to be decreasing. Even if an Afro/Caribbean Briton does initially 'make it', i.e., he is signed by a league club, then he may encounter what, as noted earlier, Garth Crooks experienced. He may well have to be a 'superspade', that is, he not only has to be as good as his white counterparts, he has to be better. A process similar to that described by Yetman and Eitzen (1972) may be at work: blacks are experiencing 'unequal opportunity for equal ability'. In rugby union, though the players tend to be better qualified and, through sponsored mobility, gain access to a potentially greater range of jobs, here too there is a cost. This cost can take several forms: enduring racist taunts and yet 'conforming'. Consider the following remarks by one élite player:

> I'm saying that your mind is attuned to being a conformist all the way up, therefore you tend not to think of yourself, you tend to just fit in ... You've striven so hard to get where you are, often against some sort of prejudice, that when you get to the top you're inclined to continue in the conformist role that you're taken up to date ...

Such conformity may in part explain the hesitancy of those involved to speak out publicly. Although, therefore, there are examples of Afro/Caribbean Britons playing at the top level, this should not be seen as confirming that sport provides a realistic and long-term opportunity for social mobility. Why should this be so? After all, as noted, Afro/Caribbean Britons make up 1.4 per cent of the population yet make up 11.5 per cent and 2.4 per cent respectively of the total number of soccer and rugby union players at élite level.

The situation is particularly clear with regard to soccer. In order to understand this situation, reference to the general experience undergone by professional footballers must be made. Work by Houlston (1982) examining the post-football occupational careers of former professionals highlights that a significant number experience downward mobility in terms of occupational status and level of income. Although Houlston did not examine the position of Afro/Caribbean footballers, it would not be unreasonable to suggest that their occupational experiences would be at least as bad and, given the experiences of black people in the labour market in general, would probably be worse.

This situation is compounded by one other factor which does not face whites. On coming to the end of their careers, players can attempt to enter coaching and management positions. At present, however, there are no role models for blacks to follow; in both rugby union and in soccer there are no Afro/Caribbean Britons in positions of managerial responsibility and their prospective employers, the owners of the clubs, are all white. On this basis it would be wise of young Afro/Caribbean Britons, especially working-class Britons to be sceptical of the claims of sport as an avenue of social mobility.

Conclusion

Clearly more work needs to be done on the issues raised. A crucial test of the contention that racial segregation exists in soccer would involve a systematic analysis of managers' and coaches' perceptions. Attention would need to focus on both their perceptions of black players and of the qualities associated with specific playing positions (Chu and Segrave, 1983; Eitzen and Tessendorf, 1978). In that way the connection with racial stereotypes and position occupancy which this study has stressed could be further substantiated. But the concept of 'stacking' is, in itself, of limited value and has been used here only to serve as a preliminary tool to tackle the subtle social processes at work.

Hence, qualitative and developmental analysis of black players' experiences needs to be undertaken. That is, consideration of their socialization into sport in general and soccer and rugby union in particular may shed light on the incipient stages in the stacking and stereotyping process which manifest itself, at a later age, at the professional level. The disengagement of this group from sports such as boxing as well as soccer and rugby union deserves attention in a more extensive study. It would also be useful to establish whether these processes are more or less evident at the recreational as well as at the élite level. The analysis also needs to be extended to consider the experience of Afro/Caribbean women in such sports as athletics and basketball.

Reference has also been made to mainland European soccer. A study along the lines so far undertaken, coupled with the suggestion just made, would provide a valuable comparative perspective. Racist stereotypes of the form highlighted may be part of the fabric of European culture.

On the basis of the evidence presented here one cannot be optimistic about the experiences of current or potential Afro/Caribbean soccer or rugby union players. In soccer, they are under-represented in central positions, and in both sports racial stereotyping does appear to be at work. Their position as 'outsiders' in soccer and rugby union may also reflect their status in British society in general. One also remains pessimistic about the extent to which the issues raised will be addressed. The task outlined requires a collective effort but given the ideological, time and financial restraints within which those interested in the sociology of sport in Britain have to work, one suspects that this task may well continue to be neglected. Yet, perhaps the work contained within this set of readings may, in some small way, change the situation described.

Notes

1 Unless otherwise stated, the quotations of English football league managers are drawn from the appendix of Wolff, D.J. (1989) *Racism and Football*, BSc undergraduate dissertation, Loughborough University.
2 Unless otherwise stated, the quotations of Afro-Caribbean rugby players are drawn from the appendix of Wedderburn, M. (1989) *You're Black, You're Quick, You're on the Wing: A Sociological Analysis of the Experience of England's Elite, Black, Rugby Union Players*, MSc postgraduate project, Loughborough University.

References

Bale, J. (1982) 'Get out of the ghetto', *Sport and Leisure* (23), p. 34.
Banton, M. (1972) *Racial Minorities*, London, Fontana.

BEAUD, S. and NOIRIEL, G. (1990) 'L'immigration dans le football', *Vintienne Siecle* (14), pp. 83–96.

BIRRELL, S. (1989) 'Racial relations theories and sport: Suggestions for a more critical analysis', *Sociology of Sport*, **6**, pp. 212–7.

BROWER, J. (1972) 'The racial basis of the division of labour among players in the NFL as a function of racial stereotypes', paper presented at Pacific Sociological Association Conference, Portland, Oregon.

CARRINGTON, B. and LEAMAN, O. (1983) 'Work for some and sport for all', *Youth and Policy*, **1**, pp. 10–16.

CARRINGTON, B. and WOOD, E. (1983) 'Body talk: Images of sport in a multi-racial school' *Multi-racial Education*, **11**, pp. 29–38.

CASHMORE, E. (1982) *Black Sportsmen*, London, Routledge.

CHU, D. and SEGRAVE, J. (1983) 'Leadership recruitment and ethnic stratification in basketball', *Journal of Sport and Social Issues* (5), pp. 13–22.

COAKLEY, J. (1986) *Sport in Society*, St. Louis, Mosby.

CURTIS, J. and LOY, J. (1978) 'Position segregation in professional baseball: Replications, trend data and critical observations', *International Review of Sport Sociology* (4), pp. 5–21.

DUNNING, E. (1970) 'Dynamics of sports groups with special reference to football' in DUNNING, E. (Ed.) *Sociology of Sport*, London, Cass.

DUNNING, E. (1972) 'Dynamics of racial stratification: Some preliminary observations', *Race* (13), pp. 415–34.

DUNNING, E. and SHEARD, K. (1979) *Barbarians, Gentlemen and Players*, Oxford, Robertson.

EDWARDS, H. (1973) *Sociology of Sport*, Chicago, Dorsey.

EDWARDS, H. (1974) 'The myth of the racially superior athlete', in SAGE, G. (Ed.) *Sport and American Society*, Reading, MA, Addison-Wesley.

EITZEN, S. and TESSENDORF, I. (1978) 'Racial segregation by position in sports: The special case of basketball', *Review of Sport and Leisure* (2), pp. 109–28.

ELIAS, N. (1978) *What is Sociology?*, London, Hutchinson.

FEDERATION OF INTERNATIONAL FOOTBALL ASSOCIATIONS (FIFA) (1974) *World Cup Technical Committee Report*, London.

GRUSKY, O. (1963) 'The effects of formal structure on managerial recruitment: A study of baseball organization', *Sociometry* (26), pp. 345–53.

HALLINAN, C. (1991) 'Aborigines and positional segregation in Australian rugby league', *International Review for the Sociology of Sport* **26** (2), forthcoming.

HAMMOND, M. (1988) *The European Football Yearbook*, London, Facer.

HAWES, R. (1987) 'Race and Sport in Britain', unpublished dissertation, West Sussex Institute of Higher Education, Chichester.

HILL, D. (1989) *Out of Your Skin: The John Barnes' Phenomenon*, London, Faber and Faber.

HOULSTON, D. (1982) 'The occupational mobility of professional athletes', *International Review for the Sociology of Sport* (17), pp. 15–26.

LAPCHICK, R. (1984) *Broken Promises: Racism and American Sports*, New York, St. Martins.

LOY, J. and MCELVOGUE, J. (1970) 'Racial segregation in American sport', *International Review for the Sociology of Sport* (5), pp. 7–22.

LOY, J., MCPHERSON, B. and KENYON, G. (1978) *Sport and Social Systems*, Reading, MA, Addison-Wesley.

MAGUIRE, J. (1988) 'Race and position segregation in English soccer: A preliminary analysis of ethnicity and sport in Britain', *Sociology of Sport* (5), pp. 257–69.

MEDOFF, M. (1986) 'Positional segregation and the economic hypothesis', *Sociology of Sport* (3), pp. 297–304.

MOORE, R. (1975) *Racism and Black Resistance in Britain*, London, Pluto.

OFFICIAL CENSUS (1981) London, Her Majesty' Stationery Office.

REX, J. (1983) *Race Relations and Sociological Theory*, London, Weidenfield.

REX, J. and MASON, D. (1986) *Theories of Race and Ethnic Relations*, Cambridge, Cambridge University Press.

SARGEANT, A. (1972) 'Participation of West Indian boys in English sports teams', *Educational Research* (14), pp. 225–30.

TROYNA, B. and SMITH, D. (1983) *Racism, School and the Labour Market*, Leicester, National Youth Bureau.

WALVIN, J. (1984) *Passage to Britain: Immigration in British History and Politics*, Harmondsworth, Penguin.

WEDDERBURN, M. (1989) 'You're Black, You're Quick, You're on the Wing: A Sociological Analysis of the Experience of England's Elite, Black, Rugby Union Players', MSc postgraduate project, Loughborough University.

WILLIAMS, R. and YOUSSEF, Z. (1979) 'Race and position assignment in high school college and professional football', *International Journal of Sport Psychology* (10), pp. 252–8.

WOLFF, D.J. (1989) 'Racism and Football', BSc undergraduate dissertation, Loughborough University.

YETMAN, N. and EITZEN, S. (1972) 'Black American in sports: Unequal opportunities for equal ability', *Civil Rights Digest*, 5, pp. 20–34.

Chapter 6

Athletics and Academics: Contrary or Complementary Activities?

Othello Harris

Sport and Academics

An area that has prompted a great deal of debate in the sociology of sport literature is that of the relationship between sport and academics. This debate stems from the fact that much of the sporting activity in American society, especially for adolescents and young adults, is organized around the educational institutions and sports are often included in one's academic training. One view of athletic participation suggests involvement in sport has positive consequences for participants and society as a whole. Among the positive consequences associated with sport is its function as a transmitter of social values. Through athletic participation, it is argued, one not only learns to play a specific sport but how to 'play the game of life' (Snyder and Spreitzer, 1983). Sport presumably transmits, among other values, the importance of hard work, character development and team work values that are complementary to those necessary for success in academic life. Sport, therefore, has been traditionally viewed as beneficial to the achievement of academic goals.

While the value of athletics to academic success historically has been taken for granted by many Americans, some social scientists have commented on the deleterious effects that the pervasiveness of sport has on academic performance. Veblen (1953) considered the increased attention to sports in colleges to be detrimental to scholarly pursuits. More recently, Coleman (1961) expressed his concern that high schools give the appearance of being organized around sport rather than academics as indicated by the visibility of symbols of athletic achievements (for example, displays of athletic trophies in school lobbies) and the relative invisibility of symbols of academic accomplishments (for example, an absence of displays of scholarly awards). Furthermore, athletes were accorded higher status in high schools than scholars or bright students as indicated by the backgrounds of members of the high schools' leading crowds. This notion of sport as a threat to academics has led to the conceptualization of the athlete as an individual interested in athletics but not academics. This stereotype encompasses the idea that time and energy spent on athletics is time and energy taken away from the pursuit of academic concerns. Because athletic excellence requires an enormous amount of time and energy — for practices, team meetings, home and away games, time to reflect, etc. — university athletes have little time to spend refining their academic skills. This stereotype has given rise to the dominant ideology that athletes are poor students.

Yet, more recent studies of the academic orientation of athletes seem to indicate that they are not poorer students than non-athletes. Schafer and Armer (1968), in a study of high school boys, found a positive correlation between athletic participation and academic performance; athletes had a higher mean grade point average than non-athletes. Also, athletes had higher educational expectations than non-athletes. They were more likely than non-athletes to report that they planned to complete two years or four years of college.

Among the explanations offered by Schafer and Armer for the above are:

1   that athletes may be graded more leniently, because teachers see them as special or more deserving;

2   that exposure in the sports subculture to effort, hard work, persistence, and winning may spill over into non-athletic activities such as school work;

3   that the superior physical condition of athletes may improve their mental performance;

4   that some athletes may strive to get good grades to be eligible for certain sports;

5   that the attraction of a college career in sports may motivate some athletes to strive for good grades;

6   that the higher prestige that students obtain from sports may give them a better self-concept and higher aspirations in other activities such as school work; and/or

7   that athletes may benefit from more help in school work from friends, teachers, and parents.

The positive relationship between academics and educational expectations, however, holds mainly for lower-class boys, i.e., those least disposed to attend college (Picou and Curry, 1974; Rehberg and Schafer, 1968). Boys from higher social class backgrounds who perform well academically are likely to go to college whether they are involved in sports or not. For boys from lower-class backgrounds who do not perform well academically, athletic involvement is related to educational aspiration. Those who are marginal students and involved in sports are more likely than marginal students who are non-athletes to expect to attend college. Thus sport involvement appears to increase educational aspiration and may improve academic performance.

Other writers have contended that sport and academics are, for most athletes, incompatible (Edwards, 1979; Meggyesy, 1971; Scott, 1971). In both high school and college, athletes are often exempt from some of the usual requirements of the student role. Because the schools are interested in athletes primarily for their contribution to the athletic reputation of the school, and because athletic involvement is often very demanding on the students' time and energy, the academic side of the student-athletes' lives is often left underdeveloped. Consequently, athletes are given special programmes and privileges and shielded from demanding academic courses and programmes. They are often exempt from any academic responsibilities beyond maintaining eligibility. Even the maintenance of academic eligibility is often fraudulently achieved by athletic advisors and universities awarding athletes false credits (for example, giving athletes credits for extension courses from community colleges and universities they never attended) and directing them toward less rigorous/demanding courses and programmes (Edwards, 1969).

The issue of athletics and academic eligibility is of particular interest with regard to American black athletes. Edwards (1979) asserts that black athletes are used by colleges for four or five years, until their athletic eligibility is used up, and then discarded without college degrees.[1] Black athletes, it has been argued, are less likely to graduate from college than white athletes (Edwards, 1979; Tolbert, 1976). In part, this results from inadequate academic preparation, inadequate counselling, lack of interest in the academic achievement of black people by athletic department personnel, racism and a white middle-class cultural bias within the educational system (Edwards, 1979). Yet, college coaches and administrators have been quick to point out that the problem with non-graduation of athletes in general, and black athletes in particular, begins in and resides with the secondary schools. In general, there is a neglect, perhaps especially of black athletes, of the kind of academic preparation that means either success in college or success in life after college.

In this research, we examine the question of whether sport reinforces or undercuts academic performance and look for possible race differences in the athletic/academic nexus. We investigate whether there are race differences in student-athletes' academic performance and in their significant others' valuation of academics and athletics. Our concern is with whether sport participation enhances or detracts from academic performance for blacks more than for whites, and whether black student-athletes value athletics at the expense of academics more than white student-athletes. Are athletics and academics complementary or contrary activities for black compared to white high school athletes?

The Sample

The data for this study were collected from two male high school summer basketball leagues in Washington, DC. These leagues attract the top area teams in the top college basketball producing area in the United States (Rooney, 1990). Questionnaires were delivered to all coaches whose teams participated in the Sidwell Friends and Jellef Boys Basketball leagues during the summer of 1985. A total of twenty-three teams — all of the teams in both leagues — agreed to participate in the study. The teams included both public and private schools. Data were obtained from nineteen of the teams. The participation rate for the two leagues was 64.3 per cent.

The sample consists of 187 basketball players in grades nine through twelve. One hundred and sixteen (63.4 per cent) were black and fifty-nine (32.3 per cent) were white. Twelve (6.4 per cent) were neither black nor white. (Because of the small number of cases and the variation in this category, they were not analyzed). Eight (4.6 per cent) were ninth graders, twenty-five (14.5 per cent) tenth graders, fifty-nine (34.1 per cent) eleventh graders, and eighty-one (46.8 per cent) twelfth graders. Both structured and open-ended questions were used to investigate the self-images, aspirations and family background of the students. All students who participated did so voluntarily and were assured of anonymity.

Much of the research in the literature review (for example, Braddock, 1980) suggests there is something distinctive about sports involvement for blacks. Are there, in fact, race differences? We turn now to a discussion of the issues, research questions and measures used to investigate academic concerns among black and white male high school basketball players.

Research Questions and Measurement

In this study we use two types of measures: single items and a Guttman-type scale. Guttman scaling assumes *a priori* ordering of the items; knowing one's total score should allow us to predict responses to each individual item (Guy, Edgley, Arafat and Allen, 1987). The items used for our scale fit the assumption of a cumulative continuum making the Guttman scale a practical choice. The coefficient of reproducibility and the coefficient of scalability were calculated for the scale. They are reported in the text following the scale items.

Sport, Race and Academic Performance

At issue, particularly pertaining to American black men's and women's sporting involvement, is the possible tension between sport and academic success. Does sport reinforce academic values and contribute to the development of traits, such as hard work and self-discipline, that contribute to academic performance? Or does sport detract from academic priorities and interfere with school work? This research addresses several specific questions bearing on the relationship between sport and the academic success of the student athletes we studied.

— Are black people more likely to receive low marks in school?
— Are black people more likely to consider being good at sports more important than being a good student?
— Do black people have different perceptions than whites of the value placed by parents and others on athletic and academic performance?
— Are black people more likely to perceive themselves to be 'star' players?
— Do black people perceive distinctive advantages or disadvantages as a consequence of being involved in basketball?

The Variables

Academic Performance

To measure academic performance, responses to the following question were examined: 'What marks do you usually get on your report cards?'. The grades were coded 'A' (excellent) through 'E' (failing). Fifty-six per cent of the student-athletes reported receiving As and Bs while 44 per cent reported receiving Cs, Ds and Es.

Personal Values

To measure the student-athletes' values on athletic and academic performance we asked: 'How important is it to you that you do well in your school work?' and 'How important is it to you that you do well in sports? Is it very important, pretty important, not very important, or not at all important?'. Most of the respondents said it was very important to do well in school work (85 per cent) and in sports (74 per cent).

Others' Values

Perceptions of significant others' values of athletic and academic performance were determined by the following questions: 'How much do your parents care how smart you are?' and 'How much do your parents care how good at sport you are? Do they care very much, pretty much, not very much or not at all?'. The same questions were also asked about the student-athletes' friends, teachers and coaches. The responses to these questions are reported in Table 6.4.

The Star-Player Scale

We selected and combined four items to create a 'star-player' scale. The following four items were selected:

1 Do you play ball for your high school? (no or yes).
2 (If yes): Are you a starter? (no or yes).
3 When you play ball in pick-up games, are you usually among

the first chosen, somewhere in the middle, or among the last chosen?

4 How sure are you of receiving an athletic scholarship? Very sure, pretty sure, not very sure, not at all sure?

The items were then dichotomized with yes equals one, no equals nil for questions one and two. For question three, among the first chosen equals one, all other responses equal nil. For question four, very sure equals one, all other responses equal nil. We then added the scores across items which produced a Guttman scale with scores ranging from nil to four. Three per cent of the respondents scored nil on the scale. Twenty per cent scored one, 31 per cent scored two, 37 per cent scored three, and 9 per cent scored four. The coefficient of reproducibility is 94 per cent; the coefficient of scalability is 72 per cent.

Consequences of Playing Basketball

Student-athletes were asked two sets of questions about the consequences of basketball for other areas of their lives. The first set of questions, which assess how basketball helps or hurts in a variety of areas is: 'Do you think that being a member of a basketball team:

1 helps one get ahead in life?
2 helps only if you get a college scholarship?
3 helps you learn the value of teamwork?
4 hurts you if you do not take time to study?
5 hurts you if you do not have time for dating?
6 hurts if your team loses its games?'

The second set of questions explores ways in which student-athletes believe basketball influences their lives. More specifically: 'Would you say that playing basketball has influenced your life because:

1 it helps make me popular with girls?
2 it keeps me from getting into trouble?
3 it pushes me to keep my grades up?
4 it improves my self-respect?
5 it helps make me popular at school?

6   teachers care about me as a student?

7   some teachers give me a break on grades?'

For both sets of questions the responses offered were 'very much', 'pretty much', 'not very much' and 'not at all'.

Selected Sample Characteristics

Table 6.1 presents percentage differences by race for three family background variables and five measures of racial composition of different aspects of the students' lives. Per cents and Pearson rs are presented for all students and then separately for those in the public and private schools.

As Table 6.1 shows, a slightly higher percentage of blacks than whites (67.2 per cent to 59.3 per cent) attend public schools. The data on family background suggest that blacks are more likely to come from less privileged settings. They are much more likely to live in a father-absent household, and are less likely to have mothers or fathers with formal education beyond a high school diploma. This race difference is especially pronounced among those in public schools. The private school context appears to include students from higher status backgrounds and race differences among these students are significantly different only on father's education. Here nearly all (96 per cent) of the white students have fathers with some college training while about two-thirds (65 per cent) of the blacks have fathers with some college training.

The data on racial composition suggest blacks and whites live in quite different social worlds. Very few whites live in mostly black neighbourhoods, attend mostly black schools, or have black teachers or coaches. The white students do report more contact with blacks as members of basketball teams where nearly 30 per cent report most of the members of their high school team are black.

Black students experience much more variation in the racial composition of their social worlds. Most black students are members of largely black basketball teams and come from mostly black neighbourhoods, although fewer blacks do report having mainly black coaches or attending a mostly black high school (50 per cent and 46 per cent, respectively). Finally, most black students report having predominantly white teachers. Only 35 per cent of the black students say their teachers are mostly or all black. These composition differences, like the family background differences, are greatest in the

Table 6.1: *Race by selected family and integration control variables*

	All			
	Per cent		N	
	White	Black	White	Black
Father absence	10	46	(55)	(93)
Mother's education (high school)	75	52	(59)	(109)
Father's education (high school)	86	52	(59)	(109)

	Public School				Private School			
	Per cent		N		Per cent		N	
	White	Black	White	Black	White	Black	White	Black
Father absence	9	56	(32)	(63)	9	27	(23)	(30)
Mother's education (high school)	71	39	(35)	(71)	79	71	(24)	(38)
Father's education (high school)	80	44	(35)	(71)	96	65	(24)	(37)

	All			
	Per cent		N	
	White	Black	White	Black
Mostly/all black				
Neighbourhood	3	71	(59)	(116)
High school	2	46	(59)	(116)
Teachers	2	35	(59)	(116)
Coaches	5	50	(59)	(116)
Team	29	80	(59)	(116)

	Public School				Private School			
	Per cent		N		Per cent		N	
	White	Black	White	Black	White	Black	White	Black
Mostly/ all black								
Neighbourhood	3	74	(35)	(78)	4	63	(24)	(38)
High school	3	64	(35)	(78)	0	8	(24)	(38)
Teachers	3	49	(35)	(78)	0	0	(24)	(38)
Coaches	3	64	(35)	(78)	8	21	(24)	(38)
Team	23	82	(35)	(77)	37	76	(24)	(38)

public school context. Public school whites have little exposure to predominantly black worlds, except on the basketball team, and public school blacks are most likely to live in black worlds.

In the private context, more complex patterns appear, especially for the black students. Private school whites are much like public school whites with exposure to blacks limited to the basketball team. Private school blacks are markedly different from whites only on the neighbourhood and basketball team members measures; they are more likely to come from neighbourhoods and play for teams that are mostly or all black. And, looking at public and private school blacks, it is clear that private school blacks are less likely to attend mostly black schools and have teachers and coaches that are of their racial group.

Another key feature of the private context which was not measured in our study is the obvious fact that private schools have selective admission policies. While public schools take virtually all eligible persons within a given geographical area, private schools are, by nature, selective with regard to measures of academic performance and/or potential, financial capability, religious beliefs, etc. As a result, not only are private schools higher status and more racially integrated schools — because students tend to come from different and distant neighbourhoods — but they choose their students differently than do public schools. Private schools draw black students from mostly black neighbourhoods but create a higher exposure to white students, teachers and coaches.

Data Analysis

The format of data presentation is percentage distributions of questionnaire item responses by race, with a summary statistic, Pearson r, that indicates the strength and significance of any differences. After comparing blacks and whites in the total sample, we stratified the sample by type of school and looked again for race differences. That is, we asked, 'Are the differences or lack thereof conditional by school context?'. We also examined school context differences after stratifying by race to see if there are significant differences within a race group by school context. This gave us the following comparisons:

1 black/white comparisons for the entire sample;
2 black/white comparisons for public schools and for private schools; and
3 public/private school comparisons for blacks and for whites.

Table 6.2:   School marks by race

| | Race | |
Marks	White % (N)	Black % (N)
Cs and Ds	7.0 (4)	10.1 (11)
Cs	3.5 (2)	22.0 (24)
Bs and Cs	26.3 (15)	44.0 (38)
Bs	10.5 (6)	6.4 (7)
As and Bs	38.6 (22)	16.5 (18)
As	14.0 (8)	0.9 (1)
		$r = -.39$***

***$p < .001$.

Findings

We investigated black and white high school basketball players'
responses to questions pertaining to sport and academics to learn if
blacks are distinctive in their academic performance and academic
values. Following the examination of race differences we will stratify
the sample by type of school — private or public — in an effort to
elaborate on the findings in the general tables.

One issue regarding race and sports is whether black and white
student-athletes perform differently in the classroom. Do black high
school basketball players receive lower grades than white high school
basketball players?

Table 6.2 reports the students' self-reports of school marks by
race. This table indicates black students receive lower grades in school
than white students. Only 24 per cent of black students compared to
63 per cent of white students reported receiving mostly As or Bs on
their report cards. The Pearson r for this relationship is $-.39$ and is
statistically significant beyond the .001 level.

Does this race difference in academic performance result from
a difference in academic and athletic values? Do black high school
basketball players, more than their white counterparts, place a high
value on sports competence to the exclusion of academic competence?
To examine this, we cross-tabulated race with two variables:

Table 6.3: *Importance of doing well in school and sports by race*

	Well in School		Well in Sports	
Response Categories	White % (N)	Black % (N)	White % (N)	Black % (N)
Not at all important	0.0 (0)	0.0 (0)	0.0 (0)	0.9 (1)
Not very important	1.7 (1)	0.9 (1)	1.7 (1)	2.6 (3)
Pretty important	23.7 (14)	12.1 (14)	25.4 (15)	21.6 (25)
Very important	74.6 (44)	87.1 (101)	72.9 (43)	75.0 (87)
	$r = .15*$		$r = -.00$	

*$p < .05$.

1 attitudes about the importance of academic performance; and
2 attitudes about the importance of athletic performance.

The question we posed was, 'Are black high school basketball players more likely than white players to hold values that focus on athletic rather than scholastic activities?'.

Table 6.3 presents student-athletes' reports of the valuation of academics by race. The students were asked, 'How important is it to you that you do well in school?'. These data indicate that blacks are more likely than whites to say it is important to do well in school. Eighty-seven per cent of blacks compared to 75 per cent of whites said it is very important that they do well in school. The r for the relationship is .15 and is statistically significant beyond the .05 level.

Apparently, the reason blacks receive lower school marks is not because they do not value academic performance. Perhaps they value the importance of athletics too much and this overemphasis on sports leads to an excessive expenditure of time and energy to the exclusion of academics.

Table 6.3 also presents the race comparison on the valuation of sport. Here we find virtually no difference between blacks and whites on the valuation of sport. Seventy-five per cent of blacks and 73 per cent of whites said it is very important that they do well in sports. Thus, these data do not indicate that, compared to whites, blacks are likely to see athletics as more important than academics.

The comparisons suggest that blacks are more concerned about academics but not more concerned about athletics than whites. Hence, we find no difference in athletic values that would explain the lower academic performance of blacks.

If the student-athletes' own values do not point to an explanation of the poorer academic performance of blacks, maybe there are differences in others' values that do. Next, we investigate whether significant others in the home and school environments — parents, teachers and coaches — are more concerned with players' athletic performance than their academic performance and if this differs by race. Perhaps black basketball players are under more pressure to neglect scholastic activities for sports activities.

Turning to Table 6.4 we find no statistically significant race difference in student-athletes' perceptions about how much their parents care how smart they are, but black athletes are more likely to report that parents care how good at sports they are. Thirty-three per cent of blacks and 20 per cent of whites report that their parents care very much how good at sports they are. Black student-athletes are also more likely to report that friends care very much how smart they are, by a difference of 11 per cent to 3 per cent, and how good at sports they are by a difference of 22 per cent to 7 per cent.

When asked about teachers' concerns, the pattern for student-athletes was the same as for friends. Sixty-four per cent of blacks compared to 41 per cent of whites reported that teachers care very much how smart they are. And, for the question of sports competency, 8 per cent of blacks compared to 2 per cent of whites said teachers care very much how good they are at sports.

Blacks were more likely to say that their coaches cared very much about how smart they were (60 per cent to 25 per cent). But, curiously, there is no evidence of a statistically significant race difference in reports of coaches' concerns about how good at sports student-athletes are. Nearly an equal number of blacks as whites reported coaches to be concerned about their sports competency. Thus, we have found mixed results in student-athletes' perceptions of significant others' values. Compared to whites, blacks report that parents, teachers, and friends are more concerned about how good at sports, and teachers, friends and coaches are more concerned about how smart they are.

To summarize the general comparisons, we find that blacks

1 report receiving lower grades than whites;
2 value academics but not athletics more than whites; and
3 are more likely to say parents care how good they are at

Table 6.4: *Perceived caring by significant others of how smart and how good at sports respondent is by race*

Response Categories	Parents care				Teachers care			
	Smart		Good at Sports		Smart		Good at Sports	
	White % (N)	Black % (N)	White % (N)	Black % (N)	White % (N)	Black % (N)	White % (N)	Black % (N)
Not at all	0.0 (0)	1.7 (2)	5.1 (3)	5.2 (6)	1.7 (1)	1.7 (2)	27.1 (16)	13.8 (16)
Not very much	3.4 (2)	5.2 (6)	30.5 (18)	18.1 (21)	8.5 (5)	4.3 (5)	55.9 (33)	41.4 (48)
Pretty much	30.5 (18)	8.6 (10)	44.1 (26)	44.0 (51)	49.2 (29)	30.2 (35)	15.3 (9)	37.1 (43)
Very much	66.1 (39)	84.5 (98)	20.3 (12)	32.8 (38)	40.7 (24)	63.8 (74)	1.7 (1)	7.8 (9)
	r = .10		r = .14*		r = .19**		r = .28***	

Response Categories	Coaches Care				Friends Care			
	Smart		Good at Sports		Smart		Good at Sports	
	White % (N)	Black % (N)	White % (N)	Black % (N)	White % (N)	Black % (N)	White % (N)	Black % (N)
Not at all	0.0 (0)	2.6 (3)	0.0 (0)	0.9 (1)	8.5 (5)	8.6 (10)	3.4 (2)	6.0 (7)
Not very much	11.9 (7)	6.9 (8)	3.4 (2)	3.4 (4)	66.1 (39)	37.9 (44)	49.2 (29)	25.0 (29)
Pretty much	62.7 (37)	30.2 (35)	35.6 (21)	36.2 (42)	22.0 (13)	42.2 (49)	40.7 (24)	47.4 (55)
Very much	25.4 (15)	60.3 (70)	61.0 (36)	59.5 (69)	3.4 (2)	11.2 (13)	6.8 (4)	21.6 (25)
	r = .23***		r = −.03		r = .22**		r = .20**	

**p < .01.

sports, coaches care how smart they are and friends and teachers care about both.

It is worth noting that although there is a race difference on the question of how much parents care how good students are at sports — blacks are more likely than whites to say parents care how good at sports they are — both blacks and whites are nearly three times more likely to say that parents care how smart they are than parents care how good at sports they are. We will now look at these comparisons by school context.

Table 6.5: *Race differences in academic performance and values: Black/white differences within school contexts and school context differences within race groups*

	All	B/W Differences		Pub/Prv Differences	
		Public	Private	Whites	Blacks
Marks	−.39***	−.42***	−.32**		Prv
Well in School	.15	.23***	.03		Pub
Well in Sports	−.00	−.00	−.04		Pub
Parents Care (smart)	.10	.23**	−.02		Pub
Parents Care (sports)	.14	.08	.19	Pub	Pub
Teachers Care (smart)	.19**	.31**	.00		Pub
Teachers Care (sports)	.28***	.30**	.20		Pub
Coaches Care (smart)	.23***	.34***	.06		Pub
Coaches Care (sports)	−.03	.00	−.08		
Friends Care (smart)	.22**	.27**	.10		Pub
Friends Care (sports)	.29**	.28***	.05		Pub

$**p < .01; ***p < .001$.

Academics and School Context

We found that blacks get lower grades than whites but not because of differences in the valuation of academics and athletics. What effect, if any, does school context have on this relationship? Turning to Table 6.5, we find that blacks get lower grades than whites in both school contexts but the relationship is stronger in the public schools ($r = .42$, $p < .001$) than in private school ($r = .32$, $p < .01$). The within–race comparison indicates that blacks get higher grades in private than public schools (see column five). It is blacks in the public schools that are most distinctive; they get the lowest grades of all four categories. In the general comparisons we found no evidence that low grades are due to blacks valuing sports but not academics. Is there, however, a difference in school context that would point in this direction?

Among public school students, blacks are more likely than whites to say it is important to do well in school ($r = .23$, $p < .001$). There is, however, almost no race difference in private schools ($r = .03$). And, there is little or no race difference in either school context on the importance of doing well in sports. However, public school blacks are significantly more likely than blacks in private schools to endorse both items — it is important to do well in school and in sports. Again, we find no evidence that the poorer academic performance among blacks is linked to a difference in student values.

In examining significant others' values by school context, we find a pattern nearly identical to the one found in the general comparisons only in public schools. As Table 6.5 indicates, in public schools black student-athletes more than white student-athletes reported that friends care more how smart they are (r = .27) and how good they are at sports (r = .28), teachers care how smart they are (r = .31) and how good they are at sports (r = .30), and coaches and parents care how smart they are (rs = .33 and .23, respectively). (All of the above Pearson rs are statistically significant beyond the .01 level). In the private context, the relationships are all smaller and none is statistically significant. We find no statistically significant race difference in significant others' values of sport or academics. It appears, then, that school context makes a difference in significant others' values of student-athletes' athletic and academic performance but only in public schools; it is in this school context where race differences in others' values are most apparent. Compared to whites in public schools, public school blacks are more likely to report that all of the significant others care more about how smart they are and teachers and friends care more about how good at sports they are.

Within race groups there is no difference between public school whites and private school whites on any of the variables except parents' valuation of sport competency. (Public school whites are significantly more likely than private school whites to say their parents care how good at sports they are). For blacks, however, those in public schools are more likely to say all of their significant others value both sports and academics except in the case of coaches' valuation of sport where there is no statistically significant difference.

To summarize this section, we have found that blacks receive lower grades than whites; there is no difference in student-athletes' values of sports and academics that would explain the lower grades by blacks; significant others do not appear to value sports but not academics for blacks more than for whites; and public school blacks, who report receiving the lowest grades, are more likely than the other three groups to say significant others value sport and especially academic competence.

Sport Involvement

In the preceding section we found evidence that black high school student-athletes do not perform as well academically as white high

Table 6.6: *Star-player scale by race*

| | Race | |
| | White
%
(N) | Black
%
(N) |
Star-Player Scale		
Low 0	3.4 (2)	2.7 (3)
1	23.7 (14)	18.2 (20)
2	35.6 (21)	29.1 (32)
3	35.6 (21)	37.3 (41)
High 4	1.7 (1)	12.7 (14)
		r = .15*

*p < .05.

school student-athletes. We turn now to the other side of the student-athletes' lives. If black student-athletes are not as good as whites as students, are they more likely to be star basketball performers? Is there evidence that blacks are distinctive in regard to their sport involvement and the experiences they report concerning the ways basketball fits into their lives? We begin this analysis by looking at black/white differences in the 'star-player scale'.

Table 6.6 shows that blacks are more likely to report patterns that we classify as indicating exceptional or 'star' level of basketball performance. They are more likely to be members of their high school basketball teams, more likely to say they are chosen first during informal pick-up games, more likely to be starters on their high school teams, and more likely to be very sure they will receive a college scholarship for playing basketball. Thus, blacks were represented more than whites at the highest level of the star-player scale — level four. The Pearson r for the relationship is .15 and it is statistically significant beyond the .05 level.

Turning to other aspects of basketball involvement, we examine two different sets of questions posed to students. One set explores their assessments of the advantages or disadvantages of being a member of a basketball team; the other set probes the way playing basketball has affected their lives.

Examining Table 6.7 for race differences we found blacks were nearly twice as likely as whites (61 per cent to 33 per cent) to say it is

Table 6.7:   *Advantages/disadvantages of playing basketball by race*

Response Categories	Value teamwork		Hurts study		Helps ahead	
	White % (N)	Black % (N)	White % (N)	Black % (N)	White % (N)	Black % (N)
Not at all	0.0 (0)	1.7 (2)	8.6 (5)	7.9 (9)	1.7 (1)	5.2 (6)
Not very much	0.0 (0)	0.9 (1)	17.2 (10)	12.3 (14)	6.8 (4)	17.4 (20)
Pretty much	27.1 (16)	21.6 (25)	41.4 (24)	19.3 (22)	64.4 (38)	49.6 (57)
Very much	72.9 (43)	75.9 (88)	32.8 (19)	60.5 (67)	27.1 (16)	27.8 (32)
	$r = -.01$		$r = .17*$		$r = -.11$	

Response Categories	Hurts to lose		Helps scholarship		Hurts dating	
	White % (N)	Black % (N)	White % (N)	Black % (N)	White % (N)	Black % (N)
Not at all	20.7 (12)	25.0 (28)	44.1 (26)	19.8 (23)	25.4 (15)	29.8 (34)
Not very much	24.1 (14)	25.0 (28)	35.6 (21)	36.2 (42)	42.4 (25)	48.2 (55)
Pretty much	37.9 (22)	21.4 (24)	11.9 (7)	22.4 (26)	18.6 (11)	16.7 (19)
Very much	17.2 (10)	28.6 (32)	8.5 (5)	21.6 (25)	13.6 (8)	5.3 (6)
	$r = .01$		$r = .28***$		$r = -.12$	

$*p < .05; ***p < .001.$

very true that being on the basketball team hurts if you do not have time to study ($r = .17$, $p < .05$). Blacks were also more likely than whites (22 per cent to 9 per cent) to say it is very true that being on a basketball team helps only if you get a scholarship ($r = .28$; $p < .001$). Note that only two items registered a black/white difference. One suggests there may be tensions between athletic involvement and academics — it hurts if you do not have time to study. The other sees basketball in strictly pragmatic, instrumental terms — it helps one only if it yields a college scholarship.

Turning to the way playing basketball has influenced the students' lives, Table 6.8 indicates black high school basketball players are much more likely than white school basketball players to say it is very true that playing basketball pushes them to keep their grades up (60 per cent to 15 per cent), helps keep them out of trouble (47 per cent to 10 per cent), that teachers care more about them (35 per cent to 12 per cent), and that playing basketball makes them popular at

Table 6.8: *The ways basketball has influenced student's life by race*

Response Categories	Grades up White % (N)	Grades up Black % (N)	Self-respect White % (N)	Self-respect Black % (N)	Out of trouble White % (N)	Out of trouble Black % (N)
Not at all	8.5 (5)	6.0 (7)	0.0 (0)	5.2 (6)	34.5 (20)	16.4 (19)
Not very much	37.3 (22)	6.9 (8)	16.9 (10)	11.2 (13)	22.4 (13)	12.1 (14)
Pretty much	39.0 (23)	27.6 (32)	57.6 (34)	32.8 (38)	32.8 (19)	25.0 (29)
Very much	15.3 (9)	59.6 (69)	25.4 (15)	50.9 (59)	10.3 (6)	46.6 (54)
	r = .40***		r = .12		r = .34**	

Response Categories	Teachers care White % (N)	Teachers care Black % (N)	Popular at school White % (N)	Popular at school Black % (N)	Popular with girls White % (N)	Popular with girls Black % (N)	Teachers give break White % (N)	Teachers give break Black % (N)
Not at all	20.3 (12)	9.5 (1)	13.6 (8)	8.6 (10)	22.0 (13)	20.7 (24)	76.3 (45)	62.1 (72)
Not very much	35.6 (21)	23.3 (27)	35.6 (21)	31.9 (37)	49.2 (29)	38.8 (45)	13.6 (8)	25.9 (30)
Pretty much	32.2 (19)	31.9 (37)	39.0 (23)	33.6 (39)	23.7 (14)	26.7 (31)	8.5 (5)	8.6 (10)
Very much	11.9 (7)	35.3 (41)	11.9 (7)	25.9 (30)	5.1 (3)	13.8 (16)	1.7 (1)	3.4 (4)
	r = .27***		r = .14*		r = .11		r = .11	

* $p < .05$; ** $< .01$ ***$p < .001$.

school (26 to 12 per cent). All of the above differences are statistically significant beyond the .05 level. In addition, blacks are somewhat more likely to say that playing basketball improves their self-respect, makes them popular with girls and that sometimes teachers give them a break on grades, though none of these differences is statistically significant.

All told, blacks are more likely to see basketball as influencing their lives, and in four of the seven possible areas of impact, the differences are substantial. Two of the three differences suggest basketball has motivational significance — it helps to keep grades up and keeps students out of trouble — as opposed to simply improving their self-respect. Blacks also see basketball as improving their image in school, in that it increased their popularity and makes teachers care more about them as students.

Table 6.9: Race differences in star-player scale and basketball involvement: Black/white differences within school contexts and school context differences within race groups

	B/W Differences			Pub/Prv Differences	
	All	Public	Private	Whites	Blacks
Star-Player Scale	.15*	.09	.26*		
Value teamwork	−.01	−.08	.06		
Hurts study	.17*	.17*	.15		
Helps ahead	−.11	−.08	−.15		
Hurts to lose	.01	.10	−.18		
Helps scholarship	.28***	.32***	.19		
Hurts dating	.12	−.10	−.16		Pub
Grades up	.40***	.53***	.18		Pub
Self-respect	.12	.25**	−.12		Pub
Out of trouble	.34***	.39***	.23*		Pub
Teachers care	.27***	.33***	.15		Pub
Popular at school	.14*	.24**	−.05		
Popular with girls	.11	.11	.10		
Teachers give break	.11	.15	−.01		Pub

*p < .05; **p < .01; ***p < .001.

In summary, there are a number of differences between blacks and whites in how basketball figures in their lives. Apparently, basketball is seen as an area of endeavour that has influence. We now turn to the examination of these basketball experiences by school context.

Sport Involvement and School Context

We found that blacks were more likely than whites to see themselves as star players and that there were race differences in the kinds of experiences the players have as a result of their involvement in sport. Do these differences hold by the type of school student-athletes attend? The first two columns of Table 6.9 report the Pearson rs for the black/white differences we have already discussed.

As Table 6.9 shows, in private schools, blacks are more likely than whites to see themselves as athletic stars (r = .26, p < .05). The race difference in public schools, while in the same direction, is smaller and not statistically significant. Columns two and three of Table 6.9 show that only in public schools are blacks more likely to say playing basketball hurts if you do not have time to study and it helps only if you get a scholarship (r = .17, p < .001). There is no marked black/white difference in the private context. Black students in public schools are most distinctive in viewing basketball as helping only if one gets a scholarship — they are more likely than blacks in private schools to endorse this item and this difference is statistically significant. The differences found in the general comparisons tend to be specific to the public school context, with black distinctiveness more associated with seeking a scholarship as the payoff to playing basketball. This is a dramatic dimension of the public school context.

Turning to the second dimension as shown in Table 6.9, we find still more evidence that it is blacks in public school contexts that see basketball as having a clear impact on their lives. All four differences found in the general comparison plus one ('improves self-respect', $r = .25$, $p < .01$) indicate that black public high school student-athletes see basketball as having an impact. Only in the case of keeping out of trouble is there a dramatic black/white difference in the private context.

The last two columns of Table 6.9 indicate where there is a marked difference among blacks or whites across two school contexts. The public/private comparison among blacks shows clear differences in five of the seven areas. The only difference not found in earlier black/white comparisons is the finding that black public student-athletes are more likely than their private school counterparts to report teachers give them a break on grades.

To summarize the school context differences, we find the private school context is distinctive in two areas; blacks are more likely to be stars, and more likely to feel basketball keeps them out of trouble. In the public school context, we find considerable evidence of something distinctive about black student-athletes. While they are not more likely to be stars, they are different from public school whites on seven of the thirteen items — playing basketball motivates them to keep grades up and to stay out of trouble, it makes them popular at school, teachers care about them, it improves their self-respect, it hurts if they do not have time to study and it helps only if one receives a scholarship. Public school blacks are different from private school blacks on six of the thirteen items including nearly all of the above-mentioned items. And, as mentioned above, blacks in public school are more likely than blacks in private school to say teachers some-times give them a break on grades if they play basketball.

Academics and Sport Involvement

We have found that blacks report different patterns than whites on their involvement in basketball; blacks are distinctive in their reports

Table 6.10: Race differences in academic and athletic performance by school context and school context differences within race groups

	B/W Differences			Pub/Prv Differences	
	All	Public	Private	Whites	Blacks
Marks	−.39***	−.42***	−.32**	.08	.24**
Star-Player Scale	.15	.09	.26*	−.04	.11

*p < .05; **p < .01; ***p < .001.

Table 6.11: Correlation of academic performance (marks) and athletic performance (star-player scale) for various categories

All Students	Whites	Blacks	White Public	White Private	Black Public	Black Private
−.13	−.10	−.08	−.20	.16	−.01	−.27*

*p < .05.

of the advantages and/or disadvantages of playing basketball and the ways it has influenced their lives, especially for public school blacks. We have also found that blacks score significantly higher on the star-player scale, but further investigation shows that difference to be confined to private schools. We now turn to the question of whether or not there is a 'tension' between academic and athletic performance. That is, are 'star athletes' poor students and good students poor athletes? To examine this we will correlate measures we have presented earlier. Marks usually received in classes is the indicator of academic performance and the star-player scale is the indicator of athletic performance. Table 6.10 reminds us that blacks get lower grades in school than whites, especially in public schools, and blacks are more likely than whites to be stars, especially in private schools.

Table 6.11 shows us where the 'tensions' are when the two measures are correlated. For all students there is a negative correlation ($r = -.13$) between academic and athletic performance. Stars tend to receive lower grades, but the difference is not statistically significant. Subclassification by race shows this negative correlation is found among both blacks and whites. And, looking at each of the four race-school groups, there is a positive relationship between grades and being a star only for whites in private schools. For blacks in public schools the measures are not correlated ($r = -.01$) while for whites in public schools ($r = -.20$, not statistically significant) and especially blacks in private schools ($r = -.27$, statistically significant beyond the

.05 level), the measures are negatively correlated. It appears that the tension between academic and athletic performance is especially acute for blacks in private schools.

Conclusions

The empirical analyses were designed to examine race differences in high school basketball players' athletic and academic perceptions and performance. In most areas, we found evidence that the experience of blacks and whites is, in fact, different; but how do sport and scholastics fit into the worlds of black student-athletes?

Some view sport in the black community as a character builder and bridge to the larger opportunity structure. Through sport, young people learn discipline, teamwork, and self-confidence. These traits contribute to academic and future occupational achievement. Sport also generates incentive, for doing well in school and going on to college, and, for some, provides needed scholarships. It also may lead to valuable contacts with potential sponsors and employers. As some of the most popular sports in America are dominated by black Americans and as black Americans tend to be represented among the working and lower classes more than whites — percentage-wise — the positive association between athletics and academics is especially consequential for blacks.

Others see sport as a misguided priority among black youth, and believe that the black community, particularly the black family, pushes its children to excel in sports rather than in school. The emphasis on sports, presumably, fosters aspirations and identities that rest on athletic performance and the perception that education is less important, if not relatively unimportant, for their futures. This creates a tension between academics and athletics; blacks find themselves in academic institutions being rewarded for athletic, not academic, accomplishments. The message is that the success route is markedly different for them than for most others.

Our data do not clearly confirm either scenario but, instead, suggest a more complex picture of the consequences of sport for black youth. On the one hand, the data in this study yield patterns which suggest that athletics and academics are not more incompatible for black than white student-athletes. Most student-athletes feel it is important to do well in school *and* in sports and blacks are more likely than whites to indicate the importance of doing well in school. Also, significant others care about both activities, but black Americans feel their significant others are concerned about these activities more than white Americans. These findings are the opposite of that predicted by those who find school and sport activities incompatible for blacks. There is, in other words, no apparent substitution of emphasis on athletics for concern with academics by the athletes nor by their significant others. And, overall, there also is not a greater tendency for performance in athletics and academics to be negatively correlated for blacks, although a significant negative correlation between perceived 'star' status and school marks is found among blacks in private schools.

On the other hand, black student-athletes are more likely to receive low marks in school than whites. Though blacks attribute the same value to academics as whites, they clearly do not perform as well. The lowest marks are found among blacks in public schools, but the blacks in private schools also fall behind their white counterparts. While black basketball players do not devalue academics, basketball has a unique centrality in their experience. These data patterns suggest that blacks rely more on basketball as a mechanism for finding a place in the world of high school and beyond than whites. Insofar as school marks are an indicator of academic assimilation, this reliance on basketball is not highly effective.

While the greater involvement with sport for black basketball players is evident among both public and private school students, there are important differences between the black athletes in the two settings. For those in public schools, sport involvement seems to be highly normalized, and blacks do not feel exceptional for being basketball players. Their academic performance is the lowest of all four groups studied, and they do not tend to be 'stars' on the basketball court.

This pattern is consistent with the finding of Rehberg and Schafer (1968) and Picou and Curry (1974) that for those black youth least disposed to attend college — in this case, those with low grades — there is a positive association between athletics and educational aspirations. For young people who would not normally have access to higher education, basketball seems to provide an opportunity to compete for a place in college and the professional world. The black student-athletes in this sample are more likely than others to see basketball as a way to obtain an athletic scholarship.

Although the sport experiences of black and white student-athletes are different, there is too little evidence to suggest blacks are 'hooked' on sport to the exclusion of academics more than whites. Still, it is apparent that blacks suffer more scholastically from their participation in sport. However, the reasons for this are not due to emphasis on sport to the exclusion of scholastics. Perhaps it is because the black athletes tend to come from less wealthy backgrounds (see Table 6.1), and those from poorer backgrounds are less likely to do well academically (Banas, 1990). The black athletes are not poorer performers academically because of a disinterest in academics by themselves or their significant others but, rather, because they lack the resources — good schools, good programmes, etc. — to compete with their white peers. This certainly is the case in this study, for blacks in both public and private schools. In this sample, blacks in private schools come from the same background as blacks in public schools, but they are often 'recruited' by prestigious schools because of their athletic skills.

Although we cannot conclude from this study that athletics and academics are complementary activities for blacks more than for whites, there is evidence to suggest that these activities are not more incompatible for blacks than whites. Perhaps for some of the star athletes, academics suffer as a result of their participation in sports. We have found this to be true for most stars in our sample. However, we see little to indicate that race is a factor in the compatibility or incompatibility of athletics and academics.

Note

1 The race difference in graduation rates is not confined to athletes. Blacks, in general, are less likely to graduate from college than whites. For example, in a study of retention rates, it was reported that only 41 per cent of blacks compared to 61 per cent of whites who enroll in college actually complete a degree (Myers, 1982). In 1984, while the enrollment rate for black undergraduates in institutions of higher education was 9.5 per cent, they received only 5.9 per cent of the baccalaureate degrees (United States Department of Education, 1988).

References

BANAS, C. (1990) 'Grades tied to school district property values', *Chicago Tribune*, 21 June, Sec. 1, p. 3.

BRADDOCK, J.H. (1980) 'Race, sports, and social mobility: A critical review', *Sociological Symposium*, **30** (Spring), pp. 18–38.

COLEMAN, J. (1961) *The Adolescent Society*, New York, Free Press.

EDWARDS, H. (1969) *The Revolt of the Black Athlete*, New York, Free Press.

EDWARDS, H. (1979) 'Sport within the veil: The triumphs, tragedies and challenges of Afro/American involvement', *The Annals of the American Academy of Political and Social Science*, **445** (September), pp. 116–27.

GUY, R.F., EDGLEY, C.E., ARAFAT, I. and ALLEN, D.E. (1987) *Social Research Methods: Puzzles and Solutions*, Boston, Allyn and Bacon, Inc.

HARRIS, O. and HUNT, L. (1982) 'Race and sports: Some implications of athletics for black and white youth', *Journal of Behavioural and Social Sciences*, **28** (Fall), pp. 95–106.

MEGGYESY, D. (1971) *Out of Their League*, New York, Paperback Library.

MYERS, M.M. (1982) 'Total, black, and Hispanic enrollment in higher education, 1980', *Trends in the Nation and the South, 1982*, Atlanta, Southern Regional Education Board.

PICOU, J.S. and CURRY, E.W. (1974) 'Residence and the athletic participation-aspiration hypothesis', *Social Science Quarterly*, **55** (December), pp. 768–76.

REHBERG, R.A. and SCHAFER, W.E. (1968) 'Participation in interscholastic athletics and college expectations', *American Journal of Sociology*, **73** (May), pp. 732–40.

ROONEY, J. (1990) 'America needs a new intercollegiate sports system', paper presented at Miami University, Oxford, Ohio, 2 April, 1990.

SCHAFER, W.E. and ARMER, M. (1968) 'Athletes are not inferior students', *Transaction*, **5** (November), pp. 21–6 and 61–2.

SCHAFER, W.E. and REHBERG, R.A. (1970) 'Athletic participation, college aspirations and college encouragement', *Pacific Sociological Review*, **13** (Summer), pp. 182–6.

SCOTT, J. (1971) *The Athletic Revolution*, New York, Free Press.

SNYDER, E.E. and SPREITZER, E.A. (1983) *Social Aspects of Sport*, 2nd Ed. Englewood Cliffs, NJ, Prentice-Hall.

TOLBERT, T.M. II (1976) 'The black athlete in the southwest conference: A study of institutionalized racism', unpublished doctoral dissertation cited in EDWARDS, H. 'The collegiate athletic arms race: Origins and implications of the 'Rule 48' controversy', *Journal of Sport and Social Issues*, **8** (1), pp. 4–22.

UNITED STATES DEPARTMENT OF EDUCATION, NATIONAL CENTRE FOR EDUCATION STATISTICS (1988) *Digest of Education Statistics, 1988*, Washington DC, United States Government Printing Office.

VEBLEN, T. (1953) *The Theory of the Leisure Class*, Chicago, University of Chicago Press.

Chapter 7

Sport and the Black Experience

Jose Parry and Noel Parry

The rise to prominence in recent years of black sportsmen and women in British society is pre-dated and to some extent pre-figured by the American experience which has been examined by a number of authors (for example, Boyle, 1971; Eitzen and Yetman, 1982; Hoch, 1974; Mousinho, 1978; Snyder and Spreitzer, 1983). Anglo-Saxon culture is in many ways obsessed with sport and, from the late eighteenth through the nineteenth centuries, produced many of the formalized sports now adopted world-wide, and played according to standard rules (Holt, 1989).

In the last century, following a brief period of participation, black sportsmen in the United States of America became barred. For example, in the case of baseball, black players were participating alongside whites in the early 1860s. In 1867, however, they were excluded as a result of the decision of the National Baseball Association. In response to this move the blacks formed their own teams and leagues, though now and then the 'colour line' was bent slightly. Life in the black leagues was hard (Boyle, 1971, pp. 260–2).

This black participation in sport about the time of the Civil War was associated in the Northern states with a surge in manifest liberal values on the race question. Northern public opinion became increasingly anti-slavery and pro-Union during the Civil War of 1861–1865 against the South. The victory of the Union side over the rebel Confederacy led immediately to the formal abolition of slavery in the South, where hitherto segregation had been total. Blacks quickly found that formality was one thing but the reality of continued racism and discrimination quite another. An ironic corollary of the victory was that when many blacks migrated to the North in search of freedom and jobs, a white backlash was stimulated which itself in turn gave rise to informal but nevertheless powerful forces of segregation.

The period of segregation instigated by white society lasted — so far as sport is concerned — for some sixty years, but it was never total. In certain sports, such as boxing, when black fighters were admitted to the ring it was often on the basis that they would agree to lose. Early signs of the breakdown of segregation could be observed during the more liberal era of President Franklin D. Roosevelt, elected in 1932. It was the phenomenal success of the black American athlete Jesse Owens in the Olympics at Berlin, in 1936, which caused such offence to Hitler and his Nazi Aryan racist philosophy. At the same time it gave a powerful boost to American nationalism and made a black American a national hero.

It, however, was not until after the defeat of Hitler in 1945 that what has been called 'the thaw' began to set in. For example, in 1946, Jackie Robinson became the first black sportsman in modern times to be signed up by a major league 'ball club'. After Robinson's entry to mainstream professional baseball, major league clubs began 'to pick the black leagues clean', black teams scarcely making anything from the sale of players to the majors. This so weakened the sporting and economic viability of the Negro National League that it led to its collapse.

Black sportsmen have, since World War II, made a remarkable impact in baseball, basketball, American football, athletics and boxing, but not so much in swimming nor, with exceptions, in the élite sports of tennis and golf (Coakley, 1978; Edwards, 1973). It has often been noted that certain sports tend to be linked with middle- and upper-class lifestyles, both in the recruitment of their players and their supporters. As Eitzen and Yetman point out,

> since the early 1960s the percentages of black competitors in each of the major professional team sports — football, baseball and basketball — have exceeded their proportion (11 per cent) of the total United States population. By 1979, 71 per cent of all professional basketball players were black, while they comprised more than 47 per cent of all professional football and 17 per cent of major league baseball players (1977, pp. 156–7).

Because black American sportsmen began to make their way before the big push of the Civil Rights movement in the 1960s, it has often been argued that sport is the 'great equalizer' — a meritocratic medium for promoting black social mobility, racial assimilation and integration. Indeed, more broadly, sport has been regarded as the very model of modern meritocracy — promoting the values of open competition, regular testing and measurement of ability by reference to impartial rules and objective standards. Sport is said to foster individual achievement and the competitive spirit but also the collective values of cooperation and team work. Those who take this view believe that sport represents above all the values of equality of opportunity and will function to break down barriers in society and to enhance social integration.

Optimists believed that once segregation was abolished, the key features of sporting success — youth, physical fitness and prowess — would be a potent and quick-acting meritocratic method of achieving beneficial social objectives. They affirm that when sportsmen and women are judged by frequent and repeated series of performances against others in the context of well-established universalistic rules fairness would be achieved and social divisions dissolved.

However valid in theory the arguments might be in favour of a meritocratic sports model, the reality — as in other institutions such as education — has fallen far short of the ideal. The black experience has been that the abolition of formal segregation has not led to equality of opportunity but, rather, has been replaced by other discriminatory practices which have the effect of managing and controlling black participation.

In sports with mass appeal and working-class audiences there has historically been opportunity for some white working-class social mobility. In the major sports there was always plenty of economic pressure, plus a burning desire for success, to drive promoters to recruit excellent performers from whatever background, and in the case of blacks, to risk breaking the segregation rule. Where the sports were segregated and there were parallel leagues of black and white players, there was at least some access to the game for blacks who were able to gain training and skills in their own teams. When white teams had greater prestige and provided bigger rewards the temptation was present both for the selection of first-class black players and for such players to accept selection.

However, for the black player entry to a white team does not, of itself, produce equality of treatment either in the selection process or within the team. For example, tactics such as stacking and centrality are means by which members of ethnic groups are relegated to specific peripheral rather than central team roles. In the years after segregation blacks were made to compete for a quota of places among themselves and were excluded from occupying leadership positions on the field. Such positions were reserved exclusively for white players (Eitzen and

Sanford, 1975; Eitzen and Tessendorf, 1978; Eitzen and Yetman, 1977; Loy and McElvogue, 1970; Madison and Landers, 1976; Schneider and Eitzen, 1979; and Chapter 5, this volume).

As Boyle (1971) points out, blacks were rarely employed in baseball on equal terms with whites. Their signing-on fees were generally lower and they tended to be hired and fired before white players. The racial segregation which operated in the profession meant that they could not share the same hotel accommodation with their white colleagues or go to the same places of entertainment. Faced with these circumstances they tended to form a separate and highly cohesive group, with their own slang and an informal code of rules which made prejudice easier to adjust to.

Mousinho (1978, p. 14), writing about America's black athletes and their problems in the late 1970s, has described the situation in the following way:

> blacks are giants on the field — then unwanted ... when the black athlete is through with the game, the game is through with him ... There are no black managers in the baseball major leagues. None of the National Football League head coaches is black and only three head coaches in basketball are black.

Black sportsmen, as he says, also tend to earn less through endorsements and personal appearances.

In Britain, there has never been a period of formal segregation of blacks in sport as there was in the United States. Informal barriers were soon exposed, however, after the arrival of significant numbers of Afro/Caribbean and Asian migrants in the 1950s and 1960s. As new black communities have formed and developed they have found themselves subject to a similar pattern of discrimation as that which had already been observed in the United States.

As Garth Crooks (a famous footballer) explains in a foreword to a book written by Ellis Cashmore (1982a, p. ix), the reason why blacks turn to sports is not just because of natural 'feel' or 'ability'; there are many other factors involved, particularly social issues which affect all young black people in modern society. As he says:

> everybody wants to be good at something. Black kids feel they have a much better chance of achieving something in sport than they have in other areas of society.

The former Principal Race Relations Adviser to the Greater London Council (GLC), Herman Ouseley (1983, pp. 14–20), has drawn attention to the fact that there are few, if any, famous black sportsmen and women who have not experienced or witnessed some form of racial abuse at some time or other in their careers. The selection of black players for football teams has in the past, for example, generated hostility from white fans.

It is this sort of experience which encouraged some black players during the 1980s to set up their own organizations and to form themselves into all-black teams. These teams have gone on to demand separate facilities. This strategy of separatism on the part of some black people is the result of their feelings of rejection by British society. This rejection is manifested in the lack of resources, the inequality of treatment and the limited facilities which are offered to them.

The blacks referred to so far in the United Kingdom are primarily the Afro/Caribbeans. For this ethnic minority group sport seems to represent a greater potential avenue of upward mobility than it does for the Asians. A survey of the views of young people aged between 14 and 19, commissioned by the Review Group of the Youth Service (Department of Education and Science, 1983, p. 45), revealed that 'West Indians' were more inclined to use nearly all of the facilities covered in the study, including sports centres, than 'Caucasians' or the 'Asians'. At the same time the findings show that the usage of sports centres is greater among youngsters from white-collar rather than blue-collar homes (Department of Education and Science, 1983, p. 41). The research suggests that young Afro/Caribbean blacks may be keener on such activities than their peers from similar social class backgrounds.

Asians, it may be argued, take their academic studies more seriously and they have formed their own increasingly realistic aspirations to enter other walks of life, including business and the more prestigious professions such as law and medicine. They see these occupations rather than professional sport as possible avenues to success (see Chapter 2, this volume).

Cashmore (1982a, pp. 213–21) reflects a growing concern in the black community — that increasing black success in sport, while it provides welcome role models for young blacks, also has negative stereotyping effects. Black aspirations are narrowed to focus on sport and entertainment rather than on other career opportunities. Teachers and careers guidance specialists tend to encourage these aspirations to the neglect of broader studies or careers (Cashmore, 1982a, pp. 215–6).

There is a complex constellation of attitudes and beliefs towards sport in Western societies which are related to social class hierarchies and racial perceptions. While it is true that sporting success brings prestige, especially when it is associated with the acquisition of personal wealth, there is another attitude which denigrates sporting achievement. Mere physical prowess is contrasted with intellectual ability (Cashmore, 1982b, pp. 6–7), as in the stereotype of the powerful, muscle-bound but stupid athlete. It is the contrast between 'brawn and brains'. (For a discussion of this dichotomy, see Chapter 6, this volume).

Slavery was quintessentially manual labour and represented the model of developed black physique operating under white orders and direction. After slavery blacks, as members of the manual working class, were caught up in the traditional Western disparagement of manual work. Within the perverted logic of an amalgam of the pseudo-science of eugenics and popular racism, there emerged the extreme notion of the black race as peculiarly fitted for manual labour and, by extension, physical achievement in sport. Given this stereotype it is not surprising that the anti-racist movement is deeply unhappy with the narrow linking of black aspiration and sporting achievement.

Yet another aspect of Western beliefs about sport associates it with the powerful and with the upper classes. The 'men on horseback' before the coming of mechanized warfare dominated the military and civilian worlds. In its original function the aristocracy was a military caste. Sport was a means of training and keeping the male members of that caste fit. Later, in the great English public schools, sport played a similar role of toughening and character building.

Among the élites of other Western countries, including the United States of America, sport was associated with military academies and universities. It has a continuing symbolic role in this regard. The apparently 'useless' sport of foxhunting — described by the writer Oscar Wilde as 'the unspeakable in pursuit of the uneatable' — has had the same social function. Sport gave opportunities for learning physical and emotional control. It was said to develop leadership qualities, individual prowess, team spirit and the capacity to obey and carry out orders. The Duke of Wellington was reported to have said that the battle of Waterloo was won upon the playing fields of Eton. It has also been noted that the bonds of friendship formed upon the sports field carry over into the networks of business, politics and the professions — the 'old boy' network.

Asian groups in Britain vary in their attitudes to sport generally

— as well as to particular sports. This is partly because of traditional cultural and religious beliefs and practices, and partly because some were linked with the former British Empire and others were not. There are instances where a minority of Asians engage in certain élite sports as a result of the connections forged in the past between British and Asian ruling élites: examples are squash, polo or cricket. Cricket is one case where under the Raj in British India, until independence in 1947, the game spread in the élite and drew support from among the masses.

In the successor states to British India — India, Pakistan and Bangladesh — cricket has continued to attract an enthusiastic following. Similarly, polo as an exclusive sport still binds together the ruling élites of countries which were formerly members of the Empire. In horse racing, the sport of kings, the very long mutual historical connection between the Arab world and Britain — centred on the fame of the Arab stallion — has fostered greater mutual respect. The role of the Crown and aristocracy provides the sport with much prestige, and in recent years the influx of Arab investment into the ownership of horses and studs has been significant. At the same time horse racing has a huge following and forms an important element in the gambling and media industries. Blacks are, however, scarcely noticeable among owners, trainers or professional jockeys.

A major black Afro/Caribbean heritage is an Anglophone culture which, like it or not, is generally much more closely bound up with the Anglo-Saxon traditions and beliefs, whether in their British or American forms. Black British attitudes have swung from the positive to the negative. The expectation of the early migrants was that they would fit easily into British life. Second and third generation black youths have become resentful and angry and have adopted a more strident approach in the face of British racism.

Among the younger generation of blacks in Britain are those who quite deliberately began to refer back to the historical experience of slavery rather than repressing it. They draw upon slavery as a means of raising consciousness, focusing and justifying black anger, and defining black culture — even exclusiveness — against white society. The assertion of black consciousness, black pride and black power has been a longstanding theme in black history.

The Rastafarian movement, starting in the West Indies in the 1930s and based on the image of a black African Emperor in Ethiopa bravely fighting white imperialism, gave an impetus to black consciousness and black pride (Garrison, 1979). Likewise, during the 1960s and 1970s, the adoption of Islam and of Islamic names by leading Americans, including sportsmen such as the heavyweight boxer Muhammad Ali (formerly Cassius Clay), drew strength from the centuries-old conflict between Islam and the West. This conflict linked the anti-imperialist struggle with the black struggle in America.

Muhammad Ali became world heavyweight boxing champion in 1964. He changed his name because he believed Cassius Clay to be a relic of slavery. He announced his allegiance to the Nation of Islam, the segregationist sect popularly known as the Black Muslims (Cashmore, 1982a, p. 15). Ali offended the white racist sports writers by having too much to say, and by not showing proper respect. For example, he kept asserting 'I'm the greatest' and repeating that he was a black nationalist. Finally, he committed the ultimate American heresy by saying that the US was a racist country and refused to be drafted to kill other men of colour in Vietnam (Hoch, 1974, p. 383). Rastafarianism and, in the United States, the black power movement provide examples of the use of a strategy of chosen black identity and a degree of separation from white culture as a means of strengthening black pride and black power (Cashmore, 1979, pp. 307–21).

An important black strategy has been to beat the whites at their own game. On this subject McDonald (1988, p. 13) has written about the importance of cricket in West Indian history and culture. The quintessentially English game of cricket was adopted as the national game of the West Indies. It thus became identified with the aspirations of the region and came to represent nothing less than the political movement of West Indians towards national self-determination and political independence. The first ever West Indian victory against England in 1950 was hailed as more than a great sporting event. It confirmed to the islanders that they had come of age and were ready to run their own affairs independently of British colonial administration.

When negotiations to create a broad-based self-governing West Indian Federation in the late 1950s failed, the main islands of the Caribbean each had to seek independence on their own account. This involved the break-up of a number of existing Caribbean-wide institutions, such as the University of the West Indies. McDonald pointed out that the West Indian cricket team was the only institution to survive and it has, ever since, continued to be a focus of West Indian nationalism.

McDonald attributed the importance of cricket in the West Indies to the fact that it was virtually the only activity in which a West Indian black man could 'grow to his full stature and be measured against international standards'. Alone on the field the cricketer's true worth could be seen by all; his race, education and wealth did not matter. The cricketer became the national hero. At the same time the battle concerning the overthrow of the colonial tradition, by which the captain of the West Indies team always had to be a white man, was no less important.

The first generation of West Indian migrants to Britain, according to Spackman (1988, p. 21), identified with cricket and supported the West Indian teams on their visits to England. She discerns a gulf between the younger generation and their fathers. To black boys born in a British culture, cricket 'is like tennis, a social grace, part of the Establishment's summer calendar, an admired extra-curricular activity'. Black sports organizers say that schools have neglected the game here.

Moreover, in 1987, the cricket authorities introduced new rules stopping flags, banners and 'excessive' amounts of alcohol being brought into the grounds. These actions were introduced for reasons of safety after a near riot at Edgbaston, during a one-day match between England and Pakistan. But the authorities, while they were at it, banned drums and musical instruments because they were considered a nuisance, not because of safety considerations. The new rules undoubtedly undermine the carnival flavour of a West Indies Test (as discussed in Chapter 1, this volume).

The West Indies has more in common with the 'second British Empire' in that it plays cricket. In this respect, if differs from the United States which in the form of the original thirteen colonies (the first Empire) became independent from Britain in 1776. Baseball not cricket, and American football not soccer, are the American games. Despite this difference there is no doubt that, in terms of cultural influence and role models, the long history of struggle and the example of successes of American blacks are of special importance to Afro/Caribbean and British blacks, in politics, sport and popular entertainment.

Together the black American and Caribbean cultures have had a profound international impact in sport and music. Jazz and reggae, and the plethora of musical innovations to which they have given rise, have generated a huge following and an enormous commercial market, with opportunities for blacks. For the few, it has meant an entrée to a world of glittering prizes. Through the development of a world-wide system of mass communication, black bands and individuals have been able to grow rich and famous. Likewise, sport has become part of the vast commercial international entertainments industry.

The original aristocratic and amateur ideal, which dominated the formation of modern sport in the nineteenth century, was expressed in the fundamental principles of the Olympic rules as set out by Baron Pierre de Coubertin in 1896, the year of the first modern Olympiad (Keefer, Goldstein and Kasiarz, 1983, pp. 183–4). These have largely been replaced by a thorough-going process of commercialism (Beaumont and Nichols, 1989, p. 15; *The Sunday Times*, 1989a, p. A11) and professionalism, not to speak of a competitive nationalism. These trends were the very thing which Coubertin hoped that the modern Olympic movement — with its spirit of amateurism, friendly competition, cooperation and internationalism — would overcome.

Critics of the Olympic movement, including some of the black community, have pointed out that the processes by which modern international sports were created — and continue to be run — fall short of the meritocratic ideal. The ruling bodies of sport, whether at national or international levels, are tainted by their association with the spread of Empire and the dominance of the great white powers. In this sense, they represent the self-interest of dominant cultures and classes.

Modern sport, then, has little to do with altruistic motives or genuine internationalism. Objectors to this analysis argue that a sport like football may have originated in its modern form in England, but it has become a truly world-wide game adopted alike by rich and poor countries. Its culture transcends its origins and has become part of the 'sacred', a sort of world-wide religion. In certain cases, however, sports and games associated with particular minority groups or cultures, instead of being 'universalized' like football, are often subject to the reverse process, of extinction or marginalization as in the Gaelic sport of shinty (Whitson, 1983, pp. 139–54).

Durkheim, in his study of religion, explored the functional relationship between the sacred and profane elements in society. The extraordinary prominence given to the role of sport in the modern world may make it akin to the sacred, but it also highlights the role of the profane. The pressures generated in sport give rise to the hypocrisies of 'shamateurism' (*The Sunday Times*, 1989b, p. B2). They also foster deviations from standards of law and sporting ethics, such as the use of drugs by individuals and teams and, sometimes, even the officially-inspired use of these substances for competitive advantage. The problems of regulating and controlling drug abuse are considerable, as are those of financial bribery and corruption.

The downside of intense international competition is the profane itinerant football hooligan/lager lout who seemingly also represents atavistic nationalist and racist attitudes. Just as regular football fans may be distinguished by their collective representations — flags, scarves, badges, chants and styles of dress — so too can the hooligans, with their special salutes and brutal attacks on opponents. At home, the hooligan elements among the supporters vent their spleen on black players (Crooks, 1989, p. 65; Hill, 1987, pp. 19–21; Walvin, 1986, pp. 70–80).

This type of behaviour is nothing new. George Orwell said about sport and the British that it had:

> nothing to do with fair play. It is bound up with hatred, jealousy, boastfulness, disregard of all rules and sadistic pleasure in witnessing violence: in other words, it is war minus the shooting (Quinn, 1989, p. 610).

For the *aficionados* of sport, who regard these sentiments as cynical and unfair, it is well to remember the dictum of Henry Adams about politics. Adams says 'politics as a practice, whatever its profession, has always been the systematic organisation of hatreds' (Wills, 1990, p. 3). This perspective is one which may help us to comprehend better the relationship between national governments, the media and the sporting world.

The contemporary power and significance of sport has given it an increasingly overt political role. A classic instance of the link between nationalism and sport is the case of the German Democratic Republic — now absorbed into the newly formed greater Germany. The German Democratic Republic made international sporting success a primary objective of the state. It organized its citizens for this purpose and put enormous resources behind the policy, with great success.

Sport has been used increasingly as a tool of international diplomatic and economic pressure, for example the American-inspired boycott of the Moscow Olympics in 1980. In 1968 at the Mexico Olympics, two black American athletes, John Carols and Thommie Smith, used the occasion of the award ceremony to publicize their political stance by giving the black power salute. They thus obtained world-wide publicity through the television link. Most notable, from the black perspective, is the use of a sports boycott in the struggle against apartheid in South Africa (Hill, 1990, pp. 3–5; see also Chapter 8, this volume). So far as the Commonwealth countries are concerned, this was organized internationally under the auspices of the Gleneagles agreement.

Women generally participate less in sport than do men (London

Regional Council for Sport and Recreation, 1989; Parry, 1988). Evidence shows that this is so even in countries such as Australia and the United States where sport has a high cultural value and, generally speaking, high rates of participation (Talbot, 1984). Women's rates of participation are much lower in traditional societies or those with strong fundamentalist influences. In Britain lower rates of participation are confirmed by the findings of the Department of Education and Science study (1983). There are marked differences in the black community between Afro/Caribbean women's attitudes towards sports, which tend to be more positive than those of Asian women (Lewis, 1979, p. 132). Gender-related attitudes are also connected to general difficulties faced by women when involved in activities which take place outside the home. A study by the London Borough of Hackney (Directorate of Leisure Services, 1986) highlighted the problem and quoted five reasons: a lack of money, too much work, too scared to go out at night, transport difficulties and no one to look after the children.

Asian women are particularly tied to their homes. However, they do get involved in out-of-home activities but usually under carefully controlled conditions. Carrington, Chivers and Williams's (1987, pp. 265–79) exploratory investigation into the factors influencing the lifestyles of young people of South Asian descent discovered the importance of the single-sex youth club for South Asian adolescent girls and young women. About these clubs they say it is 'a sanctuary from domestic drudgery, and a means of *resisting* the appropriation of their leisure'.

There is another interesting case of an experience in Bradford described by Dixey (1982, p. 108), where an English language class developed into a 'keep fit' class, and thence into a swimming scheme. Before such a swimming course could be put on, the organizers had to assure religious leaders (men) in the Asian community that the scheme would not offend traditional customs, and that women would be adequately supervised. The idea of women appearing scantily clothed in public is not accepted in the Asian community. Privacy was ensured by excluding men from the pool and by blocking out the windows of the hall.

Historically, women in Western countries were also subject to such traditional constraints. They, likewise, were excluded from showing themselves in the public domain — for example, in Shakespeare's day boys played women's roles and, later, women who became actresses tended to be regarded as socially disreputable. Only after the Restoration when some gentlewomen went on the stage because their families had been ruined in the Civil War did a greater degree of respectability accrue to top rank actresses.

It is only in recent years that respectable women have been able to reveal themselves in public in certain contexts (Mediterranean beaches, for example) wearing a minimum. But Western culture remains very ambivalent on this issue, and there are strong counter movements set up in reaction to these 'liberalizing' trends. Traditionalists wish to return women to their former role in the home and family, and many contemporary feminists object to the commercial exploitation of women's bodies, for example, in pornography and advertisements.

Some women use the idea of women-only groups to raise consciousness and develop women's skills in asserting themselves in a male-dominated society. This strategy has certain similarities with the Christian religious communities of women which were founded in the Middle Ages and onwards, but which have been fading in recent years for lack of recruitment. The secular form of women-only groups are reacting against the bad effects of the full meritocratic integrationist model which was dominant in the postwar decades, and which was a key feature of the postwar consensus. Just as this meritocratic model was supposedly 'colour blind' so it was assumed to be 'gender blind'.

Feminists now view the so-called sexual liberation and permissiveness of the 1960s — the unisex era — not as a genuine liberation for women, but merely a means of increasing the exploitation of women by men. In this regard there is a close parallel with the thinking of some black groups which led to the idea of all-black segregation in sport and the arts as a way of empowering black people.

Within the black community the issue of male domination has also been raised. Black women suffer the effects of a double discrimination; they face barriers of both racism and sexism which, together, are particularly difficult to overcome. Afro/Caribbean women, however, share aspirations with their black male counterparts to achieve in sport and have often been very successful, especially in track and field events where individuals like Tessa Sanderson have become household names. Nevertheless, some black women have found it advantageous to form their own black women's groups.

The development of attitudes, social movements and social policies about the role of ethnic minorities in sport has been related to broader political changes in Britain: about equal opportunities generally, and race in particular. Since the 1930s the state has become more active and interventionist in sport, as in other areas. Partly this has reflected a wider trend in Europe and America towards corporatism — the situation in which the major economic and social pressure groups (business, trade unions and the professions) come to occupy a central position in national decision-making and in return agree to cooperate with government in keeping prices down, moderating wage claims and formulating and implementing specific social policies.

Britain was successful in international sporting competition in the late nineteenth and early twentieth centuries, when the voluntary principle and private voluntary support prevailed. The major continental states, such as France and the more recently unified and centralized states such as Germany and Italy, were interventionist in sport and were keen to boost sporting success. State funding was used as a means of asserting national prestige. Given its earlier achievements under private and voluntary support, Britain saw little reason to change.

The British state lagged behind Europe in getting involved directly in sport, either in terms of having a national policy or through public funding. Moreover, Britain shared with the United States a culture of voluntary private support. The latter, however, was rapidly becoming the richest country in the world, and private support was munificent. The relative economic decline of Britain led to a relative decline in the private sponsorship of sport. For this reason, calls for public funding in sport began to grow stronger in Britain and were eventually successful.

The call for public funding of sport was part of a wider loss of faith in old-style liberalism during the inter-war years — a loss of faith in *laissez-faire* economics and non-state interventionist politics. The challenge of communism on the one hand and facism on the other undermined the belief in capitalism. The Wall Street crash and the economic slump of the 1930s generated in Britain a more modest if somewhat corporatist state intervention.

The creation of the forerunner of the Central Council of Physical Recreation in 1935 and the passage of the Physical Training and Recreation Act in 1937 marked the first stage of the advance of the state into sport. A second stage, which took place after the Second World War, came with the establishment of the Sports Council, first as an advisory body in 1965 and then as an executive organization in 1972. At the same time the reform of local government under the Act of 1972 and the Local Government (Miscellaneous Provisions) Act 1976 signalled the establishment of new comprehensive leisure departments (Torkildsen, 1986, pp. 4–38).

As a result of these acts, sport became part of the new politics of communalism in which policies about leisure and recreation absorbed sport and made it part of wider objectives and concerns. The legislation coincided with a period of rapid building of publicly-funded leisure centres and sports halls throughout the country. These were seen as a way of fostering community, taking bored youngsters off the streets — and thus reducing crime by involving young people in meaningful activities.

User surveys soon showed that such public facilities tended to have a middle-class image. Indeed, participants were disproportionately drawn from among middle-class males. The working class (particularly unskilled manual workers), blacks and other ethnic minority groups and the unemployed were among the low participants (Parry and Johnson, 1973; 1974). Local authorities believed that because public money was contributed by all sections of the population all should have equal opportunities to participate. Participation was the watchword and encouraging it became the primary concern of policy.

At the same time, from the late 1960s onwards, numerous reports had identified widespread economic and social disadvantages affecting Britain's Afro/Caribbean population. For example, they experienced higher rates of unemployment and housing problems. Governments attempted through the Race Relations Acts of 1965, 1968 and 1976 to make individual acts of discrimination unlawful. While these eliminated the more obvious symptoms of discrimination in job advertisements and notices of accommodation, such as those baldly stating 'no blacks', it did not tackle the deep-rooted forms of racism.

In attempting to remedy these problems, the official approach drew on the established and shared assumptions of the meritocratic consensus — individualistic and assimilationist in nature. As far as blacks were concerned, the official perspective regarded itself as 'colour blind' (although this was not how it was experienced by blacks themselves). This 'colour blindness' was the very thing which white liberals regarded as its chief merit.

However, in the 1960s, the postwar consensus and the meritocratic model, with its assimilationist implication, had come under attack from the political left and the far right. The student revolt of the 1960s attacked the élitism of the meritocratic model and, under the influences of feminism, the civil rights movement in the United States, the anti-apartheid campaign and the pressure for lesbian and gay rights, a political momentum was built up — especially in London.

These various elements were loosely bound together by the anti-war, pro-Campaign for Nuclear Disarmament attitudes of the youth culture manifested in music, but the whole was too fragmented to be considered a coherent political movement. The London Labour Party, tentatively at first, set out to tap and to organize this potential source of support. It was realized that Labour's traditional constituency — the white working-class community — was being eroded. For this reason London Labour attempted to put together the so-called 'rainbow alliance'. The alliance was made up chiefly of minority groups which, after Labour was elected to the Greater London Council in 1981, led to rapid changes in London Labour policy. The policy focused on equal opportunities and set out to combat racism, sexism and discrimination against people with disabilities (Parry and Parry, 1988, pp. iii–xi).

The Greater London Council was deeply affected by communalism, particularly the community work philosophy which — deriving in part from influences in the United States — was widely adopted in British local authority social work. The revolt of the inner cities in the United States in the mid 1960s had provided a warning to government in Britain. The inner city programmes with their 'communalist' rationale were the result.

In 1981 the wave of riots in British inner-city areas had a dramatic impact. Lord Scarman's inquiry was quickly set up by the government to look into the causes. His recommendations were in line with the communal approach. High unemployment and problems of racial conflict were for a short time given a higher priority on the national political agenda. But there was also the need to restrain public expenditure, which led to a cost-effective targeting approach for dealing with social problems.

Communalism offered the reason, if not the excuse, to give up universalism in public provision. The inner cities, with a high proportion of black residents and unemployed people, became target areas with target groups. Leisure and sports facilities were seen as an important instrument of targeting (Tomlinson, 1987, pp. 329–45). The new Labour Party in London seized the opportunity to make a political appeal to these inner-city groups and mobilize them for democracy, rather than simply 'state manage' them. However, it could be argued that what Labour terms 'positive discrimination' and the Conservatives label as 'targeting' are both cost-conscious withdrawals from the principle of universal provision.

In the area of sport, the Greater London Council was aware in the early 1980s of the problems about participation in sports centres and it made a conscious effort in its new sports centre in Brixton — an area with a large black community — to convey a different sort of image (Botlholo, Lewis, Minten and Shaw, 1986). Its aims were to provide sporting, social, artistic and recreational opportunities which met the actual needs of the individuals, particularly the disadvantaged and the traditionally low participant groups. These needs were to be met for both the local community and the adjacent boroughs of South West London. It went a stage further in implementing a new policy designed to attract staff from the ethnic minorities. It hoped through the careful planning of activities to promote a genuinely multi-racial use of the centre.

Another strategy, of which there are several examples, is of detached sports development and outreach work. In London, this began with the Muhammad Ali Sports Development Association initiative as early as 1974 (Stephenson, 1983, pp. 21–4). The training scheme was designed to help youngsters make the transition from participation to coaching. The scheme was an example of self-help on segregated lines. It was eventually recognized, however, that if more black and other ethnic minorities were to be drawn into sport it would be necessary to go beyond simple participation in the activities themselves, or even to entry into performance on a more serious or professional level. Job opportunities and positions would have to made available throughout the professional and supporting employment structures.

Action Sport was a Sports Council initiative in the early 1980s which aimed to demonstrate the value of sports leadership in increasing participation by non-participant target groups including ethnic minorities (Rigg, 1986). In fact, it was probably more successful in moving people up from the lower rungs of participation rather than in helping people on to the ladder in the first place. It was less successful in attracting Asians than Afro/Caribbeans, especially Asian women. Of the project Rigg (1986, p. 6) says,

> there is a clear need to develop a much higher degree of sensitivity to work in this field with training that incorporates a greater degree of understanding of cultural and religious factors as they relate to ethnic minorities.

The Greater London Council itself helped to fund a number of outreach initiatives aimed at ethnic communities such as the London Street Hockey Association in 1982 and the London Community Cricket Association, both of which are still running. The latter initiated a scheme for coaches to visit community groups and adventure playgrounds, and puts on training courses in coaching. There are strongly-held attitudes in the black community about which sports are appropriate for them. Certain sports are considered strictly 'white', for example, sailing, tennis and golf. These usually require expensive equipment and training. Sports centres need to provide areas for informal recreation for ethnic groups who may feel a lack of confidence in making use of leisure facilities, or who feel uncomfortable in the 'white environment'.

Building on the initiatives mentioned above there have been in recent years several further developments intended to promote employment among black and ethnic minorities in sport and recreation. Connected with the Brixton Recreation Centre there was a special training project jointly funded by the pioneering London Borough of Lambeth and the Sports Council. Forty students were taken on as trainees and subsequently employed at the centre. Another initiative was the Haringey Cricket College. It was set up through the London Borough of Haringey to combat unemployment among blacks and Asians by training them for work in sport — as players, ground staff or coaches. The college is now facing the threat of closure as a result of Haringey Council cutbacks (Hodgson, 1990, p. 35).

A third initiative has been the Sports and Recreation Management course started at the North London College. This course is divided into two parts: academic and coaching. The aim is to provide two distinct avenues into possible employment. A London Strategic Policy Unit (LSPU) report (Pote-Hunt, 1987a, p. 14) says of this course:

> the most remarkable feature is the ability to target itself to its prospective students. Most of the potential students for this course are in the nineteen years plus age group and the majority would be unemployed and not likely to respond to traditional methods of advertising.

Recruitment of new students has been through an informal network — talking to people in dole queues, on athletics tracks, at local football pitches. Although there are courses of similar content offered at other colleges in London, none has been designed with the direct targeting of black and ethnic minority communities in mind.

That notwithstanding, there are still all too few opportunities for blacks in professional sport. Football and boxing, like other sports, offer no financial security or proper career structure. There are relatively few opportunities for players to progress into management or coaching positions (Cashmore, 1990, pp. 10–11). At the end of their professional careers in sport — with few exceptions — most black sportsmen become downwardly mobile, face the possibility of unemployment and come up against discrimination when seeking alternative work.

When the British team went to the Seoul Olympics in 1988 there were only two black officials, although 11.9 per cent of the athletes were Afro/Caribbean and Asian. Currently there is one ethnic minority member on the Sports Council. As the London Strategic Policy Unit report mentioned above points out there is considerable under-representation of black and ethnic minorities at all levels of the structure of sport and recreation.

There is small participation by black and ethnic minorities in the voluntary sector of sport and therefore very little representation in the decision-making process. A separate report published by the London Strategic Policy Unit on local sports councils (Pote-Hunt, 1987b) found that the proportion of black and ethnic minority members was very tiny among those councils surveyed, and that black representation on executive committees of these organizations was minimal. Although access to the local sports councils is in theory not restricted to a particular group, the councils tend to operate much as they have always done because there is no publicity or targeting for new membership. Many participants in sport do not want to get involved in the administration of sport. Low expectations derived from multiple deprivation (poor housing, low pay, unemployment, etc.) can inhibit the desire to become a representative of such bodies.

Much of the work alluded to above deals with disparities and inequalities between white groups and black and ethnic minority groups in adult life. It is not surprising, therefore, to find that people look to the educational process to see whether it is helping or hindering in achieving the goals of greater participation and greater equality, or whether it is to blame for reproducing or even narrowing opportunities for some groups.

Prior to the abolition of Inner London Education Authority in 1990, a published review of examination results of schools under its control showed that the academic achievement of Afro/Caribbean pupils was still low although there has been some improvement. On the other hand, certain Asian groups perform very well. Perhaps for this reason disquiet has been expressed within the West Indian community about the often extensive commitments of their children in school sport. Many now believe that their children fail to achieve their full academic potential because they are perceived by teachers as possessing physical rather than cognitive-intellectual abilities and are thus encouraged to concentrate on activities such as sport to the detriment of their academic studies. The use of sport as a coping strategy by teachers to deal with young blacks who have side-tracked the academic mainstream serves to reinforce both academic failure and unacceptable behaviour.

Some writers have questioned the relevance of certain elements of multi-racial education such as the dialect classes, black studies and dance workshops, and argued instead for a de-emphasis on the more therapeutic components of educational programmes aimed at blacks. They believe that the alleged problems of black self-esteem should be forgotten and that teachers should raise the expectations of blacks' intellectual abilities and lower them in relation to 'natural' sports prowess.

This argument, which suggests that teachers and schools simply operate on racist assumptions and with a view to reinforcing social control, oversimplifies the position. As we have seen, there are reasons why black aspirations towards sport derive from black culture and are influenced by black role models. Similar arguments about blacks being pressed by schools into stereotypical roles in the music and entertainment industry are conspicuous by their absence. However, it is true to say that schools have a long tradition of treating sport as an activity in which pupils, particularly boisterous and disruptive pupils, can 'let off steam' in a controlled way. As the metaphor suggests, this strategy is at least as old as the Victorian age of the steam engine and was (and still is) applied in the public schools as in the state sector.

During the 1980s there was a strong tendency for Labour-controlled councils to accept the fact — previously denied — that institutional racism existed and should be overcome by anti-racist strategies. In Labour-controlled education authorities too (including the now abolished Inner London Education Authority) anti-racist policies have been pursued with some vigour.

There is evidence that the equal opportunities movement has achieved considerable formal success in so far as strategies for their promotion have been formally adopted by local authorities of whatever political complexion. These policies have also been widely adopted by funding bodies, which insist on the application of equal opportunities criteria for funding the voluntary sector. Some anti-racist groups, however, believe that the formalism is somewhat empty of real effects and that we are still only near the beginning of creating a genuinely multi-racial society.

The time has long gone when the Sports Council and the local authorities saw themselves just as the passive providers of facilities. They have moved on to devise methods of targeting and there is more monitoring of intervention and outreach work to ensure service delivery to black and ethnic minority groups. Nowadays, publicity material is commonly offered in serveral languages.

But more training opportunities are needed, for example in outreach, and more targeting of jobs in recreation services for black and ethnic minorities. There should also be adequate representation of black and ethnic minorities on voluntary sector bodies, including local sports councils, and more consultation with minority groups so that informed decisions on recreational planning issues can be made. This may require the black communities themselves to form voluntary and private clubs and groups. Finally, schools should take action to build up positive attitudes among black and ethnic minorities to participation in sport as an active and healthy lifestyle — but not at the expense of cultivating *academic* excellence.

In the United States, some blacks say that they were done a disservice by the white liberal policies of the 1960s, with their emphasis on individual mobility. This policy benefited the few. Desegregation actually undermined the traditional black community which had its own economy and in which black business people provided for blacks. The effect was that the better-educated and wealthier blacks moved out of the ghettoes. The remaining poorly-educated and more disadvantaged blacks were left behind without leadership (Barber, 1987).

A fundamental difficulty for politicians and policy makers is how to connect the universalistic and individualistic criteria of contemporary liberal secular society — which seeks to promote the notion of equality of opportunity for all women and men, irrespective of race, religion, gender or political view — with communal ideas. Modern sport may be considered quintessentially to express universalistic competitive and meritocratic values. But for this very reason the practice of sport reveals more quickly and starkly the many social impediments to the great meritocratic ideal.

Sport is, then, a source of both inspiration and aspiration to many. In this respect sport provides role models of persons who triumphed despite the odds against social disadvantages. But, by the same token, it generates anger and bitterness because of the barriers to fair play for all, on or off the field, which are known to operate. In the late twentieth century sport may be something of a world religion, but its sacred self casts a profane shadow.

Because of these drawbacks to the implementation of the Western meritocratic ideal — drawbacks which are most strikingly revealed in sport — there has re-emerged a new range of strategies and policies grouped around the ideals of community and culture. Individualism of itself is not enough; to compete effectively in a meritocratic arena such as sport people need the support of communal and cultural identities. Communalism and multi-culturalism assert not merely cultural diversity or even positive discrimination, but reaffirm the particularity of religious, racial or sexual identities. These are postulated as uniquely valuable and should not be overridden by a bland universal, secular conformity. But such a political agenda, created recently in Britain by Muslim fundamentalism creates elsewhere in society the fear of fragmentation and of a politics of warring, communal rivalries.

Public policies in Britain are with difficulty trying to justify the application of their universalistic criteria, not on the old passive basis of 'we provide the services and you can use them if you want to' but through the encouragement, development and fostering of communal strategies which will balance up perceived inequalities in participation. It is one thing to argue for the temporary promotion of groups by, say, methods of positive discrimination and segregation in order to achieve integration in the long run. It is quite another to assert as do some communal groups or fundamentalist religious bodies that they wish permanently to retain an exclusiveness which denies or rejects integration with the wider community.

Note

1 In 1987, the London Regional Council for Sport and Recreation (LRCSR) commissioned the London Research Centre to undertake some research on ethnic minorities and recreation as a basis for formulating its own regional policy on black and ethnic minority participation. The London Regional Council for Sport and Recreation (through its Black and Ethnic Minorities Working Party) was particularly concerned to gather more information about the needs of black and other ethnic minorities within the Council's target groups, to identify the constraints on participation by blacks in sport and to determine the extent of opportunities for such groups in the organized structure of sport, especially in relation to community sports leadership, coaching, sports administration, recreation management, access to sport and funding. The research project consisted of three elements — the provision of data on the distribution of black and ethnic communities in London (including population projections), a survey of the employment situation of blacks and ethnic minorities in the London boroughs' recreation and leisure services and a review of relevant literature. Jose Parry undertook the literature review, which was

published under the title *Participation by Black and Ethnic Minorities in Sport and Recreation* (1988).

References

BARBER, L. (1987) 'America's Black Paradox', *The Weekend Financial Times*, 7 November.

BEAUMONT, P. and NICHOLS, P. (1989) 'Take the money and run', *The Observer*, 20 August.

BOTLHOLO, G., LEWIS, J., MINTEN, J. and SHAW, P. (1986) *A Sporting Chance. The Work of the GLC Sports Sub-Committee 1983–85 and a Review of the Brixton Recreation Centre*, Greater London Council.

BOYLE, R.H. (1971) 'Negroes in baseball' in DUNNING, E. (Ed.) *Readings in the Sociology of Sport*, London, Frank Cass.

CARRINGTON, B., CHIVERS, T. and WILLIAMS, T. (1987) 'Gender, leisure and sport: A case study of young people of South Asian descent', *Leisure Studies*, **6** (3).

CASHMORE, E. (1979) 'More than a version: A study of reality creation', *British Journal of Sociology*, **30** (3).

CASHMORE, E. (1982a) *Black Sportsmen*, London, Routledge and Kegan Paul

CASHMORE, E. (1982b) 'Black youth, sport and education', *New Community*, **X** (2).

CASHMORE, E. (1990) 'The race season', *The New Statesmen and Society*, 1 June.

COAKLEY, J.J. (1978) *Sport in Society*, St Louis, Mosby.

CROOKS, G. (1989) 'In the penalty area', *The Sunday Times Books*, 3 September.

DEPARTMENT OF EDUCATION AND SCIENCE (DES) (1983) *Young People in the 80s: A Survey*, London, HMSO.

DIRECTORATE OF LEISURE SERVICES (1986) *Women and Leisure Services*, London Borough of Hackney.

DIXEY, R. (1982) 'Asian women and sport — The Bradford experience', *The British Journal of Physical Education*, **13** (4).

EDWARDS, H. (1973) *Sociology of Sport*, Homewood, Dorsey Press.

EITZEN, D.S. and SANFORD, D.C. (1975) 'The segregation of blacks by playing position in football: Accident or design?', *Social Science Quarterly*, **55**.

EITZEN, D.S. and TESSENDORF, I. (1978) 'Racial segregation by position in sports: The special case of basketball', *Review of Sport and Leisure*, **3** (Summer).

EITZEN, D.S. and YETMAN, N.R. (1977) 'Immune from racism: Blacks still suffer from discrimination in sports', *Civil Rights Digest*, **9** (Winter).

EITZEN, D.S. and YETMAN, N.R. (1982) 'Racial dynamics in American sports: Continuity and change', in PANKIN, R.M. (Ed.) *Social Approaches to Sport*, Chicago, Associated University Presses.

GARRISON, L. (1979) *Black Youth, Rastafarianism and the Identity Crisis in Britain*, London, ACER Project Publication.

HILL, D. (1987) 'Black on red', *New Society*, 11 December.

HILL, D. (1990) 'Mismatch of history and opportunism', *The Independent on Sunday*, 11 February.

HOCH, P. (1974) 'The battle over racism' in SAGE, G.H. (Ed.) *Sport and American Society: Selected Readings*, 2nd ed., Toronto, Addison-Wesley Publishing Company.

HODGSON, D. (1990) 'Haringey's academy falls victim to council cutbacks', *The Independent*, 5 July.

HOLT, R. (1989) *Sport and the British. A Modern History*, Oxford, Oxford University Press.

KEEFER, R., GOLDSTEIN, J.H. and KASIARZ, D. (1983) 'Olympic games participation and warfare', in GOLDSTEIN, J.H. (Ed.) *Sports Violence*, Springer Verlag.

LEWIS, T. (1979) 'Ethnic influences on girls' PE', *British Journal of Physical Education*, **10** (5).

LOY, J.W. and MCELVOGUE, J.F. (1970) 'Racial segregation in American sport', *International Review of Sport Sociology*, **5**.

LONDON REGIONAL COUNCIL FOR SPORT AND RECREATION (1989) *London Sport. Black and Ethnic Minority Participation*, London, LRCSR.

MCDONALD, T. (1988) 'Past and future in a summer game', *The Independent*, 30 April.

MADISON, D.R. and LANDERS, D.M. (1976) 'Racial discrimination in football: A test of the "stacking" of playing positions hypothesis', in LANDERS, D.M. (Ed.) *Social Problems in Athletics*, Champaign IL, University of Illinois Press.

MOUSINHO, G. (1978) 'America's black athletes — and their problems', *Sport and Recreation*, **19** (3).

OUSELEY, H. (1983) 'London against racism in sport and recreation', *Sport and Recreation in London's Inner City. Special Needs — Special Measures*, Report of a one-day seminar organised by the Greater London and South East Council for Sport and Recreation.

PARRY, J. (1988) *Participation by Black and Ethnic Minorities in Sport and Recreation*, London, London Research Centre.

PARRY, J. and PARRY, N. (1988) *Leisure, the Arts and The Community*, Brighton Leisure Studies Association, (30).

PARRY, N. and JOHNSON, D. (1973) *Leisure in Hatfield*, Report of a research study carried out on behalf of the Hatfield Rural District Council.

PARRY, N. and JOHNSON, D. (1974) *Leisure and Social Structure*, London, Report for the Social Science Research Council.

POTE-HUNT, B. (1987a) *Black and Other Ethnic Minority Sports Policy Issues*, London, London Strategic Policy Unit.

POTE-HUNT, B. (1987b) *Local Sports Councils. Comparative Study Across LSPC Boroughs*, London, London Strategic Policy Unit.

Quinn, A. (1989) 'Games people played', *The Sunday Times Books*, 23 July.

Rigg, M. (1986) *Action Sport: Community Sports Leadership in the Inner Cities. Summary Report*, London, Sports Council.

Schneider, J. and Eitzen, E.D. (1979) 'Racial discrimination in American sport: Continuity or change?', *Journal of Sport Behaviour*, 2 (August).

Snyder, E.E. and Spreitzer, E.A. (1983) *Social Aspects of Sport*, 2nd ed., New York, Prentice Hall.

Spackman, A. (1988) 'Is calypso cricket over?', *The Independent*, 5 August.

Stephenson, P. (1983) 'The Muhammad Ali Sports Development Association', *Sport and Recreation in London's Inner City. Special Needs-Special Measures*, Report of a one-day seminar organized by the Greater London and South East Council for Sport and Recreation.

The Sunday Times (1989a) 'Running into trouble. The man with the money who made Steve Ovett weep', 20 August.

The Sunday Times (1989b) 'The hypocrisy of sport', 20 August.

Talbot, M. (1984) 'Women and Sport: A Gender Contradiction in Terms?', paper delivered at the International Conference of the Leisure Studies Association, 'Leisure, Politics and People' at Falmer, Sussex, 6 July.

Tomlinson, M. (1987) 'State intervention in voluntary sport: The inner city policy context', *Leisure Studies*, **6** (3).

Torkildsen, G. (1986) *Leisure and Recreation Management*, 2nd ed., London, E. and F.N. Spon.

Walvin, J. (1986) *Football and the Decline of Britain*, London, Macmillan.

Whitson, D. (1983) 'Pressures on regional games in a dominant metropolitan culture: The case of shinty', *Leisure Studies*, **2** (2).

Wills, G. (1990) 'The politics of grievance', *The New York Review of Books*, 19 July, **xxxvii** (12).

Chapter 8

Sport, Popular Struggle and South African Culture

Grant Jarvie

The new South African politics of the 1990s has created a climate of optimism that real political change is on the agenda. Even such front line foes of apartheid as Desmond Tutu and Allan Boesak have recently conceded that 'the promise of reforms' has indicated that a new plan of action is now on the negotiating table (*The Sunday Correspondent*, 2 February 1990). Mrs Thatcher's pressure on the European Community to remove economic sanctions on South Africa and President Samaranch's suggestion that the International Olympic Committee (IOC) should consider welcoming South Africa back into the world of Olympic sport are but two indications of the growing international conservative support for South Africa's National Party. The new climate of the early 1990s has certainly given rise to some of the most basic questions that might be asked concerning South African development, culture and politics: How should we evaluate these and other reforms which have characterized the development of the South African social formation? Are the current changes essentially reformist or revolutionary? What is the role of sport within popular struggles? What combination of forces characterize the ongoing struggle to overthrow the apartheid state? What are the politics of South African sport? What is particularly significant about these problems is that they necessitate not only a tight fit between theory and evidence but also some understanding of the politics of race, class and nationalism in twentieth-century South Africa.

The Politics of South African Sport

From the vast amount of literature that has focused upon the issue of sport and apartheid at least two popular definitions are continually represented (Archer and Bouillon, 1982; Guelke, 1986; Jarvie, 1985; Lapchick, 1975; Ramsamy, 1982). The official government stance on sport is that sport, despite being regulated through the Department of National Education, is free from all statutory control (South African Yearbook, 1988, p. 659). Sport we are told is free to go its own way. In theory at least, the depoliticization of sport has been the objective of the Directorate of Sport and Recreation Advancement, a policy which has tended to be operationalized through the South African Olympic and National Games Association (SAONGA) and the South African Sports Federation (SASF). Yet such a position did not merely emerge overnight but did in fact emerge as a result of historically changing social, political and cultural tensions and conflicts. Dr Donges, Minister of the Interior, argued in 1956 that whites and non-whites should organize their sport separately within South Africa. Prime Minister Vorster broadcast a similar policy statement concerning sport in 1967 while Dr Koornhof, between 1971 and 1976, was given the responsibility for establishing a new multi-national sports policy compatible with South Africa's overall policy of separate development. This policy, although it has shifted historically to meet changing internal and external pressures, remains a corner-stone of President de Klerk's liberalization. Supporters of South Africa's official sports policy have argued on a number of occasions that sport provides an essential key to the process of integration and bridge building while critics of this position have argued that the changes are cosmetic, ideological and indeed peripheral to the lives of the majority within South Africa.

While the official government stance on sport might be loosely termed as attacking down the right, or sport is free to go its own way, those oppositional forces which have attacked down the left have tended to argue that one cannot have normal sport in an abnormal society. Aiming to create a sporting practice free from all forms of racism, sporting resistance, since the early 1970s, has been expressed through the South African Council of Sport (SACOS) and the newly formed National Sports Congress (NSC). The NSC is as vital to the resolution of the crisis in South African sport as the African National Congress (ANC) is to the solution of the crisis in apartheid society as a whole. Yet a long heritage of struggle lies behind the emergence of the NSC. The 1940s saw the emergence of the non-racial table tennis board; the 1950s witnessed the inauguration of the South African Sports Association (SASA) and the transition of many black sporting federations to a position of non-racialism; the 1960s saw the formation and expulsion of the South African Non-Racial Olympic Committee

(SAN-ROC) from within South Africa and the expulsion of South Africa from the Olympic Games in Tokyo and Mexico; the 1970s saw the development of the South African Non-Racial Sports Organization (SASPO) and the expulsion of South Africa from the Olympic Movement; while the 1980s have witnessed the ANC being involved in sporting discussions in Harrare and the development of a new militant sports organization, namely the NSC. While a number of sporting organizations have historically compromised their demands, the strength of SACOS, SAN-ROC and the NSC lies in their refusal to separate sporting demands from the broader demands for social change. As stated above, we are told one cannot have normal sport in an abnormal society. Freedom in sport, it is argued, can only materialize from true liberation which in turn necessitates the dismantling of apartheid's core statutes and policies.

In *The Politics of Sport*, Lincoln Allison has outlined three inter-related conceptions of politics all which may or may not apply to the South African context (Allison, 1986). The development of South Africa's sports policies is perhaps a clear indication of the first conceptualization, namely that a matter becomes political when the state becomes involved. A second related view of politics is that it involves matters of power, control, domination and influence over people's behaviour. In particular this view of politics as power serves as a useful reminder that sport has its own internal struggles even when governments are not directly involved. The various conflicts both between and within various non-racial and racial sporting organizations is a clear indication that historically South African sport has always had its own internal, political struggles. The final view alluded to is that politics is not just brought into being by governments or by the existence of power relations, but by disputes. In this sense politics concerns the processes by which clashes of values, interests and strategies are resolved. Clearly, there is some degree of overlap here with the previous conceptualizations since those with power are best placed to resolve or mediate conflicts. It should, however, be added that no one group, culture or organization is powerless since power is a structural characteristic which permeates all social relationships.

It is not enough to simply recognize that politics does not take place in a vacuum; it is related to the economy and society. Politics is indeed distinguishable from economics and social life but it cannot be understood as a distinct field of activity occurring in a separate realm or region of its own. Rather it needs to be grasped as an aspect of all social relations and consequently as an aspect of relative autonomy, conflict and struggle (Leys, 1983). In South Africa it is present in the power relations that influence housing, the workplace, schooling, the electoral system, the law courts, religion, sport, leisure and other facets of South African culture. In South Africa perhaps the real politics of sport revolves around the monopolistic capacity to define what sport is and what sport should be within Southern Africa. Sport, like any other aspect of culture, has always been an object of struggle within and between different social factions with each social faction having a greater or lesser degree of power (Bourdieu, 1978). This type of argument has been drawn upon by Marxists, Neo-Marxists and cultural radicals who, during the 1980s, have increasingly drawn upon such notions as ideology, hegemony, class conflict, patriarchy and cultural production to ask questions about the nature and practice of sport, power and domination within both state socialist and capitalist liberal democracies (Cantelon and Gruneau, 1982; Donnelly, 1988; Gruneau, 1983; Hargreaves, 1986; Harvey and Cantelon, 1988). The core argument here is that the politics of sport, and consequently the politics of South African sport, needs to be grasped as a mediated cultural form located within a set of social relations.

Sport, Nationalism and Popular Struggle

In seeking to develop answers to unanswered questions and provide alternative codes for understanding the past and the present, the Gramscian concept of hegemony has gained a lot of credence within Marxist cultural approaches to sport. One of the most useful contributions which Marxist cultural discourses on sport have made is to highlight the relationship between sport, power and cultural struggle. Thus the history of sport according to Gruneau (1988, p. 20) is a history of cultural struggle. In *Sport, Power and Culture*, John Hargreaves has illustrated how sport in England cannot be dissociated from the context of class relations and specific hegemonic patterns (Hargreaves, 1986). Instead of looking at sport in terms of such classical considerations as alienation, surplus-value and wage-labour relations, Hargreaves has attempted to demystify and amplify the processes of domination and struggle in English society and in particular the impinging of various sets of primary relations upon sporting life. Thus even such relatively innocent and pleasurable cultural practices, such as sport, are viewed in terms of power, inequality and social differentiation. For Hargreaves, the main set of primary relationships are not those of nationality but those of class, gender and race. Indeed Hargreaves has gone to some length to show how a Marxist cultural analysis of sport in England might proceed.

The value of this approach lies in its attention to historical context, treatment of sport as culture, its avoidance of determinism and class reductionism and its sensitivity to the tensions and contradictions that exist within and between cultural forms (Robbins, 1987, p. 581). The appropriation and development of Gramsci's ideas have helped to avoid two of the more problematic aspects of orthodox Marxism, namely determinism and class reductionism. An emphasis on the conflicting and contradictory meanings signified by sport means that it cannot be simply dismissed as an ideological state apparatus which necessarily programmes participants for their place in the mode of production. Nor, given that the power relations and social differentiation in sport have been negotiated and structured over time, can it be argued that sport reflects the straightforward interests of a particular social class.

Yet I think it is fair to say that much of the Marxist cultural work on sport has grown out of a certain reading of Gramsci's work. As Gramsci's work has become more readily available, the meanings which have been attached to the various texts have been used in many different contexts. During the early 1960s, the work on culture and class produced by left-wing intellectuals such as Raymond Williams and Edward Thompson reflected a certain familiarity with the work of Gramsci, or at least a certain reading of Gramsci (Forgacs, 1989). Thus terms such as hegemony, cultural form and experience provided a basis for explaining the relationship between culture and ideology. The value of the Gramscian theory of hegemony was that it provided an integrating framework upon which to build a field of cultural studies (Bennett, 1986). Writers who have been influenced by this reading of culture have undertaken work on sport to: 1) delve into the broader conditions and social relations through which a dominant conception of sport is made or reproduced; 2) examine how the struggles between different groups have resulted in dominant, residual and emergent forms of sporting practices; and 3) demonstrate how a particular form of sport is consolidated, contested, maintained or reproduced within the context of cultural reproduction as a whole (Clarke and Critcher, 1985; Hollands, 1984; Horne, Jary and Tomlinson, 1987). In short, Marxist cultural readings on sport have been dominated by an essentially cultural, humanist reading of Gramsci as seen through the eyes of Williams, Thompson and the cultural studies school of thought.

To paraphrase Clarke and Critcher, hegemony has become a significant concept for cultural studies because it condenses a number of major themes concerning the processes of cultural domination and conflict (Clarke and Critcher, 1985, p. 228). First, it emphasizes the field of culture as being made up of different cultures and sub-cultures. Second, hegemony stresses that cultural struggle is needed to unite aspects of these divergent cultures under the leadership of a dominant culture. Third, hegemony identifies cultural conflict as a process which does not just happen at the level of formal political ideologies but also involves common sense experiences and struggles over patterns of everyday thinking. Finally, hegemony contains the idea that cultural domination itself is always in a state of tension. Thus the theory of hegemony opens up the field of popular culture, and sporting culture as a facet of popular culture, to a number of limits and possibilities. None the less, there are some troublesome silences within this body of literature on sport, in particular the lack of concern with nationalist-popular struggles.

Gramsci's concept of national-popular struggle formed a central part of his theory of hegemony. He maintained that it was necessary for a class trying to achieve hegemony to form linkages with popular democratic struggles which were not solely confined to the antagonisms between capital and labour. By linking together the ideas of nationalist-popular struggle with the notion of counter-hegemonic struggle, Gramsci was able to impart a relatively coherent theory of social transformation (Gramsci, 1971, pp. 418–21). Contemporary examples of such popular democratic struggles are manifest in the women's movement, CND, ethnic and ecological tensions, the campaign for Scottish self-government and constitutional change and nationalist-socialist movements in African politics. For Gramsci it was crucial to both socialist transformation and future democracy to take into account the specific national context and nationalist contribution of any historic bloc driven by national popular will (Tritschler, 1986, p. 30). Clearly Gramsci recognized the necessity for a plurality of parties, alliances and organizations within the overall revolutionary process, but he also recognized that the party which linked the various interests and movements together must have a national character. Admittedly this line of development led towards internationalism but the crucial point of departure for the discussion at hand was that Gramsci recognized the nationalist contribution to the revolutionary process (Gramsci, 1971, p. 240).

The fact that there has been a relative silence within the Marxist cultural discourse on sport over the national question lies not so much in the inadequacies of Gramsci's Marxism, but in that it has been premised upon a certain reading of Gramsci, namely the cultural humanism of Williams, Thompson and the cultural studies school of thought. Alternatively the Nairn-Anderson reading of Gramsci is much more open to the place of nationalist-popular struggles within the overall revolutionary process (Nairn, 1964; 1970; 1980; Anderson, 1965; 1968; 1979; 1980). The Gramscian character of the Nairn-Anderson intervention revolves around several features. First, there is recognition of the nationalist character of history. Second, various historical analyses are used as a basis for attempting to work out some counter-hegemonic or overall total strategy for the left. Third, there is a distinct rejection of economism and class determinism and in Nairn's work in particular a rejection of the base and superstructure dichotomy. Fourth, there is a closer fusion of theory and evidence based upon the concrete realities of given historical and cultural situations. Finally, Gramsci's notion of party politics informed Nairn's critique of the labour movement in Britain during the 1960s. Yet the crucial point to be emphasized here is that nationalism and the forms in which it is constructed and celebrated needs to be given a socialist articulation rather than simply dismissed as essentially a bourgeois phenomenon (Gray, 1982).

To take a nationalist approach, therefore, is not necessarily at variance with either Marxist or socialist objectives. Over the last decade Tom Nairn has continually argued for Marxism's need to accept nationalism (Nairn, 1980; 1988; 1989). The great value of Nairn's work is that it allows us to see that there are categories of oppression, such as race and gender, which cut across nations just as the category of national oppression itself cuts across gender and class. Thus the relations between the cultural politics of various socialist movements and those of, say, feminist, anti-racist, and nationalist-popular struggles can be productively debated without their respective politics threatening either to engulf or be engulfed by potentially oppositional schools of thought.

While it is not necessary to provide a detailed account of Nairn's thesis, it is important to understand that the central tenet of Nairn's discussion on nationalism has its source in the uneven development of regions within the world as a total set of power relations. In particular, it is in the effects of the expansion of capitalism, not in its class system as such, that the roots of nationalism are to be found. While Nairn proceeds to provide a materialist theory of nationalism, the subjectivity of nationalism, he argues, must itself be approached with the utmost effort of objectivity. The real objective logic of nationalism is itself connected with the uneveness of development and the relations that arise between ethnic communities at different stages of political, cultural and economic advancement. Both result from the same uneven process, namely the dialectic of development and underdevelopment (Nairn, 1981, pp. 170–98). The solution to this problem lies in the populist mobilization of the nation and only through this strategy, Nairn argues, can the full promise of development and modernization be made to outweigh its threat. As such, nationalism itself may or may not be viewed as a tactical possibility in the move towards a more socialist society.

It is not necessary to view the position being developed here as unrelated to the South African context. Indeed Cedric Robinson's work on *Black Marxism* also develops a similar argument concerning the relationship between Marxism, nationalism and socialist theory (Robinson, 1983). With specific reference to South African sport, the problematic during the 1970s tended to be evaluated purely around the questions of race and racism (Brickhill, 1976; Lapchick, 1975). The argument here was simply that the situation in South Africa can be best explained in terms of a unified white minority subjugating and denying an undifferentiated black majority any meaningful rights by means of a combination of overtly racist legislation, a powerful administrative machine and the use of military force. Most of these writers tended to focus their evaluations purely on the question of race and thereby missed the complex interaction between broader power relations as a background to understanding the South African sporting way of life. A critique of this 1970s work on South African sport emerged during the 1980s (Archer and Bouillon, 1982; Jarvie, 1985). The central arguments here were: that sport must not be understood abstractly or simply in the context of ideas about racial prejudice, but rather in the context of the ensemble of social relations characterizing the South African social formation; and to suggest the significance of sport as a field of cultural struggle in the overall resistance to South African ruling hegemony. The concepts of class conflict, ideology and cultural struggle were used as axial principles for analyzing the nature, meaning and political significance of South African sports policy. The value of this work still remains in that it gave due attention to historical context, power relations, an avoidance of determinism and class reductionism and was an attempt to locate sport within the broader context of South African development. Nevertheless its failure to articulate clearly any nationalist-socialist strategy has proved to be troublesome and indeed problematic in the light of current developments within South Africa.

Sport, Popular Struggle and the African National Congress

The extent to which various social groups have been oppressed historically within South Africa must not give rise to the idea that this oppression was accepted without a struggle. Severe and intense struggles have been waged throughout African history. As South African capitalism has developed, men and women of different racial and class backgrounds formed numerous alliances and coalitions to try and advance their struggle for class, gender, racial and national liberation. Scarcely a decade went by without major battles being fought: the first mass black demonstrations and strikes of the 1910s, the meteoric growth of African unionization in the 1920s, attempts at forging broad African unity in the 1930s, the formation of the African National Congress's Women's League in 1943 and the Federation of South African Women (FEDSAW) in 1954, boycotts, general strikes and massive civil disobedience during the 1950s, widespread rebellion following the Sharpeville Massacre of the 1960s, labour unrest and the activities of the Black Consciousness Movement during the 1970s, the declaration of a state of emergency, media censorship, bombings and civil unrest during the 1980s and early 1990s. Throughout this heritage of struggle the politics of class, race, gender and nationalism have left a strong imprint on the demands raised and the forms of struggle undertaken.

While it is crucial not to overestimate the role which sport has played in these popular struggles, it is equally important not to view it as peripheral or meaningless. Sport as a facet of popular struggle in South Africa remains important for at least three reasons: 1) the way in which it has been used by the state as a means of suggesting to the rest of the world that egalitarian change has taken place in South Africa (sport itself was historically taken into the political sphere by the dominant culture); 2) the way in which popular sporting struggles have contributed to broader popular resistance such as through the close alliance between the ANC and the NSC; and 3) the inherent dynamics of the politics of sport itself and the way in which resistance to 'the attacking down the right coalitions' has been contested, struggled and mobilized through the actions of the non-racial sports movement. Especially during times of severe state crackdowns sport has remained one of the relatively open avenues of protest. For instance, after the response to the Sharpeville riots of the 1960s, SASA provided one of the few avenues for protest against apartheid.

External sporting pressures have certainly helped to bring pressure to bear on South Africa and provide SACOS and NSC sportsmen and sportswomen with a certain degree of security. Yet an over-emphasis on the part played by such external sporting pressures, such as the international sporting boycott, should not undermine or deflect attention from the efforts being made by the various oppositional sporting groups inside South Africa. The formation of the NSC in July 1989 was one of the most important sporting developments inside South Africa. By complementing the activities of SACOS and the ANC this tri-partite coalition was designed to bring about a broader degree of unity not only within the non-racial sports movement, but also between the non-racial sports movement and the wider national-popular liberation forces (Asmal, 1989). As such the politics of South African sport remains inextricably linked not only with the struggle for South African sport itself, but also with the struggle over Southern Africa in general. Sporting struggles may contribute to an overall war of position but the dismantling of apartheid requires a coordinated struggle involving a broad degree of unity, a degree of unity which is neither totally black nor white but consisting of a number of shifting alliances and coalitions.

Popular struggles, insofar as they represent authentic rank and file expression, cross a number of spaces and peoples. In South Africa there is not one monolithic set of 'people's struggles' but many. Labour struggles have witnessed a fusion of alliance politics under the auspices of the Congress of South African Trade Unions (COSATU) which was launched in 1985 with a view to drawing together all of those unions in South Africa which support the United Democratic Front (UDF)/ANC alliance. Urban struggles, as opposed to those at the point of production, have always been a site of resistance against the state in South Africa. These have included township groups attempting to construct viable areas of residence and recreation into decent environments. More importantly the urban struggle has often involved the struggle by rural people against their land being seized and assigned the independent status of a homeland or *bantustan* (Cobbett and Cohen, 1988). Women's struggles have also been a vital force in the mass struggle against aparthied. The launch of the UDF's Women's Congress and the revival of the FEDSAW both occurred during 1987, as did the formation of COSATU's women's section. These popular-national organizations remain committed to the basic socialist principles of non-racialism, non-sexism and popular liberation. The prominent role of Winnie Mandela should not hide the fact that many girls and women have, for example, stood in solidarity in class boycotts and numerous action demands for democratic control of education (CIIR, 1988).

Perhaps the most dramatic development of all has been the revitalization and unbanning of the ANC. Formed in 1912, the ANC has the longest history of both peaceful and violent opposition to apartheid. It led the defiance campaign in 1952 and spearheaded the 1955 Congress of the People which drew up the Freedom Charter (Meli, 1988). After the state of emergency was declared in 1960, the ANC went into forced exile whereupon it formed a military wing, *Umkhonto we Sizwe* (Spear of the Nation), based in Lusaka. During this period of exile the ANC formed an alliance with the UDF in order to give it a foothold within South African politics. The UDF, like the ANC, adhered to the Freedom Charter adopted at the Congress of the People in Kliptown, South Africa on 26 June 1955. Even before the unbanning of the exiled opposition forces in 1990, the ANC commanded the loyalty of the vast majority of the oppressed people in South Africa. If not in terms of political representation it certainly continues to command the loyalty of the majority at the level of national psyche. The Freedom Charter now more than ever forms the centrepiece of the ANC's presentation of itself.

The Freedom Charter is first and foremost a national-popular democratic document. Since its inception, the Charter has marked a noticeable swing towards a more socialist approach to popular struggle and yet it still stresses that national-liberation for the African majority is the key revolutionary path towards a national-popular democratic form of socialism. In terms of land control, popular ownership of the mines, banks, business monopolies and educational policy, the Freedom Charter holds the seeds of many radical possibilities which may provide the blueprint for the ANC's vision of the future. Furthermore, it also categorically states not only that the people shall govern and that all national groups shall have equal rights but that rent, leisure, and recreation shall be the right of all and that the colour bar in sport and other cultural areas shall be abolished (Meli, 1988, p. 211). Organizationally the ANC remains clearly dominant, but in the light of President de Klerk's liberalization, it now faces a host of testing questions.

Conclusions

The new South African politics of the 1990s has created a climate of optimism that real social transformation is now on the political agenda. Yet already a number of problems and frustrations are beginning to emerge which indicate that the presidential promises of 2 February 1990 are essentially reformist as opposed to revolutionary.

First, there is the issue of F.W. de Klerk's pledges to South Africa's right-wing coalitions since his presidential address of early February. It has been consistently pointed out that majority rule within a unitary political system is not on the political agenda. In a flat rejection of the ANC demand for majority rule, President de Klerk argues that the government are not prepared to destroy existing rights or allow them to be destroyed. The government's position remains that for the smaller groups in a multi-national country who run the risk of being dominated and suppressed, majority rule is totally unacceptable (*The Independent*, 18 April 1990). Power sharing in national-party terms refers to the process by which black voices may be heard and represented but it is envisaged that this will operate through a committee structure which protects white minority rule. The message is clear: negotiation, consensus and limited power is on the political agenda but majority rule is not open for discussion.

Second, it is important to maintain a sense of realism about the new promises and pledges. Despite an ever changing situation, the fundamental principle of apartheid, the Population Registration Act, remains unaltered. Schools still remain segregated and the Group Areas Act which regulates where people may live has been only vestigally eroded for certain social groups. Africans are still forbidden to own land in South Africa. The reaction of the South African police to civil unrest in the homelands of Ciskei and Bophuthatswana during March 1990 is indicative of the fact that South Africa's multi-national or homelands policy is still very much part of the current agenda (*The Independent*, 11 March 1990). Furthermore, in the light of this new liberalization, it is often forgotten that the same F.W. de Klerk only recently called on whites to report to the police any people of colour who broke the country's residential segregation laws (*The Guardian*, 23 June 1989).

Third, there is the issue of the ANC strategy itself. Few people would argue that Westminster-style democracy would be appropriate for Pretoria. If South Africa suddenly becomes a form of meritocracy, the educational privileges that whites have kept for themselves will ensure that power and privileges remain in white hands. On the other hand, if there is a total transfer of power and the ANC turns itself into the state and tries to nationalize the banks and mining houses in the same way as other African nations, then the outflow of capital could cause economic collapse. Furthermore, there is also the question of unity within the ANC itself. Its president, Oliver Tambo, remains ill and now veterans such as Walter Sisulu and Nelson Mandela are back in play. There are reported differences between the diplomats of the ANC embodied not only in young exiles such as Thabo Mbeki but also with no-compromise militants such as Chris Hani of *Umkhonto we Sizwe*. There is also the question of what role there will be for those who have carried the torch inside South Africa during the ANC's thirty years of exile. If the United Democratic Front (UDF) are to be disbanded, then how are its members to be assimilated into the ANC? The notion of Gramsci's modern party which links together the idea of counter-hegemonic struggles and national popular struggles, certainly provides a sense of totality and unification which is at present unclear within the ANC. The conception of totality is what distinguishes Gramsci's theory of a revolutionary party most clearly.

Finally, the complex nature of state power in South Africa means that it is important to wage political battles on a broad terrain. Sporting struggles contribute to this overall war of position within Southern Africa but the dismantling of apartheid requires a coordinated struggle involving a broad degree of unity. The efforts of the NSC and the ANC to frustrate the Gatting rebel cricket tour of South Africa in 1990 are but one small example of the increasing unity that now exists between various oppositional alliances and coalitions. In the South African situation the central role of the ANC must be to coordinate and direct the various national-socialist popular struggles taking place. The politics of race, class and nationalism are but three of the complex inter-weaving factors which still exert pressure on people's choices, options, experiences and actions in South Africa.

References

ALLISON, L. (1986) *The Politics of Sport*, Manchester, Manchester University Press.

ANDERSON, P. (1965) *Towards Socialism*, Cornell, Cornell University Press.

ANDERSON, P. (1968) 'Components of the national culture', *New Left Review*, (50) July, pp. 3–57.

ANDERSON, P. (1979) *Considerations on Western Marxism*, London, Verso.

ANDERSON, P. (1980) *Arguments Within English Marxism*, London, Verso.

ARCHER, R. and BOUILLON, A. (1982) *The South African Game*, London, Zed Press.

ASMAL, K. (1989) 'The case for continuing the boycott of apartheid South Africa', unpublished paper presented at Queen's University of Belfast International Sports Symposium, June.

BENNETT, T. (1986) 'Popular culture and the turn to Gramsci', in BENNETT, T. et al. (Eds) *Popular Culture and Social Relations*, Milton Keynes, Open University Press, pp. xi–xix.

BIRRELL, S. (1989) 'Racial relations theories and sport: Suggestions for a more critical analysis', *Sociology of Sport*, **6**, pp. 212–7.

BOURDIEU, P. (1978) 'Sport and social class', *Social Science Information*, **17**, p. 826.

BRICKHILL, J. (1976) *Race Against Race*, London, International Defence and Aid Fund.

CANTELON, H. and GRUNEAU, R. (1982) *Sport, Culture and the Modern State*, Toronto, Toronto University Press.

CATHOLIC INSTITUTE FOR INTERNATIONAL RELATIONS (CIIR) (1988) *Cries of Freedom*, London.

CLARKE, J. and CRITCHER, C. (1985) *The Devil Makes Work: Leisure in Capitalist Britain*, London, Macmillan.

COBBETT, W. and COHEN, R. (1988) *Popular Struggles in Southern Africa*, London, Currey.

DONNELLY, P. (1988) 'Sport as a site of popular resistance', in GRUNEAU, R. (Ed.) *Popular Culture and Political Practices*, Toronto, Garamond, pp. 69–82.

FORGACS, D. (1989) 'Gramsci and Marxism in Britain', *New Left Review* (176) July–August, pp. 70–88.

GRAMSCI, A. (1971) *Selection from Prison Notebooks*, New York, International Publishers.

GRAY, R. (1982) 'Left holding the flag', *Marxism Today*, 25, 11, pp. 16–19.

GRUNEAU, R. (1983) *Class, Sports and Social Development*, Amherst, Massachusetts University Press.

GRUNEAU, R. (1988) *Popular Culture and Political Practices*, Toronto, Garamond.

GUELKE, A. (1986) 'The politicization of South African Sport', in ALLISON, L. (Ed.), *The Politics of Sport*, Manchester, Manchester University Press, pp. 118–48.

HARGREAVES, J. (1986) *Sport, Power and Culture*, Cambridge, Polity Press.

HARVEY, J. and CANTELON, H. (1988) *Not Just a Game: Essays in Canadian Sport Sociology*, Ottawa, University of Ottawa Press.

HOLLANDS, R. (1984) 'The role of cultural studies and social criticism in the sociological study of sport', *Quest*, **36**, pp. 66–79.

HORNE, J., JARY, D. and TOMLINSON, A. (1987) *Sport, Leisure and Social Relations*, London, Routledge.

JARVIE, G. (1985) *Class, Race and Sport in South Africa's Political Economy*, London, Routledge and Kegan Paul.

JARVIE, G. (1989) 'Getting Gatting', *New Statesman and Society*, August, pp. 16–17.

LAPCHICK, R. (1975) *The Politics of Race and International Sport*, Westport, Greenwood Press.

LEYS, C. (1983) *Politics in Britain*, London, Heinemann.

MELI, F. (1988) *A History of the ANC*, London, Currey.

NAIRN, T. (1964) 'The British political élite', *New Left Review*, (23) January–February, pp. 19–25.

NAIRN, T. (1970) 'The British Meridan', *New Left Review*, **66**, March–April, pp. 3–35.

NAIRN, T. (1980) 'Internationalism', *Bulletin of Scottish Politics*, **2**, pp. 101–25.

NAIRN, T. (1981) *The Break Up of Britain*, London, Verso.

NAIRN, T. (1988) *The Enchanted Glass*, London, Radius.

NAIRN, T. (1989) 'The Timeless Girn', in EDWARDS, O. (Ed.) *A Claim of Right for Scotland*, Edinburgh, Polygon, pp. 163–78.

RAMSAMY, S. (1982) *Apartheid, the Real Hurdle*, London, International Defence Aid Fund.

ROBBINS, D. (1987) 'Sport, hegemony and the middle class: The Victorian mountaineers', *Theory, Culture and Society*, **4** (4) November, pp. 579–602.

ROBINSON, C. (1983) *Black Marxism*, London, Zed Press.

SOUTH AFRICAN YEARBOOK (1988) Johannesburg, Department of Foreign Affairs.

TRITSCHLER, P. (1986) 'Gramsci', *Radical Scotland*, **20**, April–May, pp. 29–32.

Notes on Contributors

Richard Burton lectures in French within the school of African and Asian Studies at Sussex University, having previously taught French at the University of the West Indies, Mona, Jamaica. His books include *Baudelaire in 1859: A Study in the Sources of Poetic Creativity* (1988) and *Baudelaire and the Second Republic: Writing and Revolution* (forthcoming). He is currently working on a full length study of literature and ideology in Martinique.

Scott Fleming lectures at the Chelsea School of Human Movement, Brighton Polytechnic. He graduated from Newcastle/Sunderland Polytechnic before completing postgraduate work at Loughborough University. Since 1986 he has been engaged on a PhD study concerned with Asian lifestyles and sports participation. He has presented papers at both national and international sport, leisure and social science conferences.

Othello Harris is an Assistant Professor at Miami University, Oxford, Ohio where he teaches courses on the sociology of race relations and the sociology of sport. He is currently working on a book which examines both the social forces which have shaped black athletes' experiences in American sport and the way in which these same athletes have also acted as social agents within American culture. He gained his PhD in sociology from the University of Maryland.

Grant Jarvie lectures at the University of Warwick. He is author of the books *Class, Race and Sport in South Africa's Political Economy* (1985) and *Highland Games: The Making of the Myth* (1991). He has taught in both physical education and sociology departments within various institutions. He gained his PhD in sociology from the University of Leicester.

Tessa Lovell graduated from the Polytechnic of Central London in politics and history. During 1989 she was engaged in a research project concerned with the sporting and leisure experiences of women of Afro/Caribbean and Southern Asian origin. She completed her MA in Sport, Culture and Society at the University of Warwick in 1990. Her main research interests are women and leisure, community education and social and political theory. She is currently a research assistant in the department of Continuing Education at the University of Warwick.

Joe Maguire lectures at the University of Loughborough. He has presented papers at both national and international sport studies and sociology conferences. He has published widely on aspects of developmental sociology, sport and American culture. He gained his PhD in sociology from the University of Leicester and is currently working on a book which examines comparative and developmental sports processes.

Vicky Paraschak has been an Assistant Professor at the University of Windsor, Canada since 1984. Her research interests include government policy, self-determination and the historical involvement of aboriginal women and men in relation to sport and recreation. She worked as a policy officer for the government of the Northwest Territories from 1980–1984. She gained her PhD from the University of Alberta.

Jose Parry is senior research officer at the London Research Centre specializing in the arts, leisure and the environment. She has written many reports and articles including 'The community arts — An arts revolution incorporated?', *Leisure, the Arts and the Community* (Leisure Studies Association, 1988); *The Capital Funding Needs of Voluntary Arts Organizations* (London Research Centre, 1986); *Participation by Black and Ethnic Minorities in Sport and Recreation* (London Research Centre, 1988); *The Greening of London: The Environmental Policies and Initiatives of the London Boroughs* (London Research Centre, 1990). She is co-author of *The Economic Situation of the Visual Artist* (Gulbenkian, 1986).

Noel Parry is Director of Research in the Faculty of Environmental and Social Studies at the Polytechnic of North London. He has also served variously as Head of the Department of Sociology and Chair and Dean of the Faculty. He has researched and published in the fields of leisure studies, the professions — in particular, health, social work, education and the arts — social stratification, the state and social policy. Joint publications with Jose Parry include *The Rise of the Medical Profession* (Croom Helm, 1976); 'Theories of culture and leisure' in Smith, M.A. (Ed.) *Leisure and Urban Society* (Leisure Studies Association, 1977) and 'Meritocrats last stand', *Times Higher Education Supplement*, 15 December 1989. Jose and Noel Parry co-edited *The Leisure Studies Association Conference Papers, Volume (3) Leisure the Arts and the Community* (No. 30, 1988).

Author Index

Abrahams, R., 16, 17, 25
Allison, L., 36, 177
Amos, V., 61, 62
Anderson, P., 181
Archer, R., 2, 176, 182
Asmal, K., 184

Bale, J., 94, 100
Ball, S., 31
Banas, C., 148
Banton, M., 95
Barber, L., 170
Bayliss, T., 36
Beaud, S., 107
Beaumont, P., 159
Beckford, W., 11
Bennett, T., 179
Birbalsingh, F., 30
Birrell, S., 2, 79, 96, 100
Borlholo, G., 165
Bourdieu, P., 178
Boyle, R., 150, 153
Braddock, J., 127
Braithwaite, T., 16
Brickhill, J., 182
Brower, J., 99
Bryan, B., 59
Burgess, R., 31
Burton, R., 7–29

Cantelon, H., 178
Carrington, B., 30, 51, 52, 94, 99, 100, 102, 108
Cashmore, E., 3, 30, 49, 51, 53, 153, 154, 155, 157, 167
Child, E., 30
Chu, D., 96, 98, 120
Clarke, J., 179, 180
Coakley, J., 51, 96, 151
Cobbett, W., 184
Coleman, J., 51, 124
Craft, A., 52
Crooks, G., 160
Curtis, J., 96, 98

Dacks, G., 76
Datar, R., 30
Davis, A., 61, 63
Deem, R., 58, 60
Dittrich, D., 80
Dixey, R., 161
Donnelly, P., 178
Dove, L., 42
Dunning, E., 95, 101, 114, 118

Edwards, H., 95, 96, 99, 101, 111, 126, 150
Eitzen, D., 99, 120, 150, 151, 153
Elias, N., 95

Subject Index

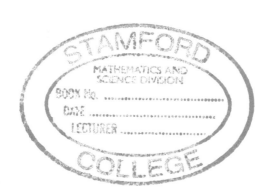